WHEN NEWS BREAKS

A memoir of love and war

by Carol Lin

THIRD RAIL PRESS

WHEN NEWS BREAKS: A MEMOIR OF LOVE AND WAR

Copyright © 2025 by Carol Lin. All rights reserved.

Published by:
THIRD RAIL PRESS LLC
P.O. Box 20285
Albuquerque, NM 87154
www.thirdrailpress.org

Paperback ISBN: 979-8-9912123-6-6
Ebook ISBN: 979-8-9912123-7-3

Cover Design: Natàlia Pàmies

Printed in the United States of America

Praise for WHEN NEWS BREAKS

"Carol Lin's chronicle of breaking news, complicated love, and life-changing tragedy stands apart. By turns raw, humorous and poignant, Lin's story resonates, revealing layers of emotion with charm and candor, and leading you to reflect on the arc of your own life against the touchstone of hers."
- Claire Chao, author of *Remembering Shanghai*

"Carol Lin writes a memoir of ambition and loss with unflinching honesty and remarkable clarity. Powerful, exhilarating, and wholly human. A writer who has walked through fire and returned with a story only she could tell."
- Farah Naz Rishi, author of *Sorry for the Inconvenience*

"I knew I would read the story of an accomplished journalist, but I also read the story of a rather remarkable woman... relatable to all women navigating the constant push-pull of our professional and personal lives. I couldn't put it down."
- Rachel Burchfield, *Forbes Magazine*

"*When News Breaks* is a testament to Lin's resilience. It shows us how telling the stories of the world can lead to stories of our own. This is a story only Lin can tell, but it is one that all of us should read."
- Joselin Linder, author of *The Family Gene*

"More than a journalist's memoir, it's a raw map of the heart, written with the same fearlessness the author once carried into warzones."
- Jason Bellini, international correspondent, *Scripps News*

"*When News Breaks* is heartful and harrowing. A riveting story of love, career, family, adventure, and grief intersecting with major world and life events, told from Carol Lin's unique and courageous perspective."
- Meredith Artley,
former Editor-in-Chief of CNN Digital Worldwide

"What a stunning memoir. I could not put it down Carol's courage, honesty and vulnerability are a gift. A must-read."
- Samantha Dockser, Reese's Book Club LA City Chapter Lead

"The greatest indulgence I've enjoyed in years."
- Diane M. Simard, author of *Unlikely Gifts Unwrapped*

"Storytelling at its finest. A must-read for anyone wanting to explore the things that matter most in life."

- **Meghan French Dunbar, author of** *This Isn't Working*

"As if a good friend was giving me a ringside seat to major events in history and her own life. I would highly recommend to anyone interested in the world."

- **Malia Mattoch McManus, author of** *Dragonfruit*

"Riveting… Offers readers an impactful narrative as richly textured and memorable as the lives that it chronicles."

- **Irene Dunlap, co-author of** *Chicken Soup for the Soul*

"This book is authentic and blunt. Carol not only navigates the realities of covering a war but also reveals the tension in the newsroom with professional detachment. Carol digs deep here, and I am humbled by her personal pain."

- **Kyra Phillips, anchor,** *ABC News*

"Carol Lin's book was one I could not put down. Perhaps it's the intrigue of a woman revealing all, unmasking the facade of perfection. Perhaps it's the emotion tied to life, love, lost and love all over again."

- **Christine Devine, anchor, Fox 11 Los Angeles**

"A raw, honest reminder that we often don't know the deepest, most heartbreaking challenges of the people we think we know. How will you ever make it without the relationship, career and labels you think define you? Carol's story shows you that the journey can indeed be messy and tear-soaked while leading you to a place so much better than you could have ever imagined."

- **Daryn Kagan, host of the** *Call me Friend* **podcast and author of** *Hope Possible*

"A stunning journey into the wilderness of first-class journalism and the unforgiving fields of heartbreak. An absolute must-read."

- **Jennifer Thym, film director and producer**

"She's covered every story imaginable, but as it turns out, the bravest story she's ever told is her own. A must-read for anyone who wants the truth about TV news, love and life."

- **Brooke Baldwin, author of** *Huddle*

For C,
because you once asked me why I don't cry,
and I wondered how it was possible to hide the tears
that led me, finally, to you.

AUTHOR'S NOTE

This is a personal recollection of people and events. I consulted and shared pages with friends and colleagues, and in some cases, I changed names to respect anonymity. There are also those who were present during specific scenes who may not be included in the book, but not at the expense of veracity. I researched locations and facts of the news events and reviewed my own reporting on video and in scripts when these editorial artifacts were available. It bears mentioning, with the advent of AI, that I wrote every word, and fellow humans, with their remarkable intuition and insight, edited this book. Unlike autobiography, this memoir is not the accounting of an entire life, but rather my recollections of a specific time. I humbly ask readers not to take my story as representative of all female journalists, Chinese immigrants, Chinese Americans, or Chinese mothers, as the latter in my life was fiercely unique!

PROLOGUE

Years later, I can still feel the rough hands on my personal belongings, rifling through my reporter notebooks, clothes, underwear; fingers poking in pockets and lifting clear Ziplocs to the harsh light of international airports from New York to London, Frankfurt to Tel Aviv. Once, in Islamabad, a female security officer working for Pakistan's version of the TSA gruffly motioned me past the metal detectors to a curtained security area and ran her ungloved hands up and down my arms, ribs, belly, hips, between my legs, and squeezed my breasts so hard that I wondered if I had been assaulted or merely searched in a specific, non-sexual way.

This was the life of a traveling network correspondent.

Search me now and it will be on the internet where a glossy bio pops up on a Wikipedia page created and curated by strangers who crowd-sourced my life based on what they saw: ABC News, CNN, and the prizes that rewarded historic moments, like my breaking the news of 9/11. I come across as accomplished, complete. Someone included a notation about a husband, a baby, a death—mentions so brief compared to the Emmys, Peabody, Alfred E. Dupont Award, and Associated Press awards that they manifest as afterthoughts.

But all of that was the story behind the headlines that I was sure I'd carry to my grave because my image-driven industry expected us to live on a high note and leave the same way. *Don't let 'em see you sweat. And for God's sake, girl, whatever you do, don't cry. Baby, you can have it all.*

After 9/11, I was at the height of my career, on assignment, descending down a mountainside to a no-man's land, and too deep into my life choices to realize that having it all was not remotely what I'd imagined.

And so we begin, on the border of Afghanistan, in a place known as the Empire of Graves.

1. CROSSHAIRS

I was on high ground, taller than the crowd of Pashtun men around me, but to the Taliban fighter, I was small, only two inches high in the crosshairs of his gunsight. I held my breath as he examined me, a woman exposed in a foreign land, dressed in denim but feeling stripped by his gaze. Across a dried-up riverbed, he rocked side to side and steadied his aim.

He wasn't bothered by the dust that swirled and dissipated in a wind that hissed more than howled. The dust, so much dust, cast an orange haze over the crowd of men around me who blocked the road. Downslope, a long, slow-moving line of ethnic Pashtuns in long cotton tunics and baggy pants weaved between makeshift guardrails that bullied chaos into a semblance of order as families moved toward the Pakistani border checkpoint, dragging alongside them sacks of farm goods and old boxes of electronics to trade at the border markets. The women looked ghostly in their blue Burqas, unmoved when their children pressed their tiny faces into their mothers' legs under the midday sun. The scene had the deceptive aura of a landscape painting. As a reporter, seeing was the equivalent of believing, but still, I wondered, just for a second, if what I saw was real.

Moments ago, I had been searching for a better view of the Chaman Border Crossing with Afghanistan when a herd of Taliban fighters had arrived in a dozen pick-up trucks, revving engines and kicking up red clouds of desert silt.

We had just arrived after a two-hour descent down a single-lane mountain road between the Toba Achakzai Mountains and Khojak Pass, designed by sadists and built for whiplash. The view from my backseat middle perch over the cracked and faded dashboard gave me no illusions; there was no way we would see a truck barreling toward us around the bend. The driver, hired by CNN only the night before, had gripped his weathered steering wheel and leaned into hairpin turns so sharp, we went airborne.

"Shit!" the photographer had cursed my clumsiness after I slammed into him.

I was sandwiched among a veteran field crew whose lives were all about the rough and tumble. Been there. Done that. They looked annoyed that I, their correspondent, clung to a broken seat belt. I looked to our fixer, Ahmed, a Pakistani translator who sat up front, for reassurance. Was this the planned route, the highway everyone took? But he was distracted with saving himself, one hand pressed against his side window.

It was October 2001, only a month after the 9/11 attacks and CNN had assigned us to the Afghanistan border to investigate US officials' claim that Osama bin Laden traveled freely between Afghanistan and Pakistan through this crossing, one of the busiest in the world. I wondered if the editors expected us to get video of some sort of terrorist morning commute. From what I saw, even the world's most wanted man could get lost in this thick shroud of humanity.

The Toyota trucks, circling now, were a favorite among terror groups around the world because they were cheap and readily available in Central Asia. Their flatbeds served as a steady launch pad for men armed with AK-47s, like the one before me now. He was tall, dressed in white, with a large scarf, or Kefiya, billowing around his neck from the back of a red pick-up stopped dead center, only a stretch of loose rock and silt between us. Fifty to a hundred yards. Not much. Not enough.

I was used to men measuring me with their eyes, gauging my value, judging whether I was special enough to be the target of their love, or worthy of their power to bestow a professional opportunity. All my life, men had shaped my self-worth with their gaze, pressing in with their judgments, like potters molding clay. Was I smart enough to make them look smarter? Did I know how to take risks that made a TV network more competitive? Was I humble enough to take criticism or quietly accept when they told me no?

Anywhere I went, it was all about who had the power. Here, it was an armed terrorist; back in the air-conditioned newsrooms I was used to, it was male news executives, with piles of resume tapes from reporters half my age who'd take my job at a quarter of my salary, who reminded me that I was never the one in control. I was replaceable. That's what it was like to be in the crosshairs of a different sort, their eyes measuring the current value of a professional climber like me at the summit of my career. The more money I made, the more excuse executives had to ask, *What is she really worth?* Of course, the bones of solid journalism mattered equally across genders, but as a female journalist, I always sensed there was something skin deep that I had to bring. Just the sight of me on the small screen had to inspire the viewers' respect but also their desire. *See me, trust me, but want me too. Keep inviting me into your home—your living room, your bedroom—day and night.*

But in these weeks immediately after 9/11, careers were made or broken. So, stay nimble and alert. Go live. Break news. But for God's sake, stay alive.

That last part depended on the terrorist before me. At least, I assumed he had a mind to kill me. I was close enough to make out his dark bearded face and the rocket-propelled grenade pointed at me. I reminded myself that I had begged CNN's international desk to assign me here, didn't think twice about leaving behind the people I love to report the news—what journalism schools declare is the first chapter of history. And, after the heady business of breaking the news of the World Trade Center attacks from CNN's anchor desk, all I wanted was to be as close as possible to the people and places party to the 9/11 plot. Yet, staring now at the tip of that grenade launcher, I never imagined I'd be this close. I froze like the guinea pig I was, believing I could become invisible even though I was an exotic creature dressed in Levi's, hiding in plain sight in a sea of men. I had to swallow my fear, shut my mouth, and project calmness to be neither a threat to this man, nor a cowering victim.

My photographer, Doug, arrived a few yards behind me.

"Shit!" he muttered as his battle-tested instincts kicked in and he began to roll video. For him, it was all about getting the shot, assuming we didn't get blown up in the process.

I whispered, "I've got your back," and then went silent to keep my voice from polluting the audio of our exclusive story.

I rationalized that the Taliban fighter might spare Doug, a man, but I was "just" a woman, a piece of property, according to Taliban law. Perhaps, to him, I wasn't even human, just easy prey caught lingering too long in the lush feeding ground of an exclusive post-9/11 story.

The rest of our team was in the satellite truck, too far away to make a run for it. Not going to lie, I was an experienced field reporter, but no gonzo war correspondent. By that point, I had reported overseas for CNN just once, covering the aftermath of the Kosovo war. The shooting was over by the time I got to Pristina.

Suddenly my cell phone buzzed twice. It was my mother calling. Again. I sent her to voicemail for the third time. I had warned her not to call today. But telling her not to call only meant she'd go to great lengths to reach me. She was the only person I knew who expected cell phone service at Afghanistan's border.

My mom had begged me not to go on this assignment. Why *this* place? Why not stay anchoring the news of the 9/11 aftermath from the safety of CNN's Atlanta studios? Wasn't that enough? She was anxious that I took risks when, after three years at CNN, I was not the highest-profile anchor on the network. Yet, I saw myself as an ambitious comet flying alongside a constellation of CNN stars instantly recognizable by their first names: Wolf, Christiane, and the up-and-coming Anderson. As the child of immigrants, I intuitively sought who had power and learned to bask in their adjacent light. It was a survival skill for people like my parents who had arrived in America as students with no long-term safety net.

Assimilation begins with *be nice*. My mainland Chinese parents had ingrained in me how important it was to be pleasing. How others viewed us, they said, shaped our destiny. Educated by Christian missionaries, they credited their prayers and my steady stream of "please" and "thank you" for my teachers as the divine difference between earning A's or settling for B-plusses. But that's not how it works in television. You never quite graduate from the real time feedback loop of agents, consultants, and of course, the audience. To get to the network, being nice undermined being badass. I witnessed plenty of journalists playing God in a newsroom, but I was on my own and had to believe I had the superpower to fly.

It took a certain kind of crazy to cross an army checkpoint into a warzone, or head toward a chemical explosion while residents evacuated. So far, I had escaped death for a living. Our news vans drove out of rising floodwaters. Earthquakes were over by the time we arrived to shoot the rubble. A wildfire hadn't caught me yet. The past was prologue, as the Bard had wisely stated. Why should this situation be any different. The Taliban fighter grinned, teasing us with the tip of his RPG.

Such hubris, but there was no other life for me. I couldn't imagine being anything but a CNN anchor and correspondent, a title so broadly international and notable, my peers finally accepted me on my own merit, as any other correspondent, instead of as the Asian-American one. My female colleagues said that feeling—of finally making it —was fleeting. *Enjoy the fun while it lasts*. Afterall, I was forty-one and fifteen years into my on-air career but more vulnerable to the bright studio lights, even as I felt ageless. Ageless was how all the forty-year-old women I knew described themselves. Yet, three years ago, when I was still cushioned in my thirties and CNN hired me, I noted the anchors departing the network were of a certain age. Why kid myself? Even the pretty glass bottles with potions that promised our youth had expiration dates.

Perhaps everything ended here anyway, with the Taliban fighter. My jeans, light blue chambray shirt, and my cameraman wearing a CNN baseball cap made us the most tempting targets. We were Americans. Surely, even a terrorist knew there would be consequences for murdering CNN journalists—all that bad press, the headlines condemning yet another cold-blooded attack on a media superpower. Then again, what did he care? The global post-9/11 headlines about the vulnerability of the United States were all a terrorist could wish for.

"This doesn't look good," Doug muttered.

"We're in it now," I said. "Don't worry. I got you."

But what could I do to defend us? My notepad and pen could be lethal to Washington, DC, reputations, where politicians only fired back in soundbites, but here, my ink-stained hands fluttered at the large scarf wrapped around my neck. The Taliban fighter didn't care about my airtime or status.

He stared at me, and I gave my best glare back. Game face on, asshole.

I wondered what the newsroom would tell my husband, Will, if I died. Before this assignment, I had reassured him, "When I get back, I promise…" Fill in the blank. Yes, somehow, we would fill in the remaining blanks. This business about starting a family—perhaps that was the right decision. I mean, would I even be in this crazy place if I had a baby? But what would a child think of me as a mother? I'm the woman who'd recite to her the origins of jazz but didn't know any songs other than Happy Birthday. I was too busy to embrace the beauty of words married to music.

"I miss you," I had told Will last night. I had put weight into the words I whispered hoarsely over the hotel phone after I had arrived in the Pakistani border town hotel where CNN had set up shop.

"Do you?" Will whispered back. Old doubts hung in the air. We were still like animals who had survived a wildfire, but the scent of danger never really went away.

"I do miss you. You know I do." I picked at the bedsheet, glad Will couldn't see me. He'd read my fidgeting as a tell, but truthfully, I was distracted by the clicking sounds on the phone line. I suspected hotel spies listened in and took notes on journalists' calls.

"Are you alone?" Will asked, matter-of-factly.

"Yes," I said softly and then paused. "Of course. No one but you."

Our latest vow. We were learning to make our bond feel less like timber and more like steel.

"No one but you," Will said back. We both knew what could happen when we were on the road because it had. I had distilled complicated stories into a ninety-second report for a living, but devotion was a tangled topic that didn't fit into a minute-thirty-second explanation. During the thirteen years since we'd met on the presidential campaign trail, our relationship had evolved into a curated collection of intense love and quiet humiliations. I loved him. Deeply. With a kind of madness that still made my heart pound when our eyes met. Yet, I had left him. Again. For another assignment.

Of course, I missed Will. I wanted to be what my husband hoped. I did. Yes. A person with a moral compass that always led me home, the wife to give him a child. But I was no longer the twenty-seven-year-old novice he fell in love with. A news producer and journalist himself, he knew what my career meant to me. I wasn't willing to commit to when I'd ever stay home. I kept flirting with "someday" or "next contract" or "in just a couple years…" How could I tell him that, for me, flying solo was when I loved him most. After almost a decade of marriage, I began to suspect it was the physical distance that bound us together.

Will had every reason to question if the woman he fell in love with understood there was more to life than work.

"When will it be enough?" he had asked me before I left on this assignment. Will wanted me to know I was more than the ratings of my next show, the status of my next assignment, and that I was much more than what I saw of myself through the distortion of a camera lens.

I assumed he couldn't understand the personal high of anchoring mornings or reporting on a big story because he worked behind the scenes. As a Chinese American anchor, I was the dependable Saturday and Sunday face for the network, while primetime weekdays largely remained snowy white. Being on assignment meant being seen in the money-making timeslots that mattered most to CNN.

"You should see yourself when the phone rings," Will prodded.

True, whenever the phone rang or my pager buzzed, my fingers curled into small pulsating fists. And when I'd hang up, I would exhale, a little more anxious than in the past when the stakes didn't feel as high. He knew that when the powers that be chose me for a new assignment, I'd always go, leaving us miles apart.

"Goodnight, Stinks," I teased. Our nickname for each other. I pressed the phone against my ear to absorb Will's response. All that he hoped to settle about our life together, if it was to go forward, had to wait.

"You're the one who stinks. Be careful out there. Call me tomorrow." Will laughed. Then he broke the connection first.

Now that my life may be on the line, the memory of that conversation stung. *No tears now, Carol. Breathe. Focus on how to report this moment: For a split second. . . One minute I'm. . . the next. . .* I was disappointed how easy it was to reduce life and death into tropes about time passing, like the obvious ways we described the sky on 9/11 when we had thought the bright blue above New York City was promising a different kind of day. Doug might have forgiven me if I had bawled.

The Taliban soldier finally lowered the tip of his RPG and laughed. Is it wrong that my first thought was that it would have made for a better story if he had fired? But missed? Nevertheless, better to be the butt of his tasteless humor than dead. When his driver peeled off in a cloud of red dust, he melted back into the sea of fighters.

"Got it!" Doug announced. This whole time, he hadn't broken a sweat. He caught me as I dabbed the tears I tried hard to hide. "What—you were worried?"

I saw his raised eyebrows, the headshaking, and I lied, "No, I'm good. Just the dust. Okay, let's get back to the truck and feed the tape. Good stuff, right?"

"Hell yeah, good *stuff*, Carol." Doug smirked and checked his camera. Cursing never felt natural to me even though swearing like a sailor would have made me more like the good ol' boys.

We jogged back to the satellite truck and heard the crew holler that 'Atlanta,' as we referred to the producers, had called and told us to go live at the top of the hour, in ten minutes. We popped Doug's video into the truck's playback machine and rewound the tape as he bragged to the crew about what just happened, like this was his big moment and not ours. Another reminder that, while I was the one on camera, it was my responsibility to make everyone else look good. The Taliban confrontation had lasted less than three minutes. It felt like a lifetime. We cued the video to the last sixty seconds and told the producers to play it raw during the live shot.

"Carol! Get over here so I can frame the background." Doug set up his camera with a wide shot of the border checkpoint.

As I fast-walked to the live shot position, I called the International Desk, anxious to share the events and practice what I'd say on the air. Really, I just wanted someone to ask me, "Are you okay?" When a senior editor picked up with a gruff hello, I chattered away about how the Taliban were show-boating, how we played tough and got away. I would have kept talking if he hadn't interrupted me.

"Don't tell me about the birth! Just show me the baby. I'll watch the live shot. Now scoot. Get ready!"

Breaking news was not the time to ask for a hug. He had booked back-to-back live shots on CNN US, International, Headline News, and CNN Radio. He had done his job and moved on, and so must I.

I ran my hand through my hair—my nervous tick. When did I start to equate good hair with confidence? I comforted myself with my live shot ritual, jotting down the first and last sentences of what I was about to say. If I knew how to begin, and where I wanted to end up, what I said in the middle took care of itself. While some reporters memorized their live shots, I also saw them crash and burn, on live TV, stumbling badly if any distraction took them off-script. Better to stay loose.

I faced the camera, tucked my earpiece in, and while I savored the familiar CNN theme music playing after the commercial, I visualized going live, speaking to millions of people who will never know me, never really understand or care how unstoppable I felt reporting the news. And with an exclusive story like this, I owned the air itself. For two minutes, I mattered. The control room team, poised, listened for my cues. The executives in morning meetings stopped to unmute their televisions and be captivated by their correspondent and the Taliban fighter who aimed for her.

"Coming to you in thirty!" Senior Executive Producer Jodi Fleisig's commanding voice was in my ear. Jodi and I had met three years before when management introduced her as the new executive to run CNN's new morning show, *Early Edition*, and since then, she'd become my best friend. A brassy New Yorker with a Long Island twist, Jodi ran the control room like she, and not the corporate bosses, owned it. Her confident voice had guided me on 9/11 when we knew nothing more than the World Trade Center was on fire. We were like sisters, and we barked at each other like them, too.

"Hey babe!" she came in through my ear. "Don't screw me. I've got a tight show. You've got sixty seconds, plus another thirty for Q and A."

But I knew being the lead meant I could mess with Jodi's timing, just a little.

"Yes, ma'am!" I said. "My exclusive life-or-death situation in ninety seconds. Copy that!"

"Don't give me that shit, Carol. Listen to me this time! Kyra's your anchor. Love you!" Jodi made noisy kissing sounds over the open line so the entire control room could hear our girl-talking smack. I laughed.

I knew Kyra Phillips from our years reporting local news in Los Angeles. She, like me, loved the hard-charging undercover stories. Her numerous contacts with the LAPD slipped her enough exclusives to remind other reporters she was more than a pretty face with a pixie brunette haircut. She regularly kicked her competition's ass. Kyra would make this live shot fun while treating the news seriously.

"Carol, baby, are you ready?" Kyra said. "We're in commercial, but are you thinking what I'm thinking?" She conspired as if no one else could hear us.

"Yup! Go for it." I listened for her introduction and began my sixty-second play-by-play when the video rolled. Kyra followed up with questions about Afghanistan's border. Then Jodi gave us a hard "Wrap it up!" in our earpieces.

But Kyra kept going, a thief stealing precious time. "So, Carol, really, tell me how you feel? What were you thinking the *whole* time?"

"Well Kyra. . . ," I replied, and both of us were off and running, hijacking the top of the show.

Jodi didn't know whether to laugh or cry, but she definitely screamed. "You're killing me, you two! Fucking killing me!"

Time was a commodity for producers like Jodi. She'd have to cut thirty seconds from the White House correspondent or from breaking news out of the Pentagon—but she did, as I knew she could, and would, for me. As a reporter, I thought time was a currency too, something I controlled and spent. I bought it, killed it, stretched it, even wasted it. For the next two years, time seemed as abundant as ever, until it ran out. For Will. For me. And I found myself willing to pay any price to have more of it.

2. DEBT

If only I had known Will and I were not forever. But love—and journalism—left me with a hunger I could not fill. Perhaps it is because my father saw in me endless potential. He was the first to tell me it was possible to possess all the knowledge in the world.

"Lo-Sen," he said, "to know everything, all you need to do is read, and you can be anything you want to be. Anything." He used my Chinese name to emphasize the importance of what he was saying, and I took note.

When I was ten, he decided I was old enough, maybe even responsible enough, to own an entire Encyclopedia Britannica set. We unboxed them together, and my dad explained that the wisdom and wonder in those dark green leather-bound books was all mine. He lined up the encyclopedias on the center bookshelf, eye-level for a fourth grader like me, in our family room. The thick books stood at attention, like wise men waiting to spill their secrets. Every day, I ran my fingers along their textured spines and admired the subtle gold lettering that titled each volume, 1 through 24. I'd tip a volume off the shelf, flip the cover open, listen for the crack of fresh binding, and thumb through the crisp creamy sheaths, cover to cover, with paragraphs and paragraphs of narrative and facts that detailed the world's creations. To this day, inhaling the woody scent of new paper reminds me of buggy summer afternoons when I laid on scratchy wall-to-wall carpet, encyclopedia in hand, and imagined the world I yearned to experience in person.

"Careful! Careful!" my dad would gently reprimand if he thought I was too rough turning the pages.

"Did you wash your hands?" he would ask, fussing over smudges.

To Po Chen Lin, the books were sacred but also expensive for our family who budgeted twenty dollars a week for groceries back in the 1960s. Even still, I understood why he treated our encyclopedias like treasure. True to his word, they explained why the sky was blue, how diamonds formed, why fish swam but rare species could also walk on land. One night I snuck one of the books to bed to read about rare seashells, pretending I was the one marching around some exotic land, collecting specimens and writing about them.

Books stoked my internal world-building, but the advent of television brought the sights and sounds of the world itself into our home. The opening animation to the CBS Evening News became the theme song of my childhood, and the scattershot sound of the Vietnam War was synonymous with dinner time. *Pow! Pow! Come to the table!*

In 1965, the news still aired in black and white, making Dan Rather and Morley Safer's battlefront reporting seem less threatening, but by 1968, we had moved on with the rest of the country to the edgy reality of color TV, and at the same time, America began to look like a very crazy place. Long-haired, bearded men and braless women protested the war by setting fire to American flags, getting tear-gassed, and being hauled away by the police. My parents thought they'd left behind scenes like this when they fled China's civil war, only to question how far they'd really come. Of course, no flags were burning at our Safeway supermarket or the discount store where we shopped on weekends in our suburban Los Angeles neighborhood, but Walter Cronkite on the CBS Evening News was the most trusted man in America, and if Walter said young people were out in droves getting arrested, it was as real to my mom as if they were marching through our backdoor.

Yet, television news also gave her a glimpse of what was possible, even if she remained suspicious. Four years after the Civil Rights Act, women were starting to make inroads as reporters. When my mother first saw Connie Chung, a CBS Washington DC-based correspondent, she thought she was hallucinating. Connie, a Chinese woman in a gaggle of male journalists, was too good to be true. Her husky voice delivered hard news with credibility, but her pretty features made her singularly different from the men around her, and thus, in my mother's mind, made Connie an outlier doomed to be consumed by the white world that might prefer to adopt the petite journalist like a pet.

Regardless of what my mother feared, at least Connie had the pert good looks of an American success story in the making. My mom, who had anglicized her Chinese name to "Joanne," viewed enough TV to understand what was important to Americans, like the physical beauty that was possible with the right products. Television models dabbed creams and lotions onto their ivory skin. Maybelline made eyes look larger, L'Oreal covered the gray, and Playtex crossed hearts, pushed up, and promised to carve a woman's body into a plush figure eight. Connie Chung was up against all of this too, but Joanne did not believe any amount of cold cream or cosmetics could transform her daughter into one of those women featured on TV, so light and beautiful, with the golden aura my mother was convinced I'd never have. All the proof she needed was in a photo I had found in a desk drawer when I was little, of a baby with a head so big that it suggested a disability.

"Who's this?" I held the picture in the palm of my small hand.

"Aiya! That's you. You were *not* a pretty baby," my mom declared with such confidence after she hijacked mine. "When you were born, we said, 'I hope she has a good personality!'" My mother chuckled. It didn't seem fair to include my dad in this conversation when he wasn't home at the moment to defend me.

"Ah, but you're prettier now," she said, though never told me by what degree. Her point was clear: I was no Connie Chung. My mom was convinced I should level-set my life expectations, even as a pre-teen, and pursue the sciences. Be a good American, meet expectations—even if they are stereotypes. Work hard. Assimilate. She was a biochemist at Children's Hospital.

However, my father had chosen my Chinese name, Lo-Sen, meaning "goddess," to remind me of my potential and our Chinese heritage. He clung to his own Chinese name, Po, which sounded like "Bo" to our Caucasian neighbors, but he also gave me my American name, "Carol," because he predicted, someday, I would be memorable, like a song. Chinese. American. I could be both.

"Above all, you are a Lin," he said. "Always remember who you are, Carol!" Somehow, he knew even if I married (if I was so lucky!), I would find a way to keep and honor our family name.

I was eleven when my childhood ended with the wail of an ambulance siren. My father had suffered a debilitating stroke. A different man, quiet and prone to sudden, angry outbursts, eventually returned home from the hospital. Even as a child, I took in the grim inventory: a mind that needed to heal; our broken hearts; a girl without her father's inspiring words. The dearth of medical remedies for stroke victims at that time left my mother caring for her depressed, volatile husband. Her paycheck alone from her lab tech work had to pay the bills, including my brother's private university tuition, and raise me, a girl filled with the dreams my father had once stoked. I was bereft without my first love, my dad, the man who first believed in me.

The man who sat in our family room, slumped in my father's favorite chair, was a stranger now. Two years of physical therapy and still my dad struggled with forming basic sentences. He stared silently at the television whose volume was perpetually on low. I watched him through the family room doorway. He was physically present but emotionally absent—except when his fiery temper flared and made him throw bowls of oatmeal and flatware off the table, crashing to the floor and creating one more mess for us to clean up as he, a grown man learning how to feed himself again, wept. Our last conversations about the beauty of art and books existed like dusty still-lifes. To join him was to be reminded that our world-building was over.

"Your father loves you," my mother said. She wiped damp hands on a faded apron. "He loves you," she repeated, but with less conviction. "Give it time." She had her own worries.

How long do I wait? I thought. I craved what he taught me about the language of love; affirmations, the time spent together. Like the electric spark of lightning, it was there—and then gone. The man who inspired me to believe in an infinite world had shrunk. Yet, as I grew, so did the ambition he had already sown in me. Perhaps in this way, my father's love moved me forward. By my senior year of high school, the journalism bug bit hard. My mother concluded she had to be the one to bite back.

My father's stroke had only hardened her biblical tendencies to expect the worst. She pointed me toward what she believed I could reasonably attain: a husband, children, a house I could make a home—tangible goals with qualifications she understood. Perhaps *someday*, another scientist or, better yet, a nice Chinese American doctor would marry me. For that, I would need to build my domestic resume, so one Sunday after church, she laid out a glass bowl of shrimp, suspiciously gray in their raw state.

"Peel them like this!" she said and proceeded to yank tail after tail loose, shucking their milky shells into a second bowl. This was the opening act for her 'famous' garlic stir fry. As hard as I tried to hold on, the slimy critters shot through my fingers and skidded across the Formica table and onto the floor. The smell of raw seafood permeated the kitchen and made me nauseous. It was remarkable I didn't become a vegetarian which wasn't yet a big thing in the 1970s. But my mother kept trying, her cooking lessons only proving that I was an equal opportunity food annihilator. I burned rice, overcooked Chinese bitter greens, and turned tofu into mush.

"Stop stirring so hard!" she would cry. I was clumsy, dropping plates and shattering mixing bowls and whining that cooking made me smell like raw ginger and garlic. My mother gave me her *What am I going to do with you?* look—her forecast of my single, childless future spent supporting myself.

"Study engineering," she said one day. "You can always get a job."

"But remember, Mom? I'm terrible at math?"

"What about being a schoolteacher? Good job *if* you have children." Her hope I'd marry still sprung like the bamboo in our backyard.

"I'm not sure I want to have kids, Mom."

"Of course you do. What kind of woman doesn't want children?"

"The kind who wants to be a journalist?"

"A journalist!" She spat as if I aspired to be a prostitute.

I knew she loved my brother and me deeply, just not with the kiss-kiss embrace of American moms. She braided her love so tightly with corrective commentary, she believed affection and damning criticism were interchangeable. When I complained, my mom reminded me she loved me enough to pay attention. In this way, I had more of her love than I knew what to do with.

The news became Joanne's sharpest parenting tool. Every day she hovered over the morning newspaper, her fingertips turning black as she ran them across the headlines and searched for the most violent stories.

"You have to be careful, Carol. You never know when these bad things will happen to you!" She meticulously looked for articles about unsuspecting victims of random crime, cut them out with her favorite red sewing scissors, and taped them to my bedroom mirror like omens. Once, she came across a front-page story about students overdosing on LSD-laced potato chips and forbade me from going to high school parties.

For all her prayers to ground me and my devil-may-care career ambitions, my dad's early encyclopedic stories still had me hungry to fly in every way. I wanted her to be wrong—about my looks, my potential, who I could become. But my mother said the devil did care and if I was not careful, there would be hell to pay for my poor choices. So, when I moved out and into my college dorm, I exercised every ounce of my American free will to defy her.

"I want to be a reporter," I declared.

"There's a difference between wanting something and actually making it happen," my mother argued. She was not up for a conversation about a woman's right to choose her own life. Joanne Lin had accepted what she considered to be God's disruptive plan for her, and of course, whatever her mother thought best, even if that was to marry my dad, an older man whom she barely knew. Comparatively, my mom thought she was reasonable, even modern, to guide me toward a practical life. As a biochemist, she believed that set equations led to predictable chemical reactions. My mother fretted that a journalism career of subjective edits of words and pictures would lead me to be used or misunderstood.

"But I love to write! I'm good at it." I pointed to my high school and college essays.

"You cannot love words!" she replied and claimed there was no Mandarin translation for the word "love." She was sure words would never love me back. To her, my desires were fiction that belonged in television dramas or novels because filial duty was a fact, even if it made for a lousy plot. She thought I owed her this consideration but the more she pushed, the more I pulled in the opposite direction. She had to be wrong, she just had to be, because if I didn't prove my father right—that we could have all the knowledge in the world, that dreams could come true in America—then who would? This was my debt to the man who first believed in me.

3. FULL PRICE

When I graduated from UCLA, my mom taped a *Los Angeles Times* article to my mirror that reported my graduation year was the toughest since World War II for college students to find a job. She urged me again to reconsider my ambitions to report the news for a living.

Local news was expanding, as was a new thing called cable TV. Media entrepreneur and owner of the Atlanta Braves, Ted Turner, gambled that plenty of Americans didn't want to wait for their news, which made him the laughingstock of broadcast journalism. His fanciful idea for a twenty-four-hour cable news network was better known in journalism circles as "Chicken Noodle News," mainly because CNN operated on a shoe-string budget with inexperienced newcomers like me or many who'd been let go from one of the big three networks for one odd, possibly sordid, indiscretion or another. A producer from a competing network likened CNN staffers to the creature characters from the bar scene in the first Star Wars movie, which I thought was a little harsh. I felt a kindred spirit with these people. Like a baby bird, I was eager to fly under the wings of a flock of industry misfits. I became an intern.

My senior year of college, on the brink of my big life, I felt bolder with each mile I drove up Sunset Boulevard from UCLA to CNN's Los Angeles bureau, a straight shot into the heart of Hollywood. *Network news*. I was sure the sacrifice of an unpaid internship would lead to a big-paying job.

When I arrived my first day, I tugged at my gray cotton skirt, creased from the forty-minute drive. Dammit. But the hem hit below the knee, a prim touch for a college girl more used to wearing Reeboks and Dolphin shorts. The elevator doors opened to the lobby where I watched a rumpled young guy lunge for a ringing phone.

"Hello. . .!" he rasped with a chain smoker's throaty hack. "Hello, CNN Los Angeles, this is Matt." He held the phone to his ear like a cold compress to ease a hangover. "Mmhmm. Yeah. Okay. I'll let Robert know." He hung up and turned his bloodshot gaze at me. "And you are. . .?"

"Carol. Carol Lin. Your summer intern?" College me spoke in question marks.

Matt scribbled on a pad. "What's your last name, Carolyn?"

Oh, God. Stop. "It's Carol. *Lin.* That *is* my last name."

Matt grunted and rubbed his head, presumably to keep himself awake. Suddenly, an old-fashioned wind-up clock on his desk clanged and he sprung to life. "Shit!" Matt dove at it like a live grenade had landed and shouted, "Incoming! The bird's up!" He ran past me and around the corner, clutching his shrieking timer.

A tall man in shirtsleeves with a gray buzz cut rounded the corner. "What the hell?! Shut the fuck up, Matt! And get a watch alarm or I'm going to throw that damn clock out the fucking window!"

Phil, who I would soon learn was the bureau chief in Los Angeles, looked nothing like the buttoned-up coat-and-tie producers you saw in *All the President's Men*. This was not to be the network news I imagined.

Over the next few months, I also learned that a "bird" was a satellite, "feeding" video meant sending it over the airwaves, and a "bridge" was when you saw the reporter in the middle of their video story. I became fluent in news-speak or else would incur Phil's wrath. No time to train the intern. Don't even bother with complaining to human resources. That department was three thousand miles away in Atlanta and basically served as paperwork processors. Phil was a Vietnam vet. I was no doctor, but his abusive hollering and sudden rages made it clear he had a problem, like undiagnosed PTSD, and yet, I had a soft spot for him. He reminded me of my dad after his stroke, emotionally damaged but, I hoped, not a real threat. After I graduated from UCLA, Phil hired me as a production assistant making a grand $9,000 a year. That was before taxes.

A sweet Italian guy named Julio ran the live truck ("Ah-low, Caroleeeen!"), setting up live shots around town for two reporters and three camera crews. I yearned to watch them in action, in the field, as they say, but instead I was tied to the research desk and assigned to two chain-smoking former magazine and radio writers who were trying to make it in television news. Elaine and Robert lived on cigarettes and sarcasm and always looked mildly irritated, as if they had boarded the wrong train and didn't know how to get their reporting careers back on track. The pair tolerated me because I was young, cheap labor whom they could work until an early editorial death.

One day, when the story broke about Vicki Morgan, the mistress of the Bloomingdale's department store scion who was suing for alimony, Robert threw the phone book at me. Literally.

"Call every goddam person named Vicki in Los Angeles," he said. "Find this fucking Vicki Morgan!"

In 1982, Los Angeles had three million residents. The task was a painful waste of time that went something like this:

"Hi, my name is Carol Lin from Cable News Network. You know, CNN? Owned by Ted Turner who owns the Atlanta Braves?" That's how new CNN was.

What usually followed was some version of the following: "Carolyn, or whatever the hell your name is, there's no Vicki Morgan here. Don't fucking call back!"

I thought I was going to die from, if not boredom with the menial tasks, then humiliation.

"Robert, I'm halfway through the phone book," I said after several hours. "There's no Vicki Morgan listed. Or at least the people who answer won't cop to it."

Robert snapped his red suspenders, a dapper uniform from his journalism heyday, put his polished leather shoes on his desk, blew cigar smoke in my direction, and sighed. "Carol, Carol, Carol. Have I told you that Mother Teresa was the only person who ever said no to me?"

He'd only told me a hundred times, but I just nodded and pretended it was the most fascinating anecdote I'd ever heard.

"I still changed her mind. Mother Teresa."

Yes, Robert. You bullied an actual saint.

These early years were a grand lesson in never say no and never *take* no for an answer. Pick up the phone. Call. Call until your fingers bleed if you have to, until someone gives you what you want.

I kept working at CNN Los Angeles for a year ripping wire copy and getting hazed with similar research requests but quit after Phil and his temper tantrums increasingly focused on me. Then I tried my luck at a struggling local news station, KCOP, but that job lasted only a year before I got fired. I was supposed to be driving my career forward, but found myself in reverse, going from CNN, technically a national network, to local news, to then being unemployed again.

At least my brother, Stan, took after my mother and fulfilled his role as the firstborn and only son, earning his PhD at Johns Hopkins University. By comparison, I, at age twenty-six, shared a two-bedroom apartment near UCLA with three other girls and still took handouts from my parents but refused their pleas for me to live at home. I was an embarrassment to my mother who listened to her Chinese friends brag about their children in the midst of applying for medical school. She responded to my job woes with "Aiyas!" which I understood to be Mandarin for "You're an idiot! Get a real job!" Afterall, what was the point of my parent's immigrant struggle and sacrifice if their American-born daughter amounted to less than nothing?

There was a time, long ago, when my parents had dreams too. In 1945, my father was a twenty-seven-year-old Chinese student earning his PhD at USC with my mother, then a seventeen-year-old bride, waiting for his triumphant return to China to teach at the local university and marry her. My grandmother had promised her, the youngest daughter and arguably the prettiest, to my father, a decade older, in an arranged marriage on the condition my mom would finish college before she married. My grandmother, the widow of a wealthy landowner, could afford her daughter's education. So, my father departed their southern port city of Fuzhou to pursue an American graduate school education on a U.S. State Department fellowship. For five years, he wrote long love letters to my mom who swooned when they arrived in the light blue "U.S. Airmail" envelope at her Christian girls' school dormitory. He vividly wrote about wealth in America: "You don't have to go to the market stalls every day. You go to a grocery store where the shelves are filled with every need. Hsi Chuan, people live in houses on hills, and at night, they see the city lights that shine like the heavens." She never thought she'd end up in Los Angeles and discover for herself that post-World War II wealth and freedom happened only for a specific few.

But in 1949, Mao Zedong declared the People's Republic of China in control, and the United States severed diplomatic ties. My father's American PhD became a death sentence and his dream of a professorship in China ended with the communists' brutal persecution of anyone with an education and ties to the West. He became desperate to get my mother to the United States, even as a new phrase—*McCarthyism*—emerged against the rise of a red China and explained why the country that only a few years prior had welcomed him with a scholarship, now turned on people like him, suspecting them of being loyal communists—even spies—for their homeland. His PhD was worthless even here. But thanks to a notable Chinese-born USC professor, my father found a foothold in this new angry white world through an introduction to a sympathetic Beverly Hills physician influential enough to offer him a journeyman job. My dad became an audiologist at Kaiser Hospital, and surely the only one with a doctorate in English Literature.

Through his U.S. Embassy contacts in Taiwan, my father was able to arrange for my mother's visa. They had not seen each other in nearly six years. A half a world away, my grandmother interrupted my mom's college studies one day and told her to pack a bag. "Quickly! You're leaving tonight." My grandmother had hired a farmer to smuggle my mother out of China, across the Shenzhen River to Hong Kong, and eventually to the United States.

It was midnight when my grandmother tearfully said goodbye to her youngest daughter at their garden gate. As the story goes, she pressed a small silk pouch into my mother's hand. Its soft folds contained ten pear-shaped green jade pieces held together with a delicate ten-carat gold chain. The Chinese gifted gold and jade, believing a woman could wear jewelry in good times but have something to sell when times turned tough.

Perhaps this was why my mother believed that double joy was inevitably followed by twice the sorrow. Whatever a woman loved, whether it was her ancestral home, her family, or this jade bracelet, her love must be ready to yield to loss. One day, my grandmother knew, my mother may need to break apart this bracelet and sell it, piece by piece, to survive.

"Come home when it's safe," my grandmother told my mother as she urged her to learn to fly alone. How deep was her sorrow at letting her daughter go? Neither could predict it would be another twenty-three years before they saw each other again.

I loved my stern mom more when I imagined that tender-hearted girl at the garden gate, with one suitcase, kissing her mother goodbye and holding faith that farewell was not forever. I could hear with more compassion my mom's modern-day pleas for me to get my act together. She didn't have choices in her life; I understood that much. But now, she was angry because I had too many and so far, had failed at each one.

Joanne Lin finally, *finally* puffed up with pride when a satellite news start-up in Washington, D.C. hired me as a field producer and assigned me to the White House. The company, named CONUS, sounded more like a weapons system than a news organization but was the first to import satellite truck technology to the United States. In 1987, my starting salary was $20,000 a year, still not enough to live without roommates, but the job paid dividends in my mother's newest bragging rights. She casually mentioned Congress, the State Department, and Capitol Hill during dinners with friends. She waited until the main course to announce I was assigned to cover President Reagan, which was not exactly true. My job as a field producer was to do the off-camera grunt work and pick up interviews that my company's in-house correspondent needed when he wasn't available. Essentially, I was a glorified gofer, taking notes and shuttling videotapes between the White House and our office on K Street NW.

"So terrible I won't see my daughter more," my mother would say, shaking her head, her eyes demurely cast down as she took a tiny sip of water during lunch with her friends. "She'll be too busy working with the President of the United States."

"When you work *in* the White House, you have to look the part," my mom explained when I packed to move for my new job. I wasn't going to be on camera, at least not yet. Still, I listened when my parents offered to take me shopping before I left.

None of us knew what 'they' wore at the White House except for what we saw on the news. All the correspondents covering President Reagan—primarily men—wore dark suits and ties. But NBC's Andrea Mitchell's colorful jackets and skirts offered some insight. I assumed my parents were talking about suits.

When we piled into our gold Chevy Impala, whose color my dad thought fortuitous, even he had a lightness in his step, which still wobbled fifteen years after his stroke. We headed toward the May Department Store, the fancy place that didn't sell hardware, tools, and kitchen appliances in the basement but had the Library of Congress's hushed tones and soft lighting. It smelled like my bejeweled Aunt Dorothy, whose gems and fragrant natural beauty were as breathtaking as her decision to marry my father's brother, a handsome sea captain based in Hong Kong.

When I was little, my mom and I would go to the May Department Store "just to look." We would take our time, strolling through the well-ordered displays of designer women's clothing as if we belonged, stopping if something caught our eye.

We'd touch the softness of a silk dress or blouse, run the fabric slowly through our fingers, or select a shoe, nonchalantly looking at the price tag before putting it back on display. Whatever the price, we were the middle-class type who couldn't afford "extras," as my dad had called them.

Today, the three of us rode the escalator up to the store's top floor where they sold coats alongside the sparkling champagne flutes and China patterns. But not just any coats. The mink coats.

"What do you think, Carol?" my dad asked, palpably proud. My parents wanted me to fit in at the White House, not for a second stopping to consider that if I wore this coat, I'd look nothing like the practical suit-and-tie press corps. But they had also put some money away in a savings account for special occasions. And each time they looked at their balance, they imagined adding another building block to their American dream.

Besides, I made the mistake of allowing my father to think I sat in the blue theater seats in the White House press room. Since graduating, I had invested years in building a new relationship with him, showing him the next volume of our encyclopedic knowledge could be written with my journalistic license to ask questions and recapture the childhood magic with my dad. The reality was that, while based inside the White House, I was squeezed against the press room wall, lacking rank to be seated during the daily briefing. My parents didn't know that their daughter, in the Washington social food chain, was the equivalent of a burger and fries. How could I tell them their mink coat gift would make me the laughingstock of the White House press corps?

My mom and dad walked down the line of soft fur on display and touched the sleeves, from chocolate browns to creamy whites. The coats were already on sale, but my dad believed you should always get something for less. "You never pay full price, Carol."

He approached the saleswoman. She peered at him over her reading glasses and then pushed them up her nose with a shiny red manicured finger. Her eyes flicked from my dad over to my mom, who was busy taking coats off the rack one by one and viewing each at arm's length as if she needed the extra space to fully appreciate something larger than life. But I saw my parents through the steely eyes of the saleswoman: my mom in her polyester cloth coat and sensible shoes, my dad dressed in his blue and red checkered button-down shirt, insufficiently ironed by my mother and tucked into a pair of baggy brown trousers.

"Can I help you?" Her tone made it clear she had doubts.

"What's your best price?" my dad said, putting his hands on his hips and pulling himself up to his full five-foot-two height.

"The price is marked." She emphasized 'marked.' I blushed in agony for my father, who didn't feel the barb of her point.

"Take another two-hundred off, and I will buy it."

"No," the saleswoman replied more firmly than necessary. "Sir. The price is the price. It's *marked*." She spoke slowly, overemphasizing each word as if my parents didn't speak English. I felt the heat of a hundred past insults like embers still burning bright.

"Daddy, let's go," I said.

I was afraid he would lose his temper, which still flared unpredictably, or that this exchange would make his blood pressure rise. Even years after his stroke, his doctors warned him his heart could only take so much. But my dad stayed cool and pretended to agree with me. He believed we were being strategic.

"I'm leaving," he declared. "I take my money with me." He was halfway off the showroom floor when he looked back and realized the saleswoman didn't care. But I did. As much as my parents had wanted to shield me as a child, as an adult, I wanted to protect them.

"Sell him the coat, or I'll call your management and say you're discriminating against your customers," I said. This got her attention. I added, hissing through my teeth, so my parents didn't hear me, "Find a store discount, and find it fast."

"Sir!" The saleswoman quickly smiled, waving her hand like she suddenly recognized my father as a long-lost friend. "It so happens that I found a store coupon you might be interested in. It offers an additional twenty percent off our sales price."

My dad took his time walking back to the counter, satisfied that his bargaining chops, honed and perfected in China's bustling outdoor marketplaces, also worked in the May Department Store in Glendale, California.

"Now, we're talking."

Where the heck did my dad learn that phrase?

My parents fully expected me to take the white mink coat with me to Washington, D.C. where they thought the coat would keep me warm but, more importantly, show my status, which was only real to them. My dad paid a little extra to have my name monogrammed on its satin lining. *Carol*, it read, in loopy letters that swooped and curled. It was more personal that way, more specific. You would know this was "Carol's" coat— no last name required.

Only a few weeks after his retail takedown at the May Department Store, my father died from a heart attack. I was about to leave my office in Washington, DC when my mom called. "You better come home," she said. Her voice sounded faraway, fragile.

The doctors tried three times to revive him, but he had gone into organ failure. I hated that word—*failure*—as if my father, who fell disappointingly short of his own ambitions, also lacked the necessary will to live.

That night, I stared at the ceiling of my childhood bedroom where I'd spent my teen years imagining my great escape from my parents' probing questions, the dull, hot summers without air conditioning, and our strange foods that none of my American friends liked. The wind howled and scolded me for showing my dad so little of my true potential.

I was still young enough to believe that sadness lived on forever, and I returned to work and dragged that mink coat around Washington, DC like a furry shroud. I slept in it for its soft embrace.

Three months later, I was still deep in this messy, miserable, vulnerable state when I first laid eyes on Will.

4. LOVE

Will was more like a missile than a man—fast, dangerous, and unpredictable. Arms flying, he charged forward and almost knocked me down the first time I met him.

"Incoming!" he shouted to no one in particular, an echo from my intern days.

It was February 1988, and the presidential race was about to kick off in Des Moines, Iowa, where I was exiled from my White House assignment after I had deeply offended an ABC News correspondent by interrupting him and asking President Reagan a question. I had been crouched on the ground in my usual position as a field producer and sound tech when the president stopped to take questions before departing for Camp David. He was so close to me, walking from the White House residence to Marine One, which had landed on the South Lawn, that I had to take my shot. Losing my dad had made me bolder and more impatient. His death was a masterclass of how I should live. Wouldn't my father want me to set aside my good girl habits and, as Americans say, go for it? But the White House press office wanted to revoke my press pass for speaking up.

The Iowa Caucus was a fresh start and a chance to show my bosses I understood boundaries. I just had to run a tight operation and uplink our client TV stations' stories. Keep the subscribers happy, including Will, the senior political producer for our biggest client, San Francisco's KRON-News. At thirty-seven, he was ten years older and had the confident stride and fast-talking pitch of someone much more experienced than me. And now, he was demanding his way, which he was not getting as long as he kept yelling at me.

"Right now! We have to feed my tape *right now*!"

Will reminded me of the preppy wonder boys of my UCLA college years who sat languidly on their fraternity balconies, shirtless, drinking cold beer high above us mortals and most definitely beyond my social reach. He was That Guy. So confident. Privileged. I was the shy, slightly boy-crazy history major, with a bad perm and twitchy habit of tugging on the hem of my running shorts. I had no hope a guy like Will might notice me. But now, I was a woman. Well, okay, twenty-six, almost twenty-seven, but I was in charge in Iowa, not him.

"Just *a minute*. I'll be *right with* you!" Like a reflex, I steeled myself against yet another man, assuming that when he told me to jump, I'd ask *how high*. Since arriving here, I had had plenty of practice ignoring people who grumbled about working with me, a novice.

"Oh my God, not you," complained a cameraman as he dropped his equipment bag with a heavy thump in the back of the truck and slammed the door. These men were veterans with twenty years or more in the trenches of field news operations and I looked every bit like the new kid, the rare female news producer in my faded jeans and black turtleneck, hiding my insecurity behind rehearsed sophistication. My press credential dangled on a chain around my neck, but I hugged my clipboard with the crew assignments like a small shield. I was not going to let them intimidate me. At least, that's what I told myself while I pulled at the strands of my long hair that kept falling in my face.

But as I watched the crew in faded jeans pushing tables together to form our workspace, I saw a dream taking shape in a city famous for Midwestern corn and presidential politics. I loved the buzzy thrill of a newsroom—here, a vast convention hall where studio tape was laid tight across thick rubber cables to keep it flat on the carpeted floor, and the clatter of wire services pumped out reams of paper copy signaling breaking news—and the tight deadlines, and the heady, exhausting eighteen-hour days spent hunting down stories. This was my new life, brewed with lousy coffee and served with cold pizza. I loved it all—and craved the companionship of a big news story, however grumpy and skeptical the journalists covering it might be.

But things had to go right. My executive producer, Joe Benton, son of Walter Cronkite's legendary producer, Nelson Benton, was not going to tolerate disorganization or unpredictability. This plan immediately fell apart when Will and I nearly collided.

I knew Will by reputation long before we met in this crowded makeshift workspace. Our crew loved to tell the tale about Will getting thrown out of the company satellite truck in North Carolina during the Pope's U.S. tour because he was late to feed his tape and had yelled at our engineer.

"What an asshole!" I had laughed at the story. "Who is this guy?"

Now that I had met him, there was something unnerving about him. Sure, he had entered the room with a bang, but the way he rubbed his hands through his long, wavy blond hair made me strangely aware that I wanted to do the same. The hint of a California tan where Will rolled up the sleeves of his faded blue shirt added to his golden aura. If only he'd stop talking.

"Hello. Hello?" Will wanted me, but not for the scene that fleetingly flashed through my mind. "I need you to feed this story to San Francisco. Right now." He shoved a plastic video cassette in my direction. "Show's in four minutes," he added as if that should make me move faster.

"Sure. No problem." I gritted my teeth as Will fell back into a swivel chair next to the playback machine I used to connect the video to the satellite uplink. He briefly swayed back and forth, looking side to side like he was testing a chair at a furniture store. Satisfied, he slouched, tipped the chair back, and plopped his mud-caked shoes on the desk. My desk. My workspace. For a split second, I had an impulse to nudge his chair and throw this man off balance.

Will pulled a toothpick from his shirt pocket and was absently sucking on it while he rifled through his reporter notebook before he leaned forward, reached for our desk phone, and called his show producer in San Francisco. He waited until after he hung up to remove his dirty feet. His elbows and shirt sleeves rested comfortably now on my desk, littered with dirt and wet snow.

"Carol. It's Carol, right?" He fished around, patting his pockets, until he finally found a wrinkled business card and tossed it across the desk at me. "Here's my number." As if I didn't already have it. "I guess I'll see ya around, huh?"

At first, I tolerated Will's disorganized chaos because it was my job. I needed to earn my way back to my post at the White House. But something else simmered, like a fire right before being declared wild. When he was near me, I caught myself licking my lips and pulling my turtleneck more firmly into place. If our eyes met, I'd glance at him, turn away, look back again, and blush like a schoolgirl. When Will needed something from me, whether to book a satellite time or check the wires for updates, I shoved my hands in my jeans pockets to keep them still because they refused to settle in his presence.

"Are you okay?" Will asked mid-sentence after our morning meeting one day. It was our second week working together. I noticed his half-day stubble in the afternoon light and wanted to touch it. *Was it rough? How would it feel. . .*

"Carol? Does that sound like a plan?" Will tapped his pen, partly to get my attention but primarily out of mild impatience.

Now I had to figure out what plan he had in mind. "Yup. Yes! Got it. No problem. But you've got to be on time. Early even."

"I'm always on time." Will winked. "Early is too much to ask."

When Will caught me working on my reporter resume tape, he asked if he could watch. I chewed on the head of my ballpoint pen when he pressed play.

"Not bad," he said. "You might want to think about slowing down your narration. Don't rush the story." He rewound and watched again. "Not many visuals when you cover the White House. So, remember, even though it's the president, to the audience, you're the star. Find ways to be memorable, a small detail or the inflection of your voice."

I turned away and pretended to write down what he said, but I didn't want him to see the tears brimming. There it was, an echo. Be memorable, Lo-Sen, like a song.

I felt a kinetic heat each time Will returned to our workspace. He brushed by me as he reached for a fresh notepad, sometimes by accident, or so I thought. I smelled the spice of his aftershave and noted the graceful way he leaned and nodded with a crooked smile, like a kid who took a snack he knew was meant for him. Will's eyes softened when I was around. We were as aware of each other in the room as butterflies to bees in a garden fully in bloom.

"Will. Will! Where's the out?" His video editor, Gary, elbowed him. He needed to know where to stop the interview for the candidate's sound bite.

"Sorry. Ten seconds in. The out is 'democracy for America.'"

Gary followed Will's gaze in my direction. "Come *on*, man." Gary rolled his eyes. "*Really*?"

On my last night in Des Moines, I sat at the hotel bar. Perched on my mink coat to add height to the old wooden stool, I started some checklists to distract me from that lonely feeling that always filled the awkward space after one story ended but before another began. By then, most everyone had packed up to head out for the New Hampshire Primary. Across the bar, the usual journalists downed whiskey shots and, when the alcohol took hold, told war stories. Even when covering the news, surrounded by action and people, I felt alone.

Will took a seat next to me. He turned an empty shot glass in circles.

"Walden Pond," he said, startling me out of my to-do lists. "My favorite book."

"What?" I asked. "Why?" Will was not a man I could see finding solace in a book about a solitary life.

"'The 'mass of men lead lives of quiet desperation.' That's Thoreau's famous quote." Will raised his empty shot glass in a mock toast and tipped its edge to kiss the rim of my club soda. For a split second, our glasses pinged. "People dream, talk a good game, but in the end, most people just settle." He looked into his empty glass, wistful and sincere. "We may never see each other again, so no harm in toasting and making a promise." He raised his eyes to meet mine and bound us in a late-night mock toast. "Promise we will never, ever live a life of quiet desperation."

I nodded and raised my soda glass.

Half-sitting on the barstool, charming and wrinkled, I could feel Will undressing me with his eyes. But then he touched the rim of an imaginary hat and said, "Good night,

Carol. Don't let that club soda go to your head." And with that, he left without an inappropriate proposition for me to bat away.

Later, I went to his hotel room, ostensibly to drop off a schedule of events fresh off the wire services. I knocked lightly and then sensed him on the other side. The door opened.

"Hi. . . ," I stammered. I could hear my father in Heaven grumbling his disapproval: *He's not for you, Carol. Not for us.* Will was a blue-eyed, freckle-faced man-boy from corn-fed Kansas roots, unlike anyone in my family. *Don't, Carol. Not this one.* Yet, I persisted.

"Um. Just wanted to drop off the schedule for tomorrow." Who cared about a schedule when the caucus was over? "Uh, it looks like Gary Hart is still hanging out in the race. He's got a photo op in the morning, flipping pancakes at the breakfast place around the corner. Pancakes! How—"

Before I finished, Will took the wire copy from my hand and pulled me into his room. He left the door open. His hands gently holding my arms, he kissed me lightly.

"Come with me to Boston," he said. His eyes sparkled. "You don't even have to travel with me. Meet me there."

I began to protest.

Will added, "It's not like that. I swear. We can have separate rooms. I just. . ."

"Just what?" I wanted him to reassure me this was not a mistake.

"I want to *know* you. I want more time." Will dropped his hands and leaned back on the dresser behind him. "Tell me you don't feel there's something between us."

Will was unpredictable, unreliable, unbelievably cocky, breathtakingly funny. I never thought someone like him, all sunshine and light, could fall for someone like me, so dark and brooding, a total rules girl. We were a study in sharp contrasts: older man, younger woman; mentor and student. Will was everything my parents wanted me to avoid, so naturally, I found him irresistible. His eyes told me I was beautiful, a girl with potential. Because I saw it, suddenly, I was all that, and more. Between the snowy corn fields of the Iowa Caucus and the Live Free or Die spirit of the New Hampshire primary, I had found my version of forever, the man I wanted to marry.

5. MY CAROL

February 21, 1988
Dear Lovely Carol,
*   There's a strange, intangible, haunting something lingering in my soul. I didn't ask for it, but it's there and somehow deeply related to you. These past four days were a wonderful time and I'm not over it yet. The rumbling from within has left me standing, arms dangling, wondering, staring ahead into the night. Two people shared and loved deeply for a bit, when the beast of poverty and war, violence and mayhem of the news rested, a least for a while. The world was clearer. It took both of us by surprise. I miss you terribly and want you. I know, I know. I'm rambling. Send pictures and remember, we may have something that is bigger than both of us.*
*   Love and Thoughts, Will*

Will's handwritten letter, scratched out on lined yellow notebook paper, arrived only days after we parted at Boston's Logan International Airport. He returned to San Francisco, I to Washington, DC. His writing was as tactile as a kiss, with a tenderness that hummed in my memory of our lost weekend. The scent of him, the weight of his body on mine, still vivid. It had been a fast four weeks since we'd met. I didn't pause, not for a second, to consider how mismatched we were or that I still grieved my father's death with an unnamed hunger. Nor did I think about the consequence of my mother living alone and her new laser focus on me. I returned to my desk in the White House press room and found it littered with "While You Were Out" pink notes and I realized over the last two weeks, I had not checked on my mom.

My desk phone rang. "Where are you?' said my mother. "What are you doing? You said you'd call me."

"Well, hello, Mom," I said.

"Why didn't you call?"

"I'm so sorry. How are you feeling? How are you doing?" I almost regretted answering the phone. I absentmindedly scrolled the wire services for any breaking news alerts I had missed during the morning briefing. My desk in the basement of the White House press room shared an open space with Bob from NPR and the other Bob from Sheridan Broadcasting. They snickered and pretended to flip through their notes when they realized I was talking to my mother. Joanne already had a reputation among some of the White House press corps after she and my dad visited, wandering off during a tour, and the press office paged me after catching them near the president's private residence.

"You don't care," she sniffed. "You were supposed to call last night. I was worried! I thought you got hit by a car!"

I ducked lower behind my desk partition and whispered, "Someone would call you if I got hit by a car."

"What? I can't hear you! Who! Who would call me?"

"I don't know, Mom. *Someone*! Why don't you worry this much about Stan?" She never questioned my brother's whereabouts. Stan led a blissfully peaceful, independent life as a scientist working in New York while our mother hunted me down like a fugitive in Washington, DC.

"He's a man. He's fine." I imagined her eye roll as if this was obvious.

"Mom, you always should worry about the *quiet* ones!"

"Aiya, Carol! You make your brother sound weird. He's doing important work!"

She understood my brother's vocation to be like hers, rooted in science where chemistry and biology led to cures, and cures led to recognition. My mother saw my job as more secretarial. I spoke to people, took notes, and told others about my notes. My White House assignment was losing its luster as her friends' children entered medical schools and PhD programs. She wanted to know when I'd move on to a 'real job' in television, like the people in front of the camera. That was a job with award-winning potential.

The press office announced over the loudspeaker that the noon briefing was about to begin.

"Got to go, Mom. I'll call you next week. Promise!"

When I hung up, the two Bobs popped their heads out of their respective sound booths. "Was mommy mad?"

"Look in the mirror, boys," I said, grabbing my notebook and pen. "You have mommies, too! Make sure you call them!"

I ran up the carpeted steps to the briefing room where there was standing room only for junior journalists. The blue upholstered seats were reserved with name plaques for established news organizations: Helen Thomas from United Press International, who traditionally asked the first question, had the seat of honor in first position to the far right; CBS, NBC, ABC, and CNN occupied the rest of the front row. I stood in the back, a feather in the room full of heavy weights, and thought one day, I would earn my place.

I didn't tell my mom about Will, even as he and I alternately flew across the country to see each other. We calendared every available weekend for the next six months. My mother would have asked too many questions, especially about where he would sleep since I lived in a studio apartment. Add 'virgin' to the long list of what she expected me to be. As the years ticked by, she must have suspected I had kicked that ball deep into the end zone, but she didn't need to know the score.

The chaste life I presented to my mom was a necessary fiction, but my goals were tangible and real. I researched and wrote scripts, did on-camera stand-ups, and mailed my practice news stories to Will, who continued to critique me. He absorbed every word and every edit and shouted a big "Yes!" over the phone each time he thought I had nailed my editorial point. I glowed under his approval.

"Boom! You got it! Yes! You're making them *feel* your words!" he'd say with pride. He taught me ways to improve my editorial pacing with cuts of ambient sound: a train whistle, a split second of traffic, or children playing to make my story more vivid.

I honed my writing and worked on my on-camera confidence. I practiced doing stand-ups in the press room while the camera crews made me blush and burn with their "Aww, so cute!" remarks but I couldn't rush work experience. Skills took time.

Other things I could control. Even though I was twenty-seven, taxi drivers often mistook me for a teen, so I chopped my long, permed hair into a short, layered cut and believed if people thought I was older, they'd assume I was wiser, too.

March 8, 1988
Hello C.L.
I think of you constantly. We've been given something extraordinary and how we use it, I suppose becomes the story. There I go again - reducing everything to 6 ½ minutes of video where I worry about the fucking "focus." Hmmmm...I think you understand.

Waiting to hold you and kiss you and laugh, talk and share, a bit of love, a spot of time. See you in 23 days.
    Love, Will

The weekends I flew to San Francisco, Will met me at the gate holding seven roses. He decided six was not enough, but a dozen was a cliché. We'd tumble into bed in the mid-afternoon in his San Francisco apartment and make love before dinner in a city that smelled like fresh coffee, caramels, and salty air, and then wake under an eiderdown quilt he'd purchased after grad school while traveling through Belgium.

I would stagger, giggling at his jokes, to the kitchen for coffee. Will would pull on sweats and go outside to buy the daily papers. We'd spread out the newsprint across the bedcovers and drink dark brew in steaming mugs thick with cream and immerse ourselves in the pages of *The New York Times*, *Washington Post*, *International Herald Tribune*, *San Francisco Chronicle*, and the *Los Angeles Times*. Our minds engaged, our eyes would lock first on the headlines, and then always, again, on one another.

"Come here," Will would inevitably say, swiping the papers to the floor and bringing my face so close that his long lashes tickled my cheeks. "Let me see you." He'd stare into my very core, and I would know he loved me. I was his, seen and known.

He would lean, lips touching lightly, then more urgently, as if he sensed time was running out. It would not be long enough if I had a hundred years to spend with him.

On my first trip to San Francisco, the afternoon sun was still bright as we laid under Will's white cotton sheets, draped like a tent over us, and held aloft by a stack of pillows. We were kids at our pretend summer camp, spilling our secrets.

"I love this," he said with an exhale, lying back and poking at the sheet above.

"What do you love?" I knew the answer but craved to hear the words.

"You. Us. Being with someone who understands me."

"Do I?" I asked. I knew I loved Will for how he made me feel, but I didn't know much yet about his past. "Why did you want to be a journalist?"

He turned and propped himself up on his elbow and stroked my cheek. "I wanted every day to be different. I guess I wanted... more."

"More than what?"

"More than what my parents had planned for me."

Journalism ran in Will's family on his mother's side. It was fine for Virginia to be a lifestyle reporter for the *Washington Post* in the 1940s, to write about "women things" as she had explained to Will, then do the thing that was expected of women and quit her job to marry. Her wholesome Oklahoma beauty and natural intelligence complemented Bill Robinson's ambitions as a prominent partner in a local law firm in Wichita, Kansas. Virginia's reporting career morphed into the job of tending the family home and raising their two children, Mary Kip, nicknamed Kippie, and Will. He, their precocious boy, was expected to follow in his father's political footsteps. Kippie was expected to marry well, like her mother, which she did, twice, first to the owner of a car dealership, and then to a doctor.

Bill ran for the U.S. Senate as the Democratic Party's candidate and lost severely against the legendary Republican, Robert Dole, who would eventually serve in the Senate for twenty-seven years, including as Senate Majority Leader. Bill's loss was so predictable, given Kansas' overwhelming Republican majority, but it hardened his expectations for his namesake and only son.

He had already decided Will, a sensitive boy, needed toughening up for a world that cared more about winners than losers. Bill Robinson thought his son's childhood was making him soft. No future senator wasted afternoons riding their banana seat bicycle with little buddies to get ice cream or daydreamed by a river on hot, humid summer days. So, he sent Will off to The Gunnery, a private school in Connecticut to be educated alongside the children of New York's elite. But no Kansas boy was going to escape private school taunting. The kids called him a low-life hick. They poured ice on him in bed and mocked him as less than human. *Let me come home*, he'd begged his parents. They replied, *Chin up*. Their support was limited to room, board, and tuition.

Seven years later, after graduating high school from The Gunnery, Will ignored his parents' urging to apply to an Ivy League. He chose Southern Methodist University in Dallas and, eventually, earned a master's degree from the London School of Economics. Bill Robinson threw up his hands when Will finished grad school and backpacked across Europe for a year working as a hotel pool boy. Will was twenty-five when he returned to the United States and took a job teaching literature at a private school in Colorado Springs. But he fell in love with journalism, watching the local news. Will used a stopwatch to calculate the lengths of different stories and learned the difference between an anchor voiceover and a reporter package. Then he sat outside the news director's office until the man agreed to meet Will, who convinced him the station needed a film critic. Will's early years as a journalist were as simple as that, so different from mine.

I felt tears well up and watched as Will, misty-eyed, turned and asked me, "Do you think I did the right thing? My dad never forgave me."

"You did the right thing." I kissed his wet eyes. "This is your life, not his."

May 2, 1988
Dear Will,

Since meeting you, I've discovered a kind of courage to do what I've wanted to do forever, be a journalist, a reporter. I just feel this incredible life force. I love you, Will. I guess that says it all, from my heart. I had a wonderful weekend. It only leaves me wanting more.

Here I am back in the nation's capital covering the heartbeat of America without you. It feels strange. The distance between us can't dampen the inner peace I feel with you. I think my executive producer senses I'm going to leave. Everyone in the office knows I can leave if I really have to. I'm not bound by this job, by children (even if I had them, I'd swing them under my arm and GO!) My point is freedom. I may get knocked around in this job hunt, mostly by my own impatience but at least I'm doing something! It makes me feel so good about you. And that makes me feel good about myself.

Love, Carol

One Friday, Will picked me up at the airport and drove us straight to his newsroom at KRON-TV. Starstruck, I held my seven roses, their wet stems wrapped in newspaper, and headed up the elevator with Will. The doors opened onto a brightly lit, cavernous space filled with the clacking of news wires that pumped out copy. I'd never been inside a big TV market newsroom where producers, anchors, reporters, and show writers worked side-by-side, their heads bent over thick notepads in meetings about the bodies police found that day and where fires burned. It was surreal, a little morbid, and I wanted it all.

Will spun me around the space to give me a tour and meet his colleagues, including the new star anchor, Sylvia Chase. I recognized her immediately as a well-known veteran network correspondent from ABC News. From her desk, Sylvia eyed me over her reading glasses, unsmiling, her finger still poised where she left off reviewing her script. Her eyes darted from Will to my roses, and then she bore into me. Her lips, caked with lipliner, flatlined, like I was a lost beauty contestant wasting oxygen and space.

"Sylvia, this is Carol," said Will. "She's working on her reporter reel. She's going to be a star!" He added that last part to annoy her.

"Hi, Sylvia. I'm such a fan," I gushed. "Congrats on the new job!" I sensed Sylvia's eyes hunting for substance. I tugged on the waistband of my fitted jeans and smoothed out the wrinkles in my long-sleeved T-shirt.

Sylvia replied, "Well, before I took this job, I considered local anchors much like flight attendants—hosting, not reporting the news. I think I can do better. Wouldn't you agree?" Will looked concerned by how Sylvia curled her lips like she wanted to eat me for dinner.

"Bye!" Will said, steering me away from her. Then he whispered, "You're just as good as she is, Carol. You don't have to take her crap." I wasn't as confident, so I leaned on Will's belief to carry me forward.

I didn't know he had driven copies of my resume tape to all five San Francisco Bay Area television stations with a handwritten note for the news directors that read, "Check out this reporter." He enclosed his KRON-TV business card as an impartial Bay Area insider. By August, just six months after we met, KNTV, the local ABC station in San Jose, interviewed me for a reporting job.

"I hear good things about you, Carol," said Tom Moo, KNTV's soft-spoken news director, offering me a seat in his office that looked more like storage for old newspapers and reporter resume tapes. He piled them on top of his desk, as well as underneath it. An enormous stack was on the floor, below a television.

"Thank you, Tom," I said. "It's great to be here." His office overlooked a small newsroom of about twenty desks crowded with phones, typewriters, and carbon copy paper for scripts. The two anchors shared the same space as the reporters.

Tom watched me absorb his cozy operation. "We're small but mighty. San Jose is the 114th TV market, but we're geographically located an hour from San Francisco," he explained. "You get a forgiving small market audience while covering big market stories. No shortage of people who want to work here."

"I'd love the opportunity, Tom. I'm excited to be here," I assured him. The stacks of resume tapes mocked me from their corner. There must've been a hundred reporter cassettes gathering dust.

As if to make his point, Tom walked over to the pile and picked up tape after tape. Like a judge in an elimination round, he gave each reporter a one-line rejection.

"Too squeaky. Too arrogant. Qualified, but not the right look. These show promise but need more seasoning. And a make-over." He tossed those cassettes in a different pile and sat on the edge of his desk and looked down at me, a classic Management 101 power move. "No shortage of reporters who want to work here."

My heart sank.

"But *you* pop on camera. And you've got the right look." I had deciphered those code words long ago. His reporter leaving for KGO in San Francisco was male but Japanese American. I was Chinese American—interchangeable. "You're still green. Let's see if you turn to gold in this market *if* you're willing to work hard enough."

"I am. Of course, I am. Whatever hours, any story you assign, I'm down for this." I knew by now that news directors wanted charisma and energy from new reporters. Still, more than anything, they wanted us eager, to relieve them from their disgruntled veterans who thought they should have made it to a bigger market by now.

June 10, 1988

Dear Sweet Carolito,

Just returned from the E. Robert Wallach interview. He didn't denounce [Reagan's attorney general] as expected but we'll start airing the interview on Monday at 11p as the big cover story with a copyright that makes all the bastard network competition have to credit our station when they take re-air soundbites. Have thought of you all day—like most days—but today with more energy and focus, realizing that indeed you will be coming this way to live, laugh and love. That gives me such a sense of life and hope and love, that we can hold each other every night, that our lives will have a chance to grow constantly and together. This is the day that I knew would come, and it has. This life is all coming together in a wonderful, strange way. Too late now to have any regrets. Time to look ahead.

Love You, Will

KNTV hired me as a significant news cycle hit, including the devastating Loma Prieta earthquake in 1989 that leveled parts of San Francisco and collapsed a section of the Bay Bridge. I was on camera interviewing a police department spokesperson about a significant arrest when the ground shook so violently, the police officer, my cameraman, Kevin, still rolling tape, and I were thrown against the cars in the parking lot. Viewing the video later, the shaking lasted nearly twenty-six seconds, long enough for buildings and freeways to collapse, and for fires to ignite across San Francisco's Chinatown and South of Market neighborhoods.

It was the first time I felt bone-deep exhaustion set in from the consecutive days of reporting. For weeks, I watched rescue workers pull people out of neighborhood wreckage while I interviewed families who'd lost everything. We profiled people killed on the collapsed section of the Bay Bridge. Fires fueled by broken gas mains continued to burn, bodies were found, victims profiled, then the blame spread like a cancer. It was someone's responsibility to prevent this scale of tragedy—the government, predictive technology, better building codes—and every station wanted to own the story with unrelenting reporting. The emotional magnitude was overwhelming. I lost track of days, dates, and time. Day was night. Night was day. It didn't matter. My station and Will's broadcasted updates around the clock for a month.

The physical toll had arbitrary but lasting effects on me. Even though I was only twenty-eight, I developed a short memory lapse that stuck with me for years, a kind of disorientation when it came to time. Days and dates eluded me. It was such a small thing, not worth mentioning to a doctor. So what if I couldn't remember? That's what watches and calendars were for. Trauma science was not a thing back then. Coping with mind-bending stress was the job.

In 1991, after only two years in San Jose, the Los Angeles Fox local station, KTTV, offered me a reporting job, shortly after the Los Angeles CBS station, KNXT, offered Will a job as managing editor. For both of us, working in the second-biggest TV market was thrilling and I was high on the perks of working in LA where I grew up. The news stories were deep and complex, the social scene more intense and glamorous.

One warm October evening, after a movie premier on the Paramount studio lot, Will and I found ourselves at an outdoor after-party under the stars. He was in a suit, and I was in an emerald silk dress, slinky and draped low. Turning on my heels, this way and that, as people called out to make introductions, I got separated from Will amid the small talk of a monied crowd, sipping martinis. I stopped and closed my eyes to quiet the chatter and sensed him near me—my man, my Will. We were intimates connected by an invisible string. What he saw, I saw. What he felt, I felt. We could never be lost to one another. *Open your eyes, Carol. Open them.* And there he was, making his way toward me.

"Hi," he whispered in my ear.

"Hi," I murmured back. Will pulled me into a slow dance and I laughed and rested my head below his shoulders. He smelled like spice. "There's no music, Will!"

And he smiled, "We don't need a song to make us dance."

By then, Will and I had dated for more than a year, and he had been promoted to managing editor and producer. Management was a good look. This was the perfect opportunity to introduce him to my mother.

"A what? What does he produce?" She scowled while I helped her pick cabbage for dinner at our local Chinese market. We tried to spend Sundays together, shopping in Chinatown for her groceries.

"The news!" I said. "Mom, you'll like him. I promise."

"He makes the news. What does that mean? Jeff is a doctor. He saves lives. You should get back together with Jeff."

My mom loved my college ex-boyfriend. I could hang Jeff's impeccable credentials from my mom's imaginary lanyard. He attended Duke Medical School and was the son of a Presbyterian minister. Even though he was not Chinese, Jeff was handsome, and his ancestry dated back to the Mayflower. She conveniently forgot he had left me for an English girl, a pop star look-alike with a mane of white curls, during his overseas internship.

I pivoted to Will's many fine points. "He comes from a good family and has a master's degree from the London School of Economics."

"*Anyone* can get a master's degree!" My mom huffed and pushed her grocery cart toward the fresh fruit to squeeze the papayas.

"*You* don't have a master's degree, Mom." Oof. That one probably hurt. "You'll love him. Give him a chance."

"Joanne! Look at you! You're *more beautiful* in person!" Will stepped out of the car, and in a single move, swept my startled mom into his arms, where she disappeared. She had finally invited him for dinner, and he rewarded her with a hug so tight, only her tiny gasp escaped his embrace.

"Ah! Will. Yes, nice to meet you, too," she said into his armpit. When he released her, she immediately clasped her hands to her heart, flustered and lost as to what to say next.

"Hi, Mom!" I leaned in to hug her, but she grabbed my hand instead.

"Aiya, let's get inside. It's cold out here. Will! Carol will show you to your room."

We spent the night at her house to make the most of a rare, slow news weekend. But shortly after midnight, the house rumbled violently. I tossed on my old bathrobe and headed downstairs. My mom pointed for me to get under the dining table where I should take cover. She moved to the kitchen and turned on the all-news radio station. Scientists were still working on the earthquake's magnitude. Will joined us from the guest room a few minutes later. He looked like he was headed to church; his hair and teeth were brushed, and he was fully dressed in a button-down shirt with cuffs, pressed khakis, a belt, socks, and shoes.

"I want to make a good impression," he shrugged as he crawled between dining chairs and joined me. We sat cross-legged, listening to the radio while my mom buzzed around, making tea. To her, appearances mattered, especially during a natural disaster that might test the limits of a mere mortal hostess. My mom shook the tea kettle and listened for the boil.

"Will, are you hungry?" She started to heat a frying pan. Both of us itched to get to our newsrooms. We didn't know the extent of the damage yet, but this earthquake could be a big story. Yet Will stayed put.

"Mom, you're not supposed to use a gas stove after an earthquake until we check for leaks."

She rolled her eyes, then smiled sweetly at Will. "That's silly! We have a guest."

My mother glided across the old linoleum floor to the refrigerator in her bathrobe and slippers. Her eyes flirted with the eggs, then the cheese. "Will, I can make you something. What would you like?" I watched a natural phenomenon that none of my dad's encyclopedias could explain. My mother was developing her own crush on Will. It was more than I could hope for; I had enough to worry about.

It was hard work establishing my own professional identity in my childhood hometown. I was the rare female Asian on the news, even though radio and TV reporter Sam Chu Lin had reported for CBS and NBC, Robert Honda reported for KGO-

San Francisco, And Ken Kashiwahara, an ABC correspondent, was a longtime fixture on the network. But Connie Chung was still The One. While I was now the one reporting in Los Angeles, Connie was three thousand miles away, back with the CBS network in New York, but it was as if she had never left LA because people genuinely thought I *was* Connie Chung.

"Connie! Connie! Look over here!"

"Aren't you Connie Chung?"

"Connie, will you sign your autograph?"

At first, I just smiled and waved. It seemed better, maybe even kinder, to let people think they had met Connie Chung, a real celebrity. It made them so happy. Connie's on-air presence probably made my journey possible, but there was no doubt that Connie owned the interstate. In this way, America accepted The One because it seemed unfathomable there might be more. There was not a single newsroom in America in 1990 that had more than one Asian reporter on the air, if they even had any.

But after a while, it felt wrong not to claim my identity. When I said I wasn't Connie Chung, people still insisted I was.

"No! No! *You're* Connie!"

"But I'm not."

"Yes, of course you are!"

"Pardon, but really. I'm not Connie. I'm Carol. *Carol Lin*."

"Huh?"

People were *so* disappointed that it was me, some unknown to them, that it wasn't Connie who had popped out of their earthquake rubble or covered their local crime. Their eyes grew wide, then their faces fell. An awkward pause followed. It took a few seconds for them to recover, only to ask, "Carolyn—what's your last name?"

At least my mother knew it was me on the air. She learned how to hook up her video recorder to the TV and pounced when the anchor said my name, "...Carol Lin with more.

Carol?" but stopped recording when someone else spoke, even if it was the crime victim. She was not interested in watching anyone but her daughter. As her collection of VHS tapes grew, so did her pride, and she lined them up on a shelf beneath her TV.

"There she is. That's my Carol."

My mother thought she saw me most clearly when I was on the news, endearing myself to look like the woman she hoped I'd be: dressed up, hair teased, a full face of makeup. She beamed with pride for the TV news version of me.

6. COLOR

In the 1990s, Los Angeles was one of the most racially diverse cities in the nation, which should have made me feel safer as an Asian American reporting on communities of color. But green was the color that mattered most in South Central, still hard hit by the 1989 recession. When a Korean grocer killed fifteen-year-old Latasha Harlin, two weeks after four white police officers viciously beat an unarmed black man named Rodney King, the tension between Blacks and Asians exploded.

Shortly after the assignment desk sent us to get a reaction to the jury verdict acquitting those officers, I was staring down the barrel of a .22 caliber at the corner of Florence and Normandie, where the predominantly black community became the flashpoint of the LA riots. The gun was just small enough to fit in the boy's shaky hand. He was, maybe, ten.

"Gun!" I shouted from the passenger seat. "Gun!" I grabbed and pulled the seat belt tighter across my chest as if Nylon could stop a bullet. My photographer stomped on the gas pedal, and our four-wheel-drive lurched forward. I heard the firecracker pop and the sound of a bullet striking metal. Thud!

"We've been hit!" I shouted, and he gunned the engine and flew through the stoplights. I patted my sides and belly and rubbed my arms, looking for blood. I tossed modesty aside and pulled at my photographer's clothes and searched for streaks of red. We were fine. The bullet must have lodged between the steel panels of our Ford Explorer.

We raced up Normandie back to our newsroom in Hollywood, past the angry mobs pouring out of apartments, houses, and stores where the televisions were on, and the jury had read its verdict. I called my news director, Jose, on a brick-shaped portable phone.

"We've been shot. Shot *at*," I quickly corrected. "I think we're okay. No blood." People threw anything they could grab at our truck as we sped through intersections—bottles, cans, bricks, scrap metal. "Heading north on Normandie. Crowds blocking intersections. We are headed back to the station."

"Be safe," Jose said. "You'll be back in no time." His calm was soothing, considering the madness around me. Jose was often our steady voice in a storm; his thick, dark mustache barely twitched when hotter personalities blasted at high volume.

We drove toward Sunset Boulevard. Through our windshield, pelted with soda cans and trash, was Hollywood Hills. Shocked and angry residents spilled into the streets. Children ran in their wake with small fists thrust into the air.

Before I returned to the newsroom, the assignment desk called to say my mother had called Marla, the senior assignment editor, to say that the station should keep me inside.

Marla had patiently tried to get my mom off the phone. "Hi, Mrs. Lin. We're a little busy right now." Calls poured in from crews situated around the city. Marla, familiar with my mom's habit of phoning the desk, transferred her to Jose.

"Jose, she needs to stay inside! Send her home. You have others!" My mom stated this with the conviction of a woman who'd survived China's war with Japan.

I flashed back to when I worked in Washington, DC and had flown to Los Angeles for a girls' weekend. My friend, Adele, found a note on her front door from the Hermosa Beach police department: "If you see Carol Lin, tell her to call her mother."

Back then, my mom had learned I was in LA after she broke the will of a seasoned journalist who answered the phone in DC, a man who once faced jail time for protecting his sources.

By the time of the LA riots, I was almost thirty-one and the featured nightside reporter. TV stations broadcasted the horrific scene of a white truck driver, Reginald Denny, getting pulled out of his truck's cab and beaten unconscious in the very intersection that I had just fled.

"Of course, I'm staying on the story, Jose. I'll deal with my mom later." I was weary just thinking about that conversation. "I'm only here to pick up a bullet-proof vest." I turned my attention to the haphazard pile on the floor outside Jose's office, where I dropped to my knees and rummaged through a pile of khaki-colored vests embedded with metal beads and plates. They smelled questionable, musty.

"Bullet resistant," Jose winked. "You mean bullet-*resistant* vest, Carol."

Holding a heavy, oversized vest, I sat on my knees and appreciated his dark humor.

"Funny, Jose. Very funny."

The vests I thought were purchased to protect us turned out to be as unreliable as the pundits pontificating during the trial of the LAPD officers. Most predicted a conviction, given the violent police tactics we all saw on the grainy amateur video of Rodney King's beating.

My photographer and I were easy targets for the angry mobs. The big van, heavy tripod, and camera gear made us vulnerable. As we exited our truck, surrounded by smoke from the trash cans rioters set on fire, he said, "Stand behind me while I set up." He felt protective but my past experience taught me a male crew's chivalry could come back to haunt me if I became locker room gossip fodder.

"I'm good. Thanks. Let me watch *your* back." It was only my gut feeling that the boy with the gun shot at me and not my white photographer. But if I dwelled on whether my race gave rioters more reason to attack, I'd lose my nerve to cover the story. I believed our camera and microphone made me a journalist with something to trade. Please don't hurt us; our nearly one million viewers will see your story.

Eventually, at two in the morning, after going live for almost ten hours, I drove home, coughing and smelling like smoke. I crept down La Cienega Boulevard, intersecting with Martin Luther King Jr Avenue, avoiding the debris and broken glass littering the streets. People were still looting shattered storefronts. They carried new sofas, mattresses still wrapped in plastic, and even washing machines down the street. Others scooped up bags and bags of groceries, boxes of baby formula and diapers, and moved boldly through crowds and streets lined with burning tires and trash.

Every local Los Angeles reporter made South Central LA their regular beat for the next year as if making up for lost time. The violence and devastation had caught us by surprise. We began hammering the LAPD with questions about police tactics and chasing down the mayor and city council members to account for the lack of funding for public schools and jobs. All the while, I questioned whether I, as a local reporter, was complicit for not looking deeper, not seeing sooner the quiet tensions building in communities rife with unemployment, poverty, and addiction.

Broadcast journalism was most potent when the audience could see historical events as they happened and hear directly from eyewitnesses. But for all the potential of television, it could also be a shallow medium. The viewer hotline, even during the riot, made it clear that my voice, apparently even my lip gloss, mattered to the audience. In general, they commented that I sounded too stern on crime stories or smiled too wide during happier features.

Jose, bless him, did his best to deflect the criticism. "We set up the viewer call line to allow the audience to vent. It's not about you." But it was very much about me, with comments that I wore too much makeup or not enough and that my hair was too short or too long. Most viewer comments focused on female journalists' appearance and tone of voice. The male reporters were praised for their journalism, with the audience 'atta-boys for that story about the gang round-up or their tough questions for the cops.

Being on camera should have made me feel validated. Instead, the exposure made me weary and wish for the confidence and breezy, blue-eyed, classic beauty of my fellow reporters, Jane Wells and Barbara Schroeder. They shared the same blasé attitude as Jose about viewer feedback. It was just information, but still, information used by stations to decide who or what boosted station profits.

Every morning, Jose posted the Nielsen ratings for the previous night's show at the newsroom entrance. The report gave the overall number of viewers for the ten o'clock news and the minute-by-minute breakdown of when viewers tuned in or out. I calculated the split second my story aired or the timing of my live shot and ran my finger along the fractional movement of a black line on a piece of paper. Did it rise or fall? Each posting was an invitation for blistering self-appraisal. I felt an urgency to take on riskier assignments, spend more money on a broader variety of clothes, and assess how I could be different but still look like I belonged, softly asking the hard questions.

I loved television's immediacy and ability for people to be seen and heard, not just quoted in a newspaper, but when I looked in the mirror and wiped the shine off my broad nose or critiqued my small, intense, brown eyes and round cheeks that begged for contour, I recalled the ugly baby in the black-and-white photo. I tried to remember these were the ethnic features that made me Chinese. Yet, no one on the air looked like me. Except Connie, whose pert nose and delicate face made her definitively pretty by American standards, even as she would complain later in interviews that male colleagues called her a lotus blossom. I felt a burning shame that even I critiqued the characteristics that made me who I was. It was the first time I questioned whether TV journalism exacted a price too high.

To competing reporters, my race gave me special privileges. "You're so marketable" was the racial dog whistle for a minority female in the 1990s, less than twenty years since the Equal Employment Opportunity Act. I knew I earned my way to the second-largest television market with a beast of a work ethic. Still, my competition acted like I arrived as management's casual affirmative action choice. These color-coded judgments had followed me all my life.

I was only four when I suspected there was more to me than how I appeared. First, there were my ghosts, according to my father, who sat me on his lap and told me Taoists believed dead ancestors lived inside us in their afterlife. I took this literally. I'd press my forehead up against my mom's full-length mirror to concentrate and see past my dark pupils. Would I see old souls dancing back there and serving tea? Of course, the closer I got, the less I saw. Everything turned black until a breathy fog erased my face.

Then, there were the kids at daycare. Every weekday, my mom and dad dropped me off at the entrance under the Disney-like Happy Land Nursery School sign where, in 1965, color established a social order. Pink was for girls, and blue was for boys. White dominated everything.

But the kids on the playground, especially the boys, were obsessed with my yellow. They were fascinated with my skin.

One morning, a gaggle of boys surveilled me from outside as I put my sweater and blankie in a cubby and then swooped and circled when I came out to the playground, where they ruled, and sat on a bench.

"Lemme see!" a boy demanded as he plunked down next to me, pinning me down by the hem of my skirt. I think his name was Tommy. But it could have been Charlie or Ben. Didn't matter. They were all the same. He raised his pale arm next to mine.

"Why is your skin so yellow?" he said. The other boys drew closer. I could smell the spicy scent of their dad's shampoo and the buttery, rich people's breakfast on their breath.

"Just cuz," I replied. "Can you *move*?" I tugged at my bumble bee print skirt.

Tommy/Charlie/Ben lowered his arm and moved from hue to shade. "You're dark. Where are you from?" He picked at a booger and flicked it toward the girls playing on the swings.

The other boys released a rowdy "Eeeeww" and ran in the same direction for a new thrill as the girls and their dresses swung higher, but Tommy/Charlie/Ben waited for my reply.

"That's a dumb question. I'm from Silver Lake. Just like you." I tugged harder and finally liberated my skirt. My mom, who sewed most of my clothes, had copied the style of the dresses sold at Sears. Silver Lake was a white suburban enclave surrounding a reservoir near downtown Los Angeles. The old guard referred to Silver Lake as a neighborhood in transition; once I had overheard the cashier at the Sav-On drug store talking about "those new people" moving in.

"Nah. You're not from around here," the boy declared as he pressed against me, daring me to push back.

"Yes, I am! Now move *over*!" Keeping territory was as crucial as claiming it. I had the bench first. The boy scooted away. It was a win—for the moment.

"Maybe you're a banana," Tommy/Charlie/Ben said. He pressed his finger to my arm, making the spot turn white before it bounced back to my golden tan.

"That's gross. I'm not a banana!"

"Oh yeah, you are. My dad says Chinks like you are white on the inside but yellow on the outside. See? You talk white, just like me." He cackled, I assumed, just like his father. They probably both liked the sound of their own voices. "Better a banana than an egg! Those are white people who are yellow on the inside. Communists!" which he pronounced *Comma-nists*. He pointed his fingers, shaped like guns, at me and made a ratta-tat-tat sound. Then he slapped my arm and shouted, "Cooties!" and ran away, and I was left alone on the playground with this new vocabulary.

These concepts were new to me—people living as bananas or eggs, objects to be peeled and consumed. Communists—I recognized that word. Those were the people my Chinese parents had fled. Chink was a new word with a metallic ring to it, like a chain.

My father spoke of natural elements that the Chinese found valuable, especially when combined. Iron for strength. Fire for warmth. Water for life. But this boy did not think I was made of metal. In this way, I learned the power of words and their multiple meanings, how people weaponized them so they hurt or closed minds. Bananas used to remind me of sunshine. I never looked at boiled eggs the same way again.

When I told my mom what these boys said, she just shook her head and muttered, "Americans!" Yet, she, of anyone, knew how important it was to present ourselves as all-American as mainland Chinese immigrants could be. She had stubbornly settled us where, in the past, Blacks and Asians had been banned from owning homes. She made excuses to her friends, who chose the robust Chinese community in Monterey Park, that she liked Silver Lake because it was close to work, but more likely, it was because she had something to prove: We were as American as anyone around us. Joanne Lin also became the rare 1960s woman contributing more than half of our family income. The extra money inspired her to adopt a taste for spaghetti and hamburgers and the occasional hair salon appointment.

But as my mother assimilated, she also clung to her traditional Chinese expectations for me. She dressed me in American-style rompers and puffy dresses and expected me to speak only English, "just like Americans," but then she demanded I be quiet and obedient "like a good Chinese girl." My mother stir-fried her judgments throughout my early life with comments like, "Stop being so loud!" or "You overthink like the Americans!" I found myself constantly slung between her Chinese past and my American present, ever and always having to sidestep between two cultures but never landing firmly in one or the other. To be white, or at least beige, was my safe bet. Walk, talk, and dress like them. Blend in.

Perhaps that's why journalism's impartiality comforted me. To be credible, I had to be neutral, color-blind. I liked to think my race made me more empathetic toward the steady stream of victims that lead local news, but a soft heart had no home in the business of hard news.

On any given day, I woke to the latest headlines screaming from my radio alarm clock and drowned my Cheerios in milk while I considered all the random people who had died the night before, usually murdered, overdosed, or in a car accident. What was their last meal? Their last conversation? The death toll was always the body of the morning show headlines before they got to weather and traffic. Los Angeles had an unprecedented bloody record in 1992. Over a thousand people were murdered, half of them in July and August alone and yet, the death count for me was routine over morning coffee. Death was a trending data point without names or faces. Compartmentalizing was part of the job.

However, there is one story that haunts me to this day. In 1994, a robber had raped the mother of a newborn in the quiet beach-adjacent town of Torrance. Her attacker had shot her husband as he tried to save his wife. Then the rapist shot her. The bullet ripped into her, then pierced her waterbed mattress. She bled and played dead as the water rose and pooled around her nose. She willed herself to be still, despite the pain, and prayed her attacker wouldn't discover her baby sleeping in the next room.

I read the wires that quoted the police report and felt weirdly transported by the grisly detail, like I was there, in that room, which of course, was impossible. My crew and I hadn't left the station. Yet, my imagination played out the crime as it unfolded. The husband had gasped for life while the wife listened to her rapist rifle through their drawers for jewelry and cash. *My baby*, she must have thought. *Please don't find my baby*. Unable to call 911, she had no choice but to lay quietly, even as her husband took his last breath. I hoped she knew she couldn't save him. She did what she had to, for herself and her child. I was rattled and asked the assignment manager to assign me a different story.

"Please. Larry. Something about this spooks me."

Larry looked at me quizzically and laughed. "Don't be ridiculous. You're the nightside reporter. Very funny." He waved me out and turned back to the show rundown. I was the lead story at 10:00 p.m.

When my crew and I arrived at the scene, yellow tape outlined the boundaries of where the young couple had started their family. The glare of the TV lights cast shadows on the white stucco and wood-framed windows with closed shades. A small heart of dried grapevines, interlaced with a blue ribbon, hung from a nail on the front door. Mike, my photographer, shot the exteriors of the performative crime scene: the slanted angles of police tape, the cop cars with strobing blue lights, and tight shots of neighbors whispering.

I had covered so many murders and deaths; I'd been to scenes where people had been buried alive in mud or crushed by buildings. But this story felt different. Perhaps it was the duality of each victim. The husband was both a father and a fallen hero. The woman was a wife and mother. The baby, an innocent bystander who escaped death but only by chance. They were a family, and fair or not, my gut told me their story deserved special care.

When the anchors tossed to me live at the scene, I tossed to soundbites with detectives and residents. "Toss it back to the anchors, Carol." The casual control room slang, friendly like beer pong at a backyard barbeque, undermined the serious eyewitness testimony. In my live shot, I avoided grandiose statements about the horror of what happened, or tropes about a community living in fear. What was the point of this story anyway? The police never caught the killer.

I imagined Will's gentle nudge that it's just the news business and sure enough, when I returned to the station, I found a note on my desk: *Remember, punch the delivery. You've got to sell the story.*

What was I—a circus barker for ratings? I wanted to punch back, but the note wasn't signed.

I called my mom on the way home—why, I don't know. Her reply left me even more uneasy. "Good fortune never travels in a straight line, Carol. What do you expect?" She believed that bad things happened to good people every single day. The yin and yang of the three of us was dizzying, my mother so black in her thoughts, Will so light in his general optimism and I, affirmed that if it bleeds, then that story will be the lead.

That night, I laid in bed, curled up against Will and tried to shake off the night. He lifted my chin, moved my bangs aside, and our eyes met. "Come here. It's alright, Carol." He saw I was still anxious and kissed me lightly on my nose, wrapping his arm around me.

"There was a baby," I said.

"Hmm?" Will made a sleepy noise.

I propped myself up on my elbow. "They had a baby. And I think. . . I think about how they just started this whole other part of their life." I wasn't sure where I was going with this. Will and I had never talked about babies. People like us, conditioned to live day to day, story to story, didn't make plans. We didn't even make dinner reservations.

"Carol, what are we talking about. . .?" Will shifted in bed and looked confused. "We're not even married yet."

Ah, that quaint notion that life happens in sequence.

"But. . . and I'm talking someday. . . should we have a baby? Is that something we just. . . decide?" I was only thirty-two and was pretty sure the clock ticking in my head was not the biological one. It was the ambitious one. I didn't even want a baby, at least, not right now. Maybe not ever. But what if Will and I made a conscious choice, here and now, and committed to creating a human life? Perhaps my mother's god would smile upon us. We could create our own luck. Manifest, manifest, manifest. Will and I had already become our own blessing.

"Let's talk about it." Will yawned and patted the pillow. "But not now. We've got time." He turned.

Click. The room went dark, the dim orange glow from the digital clock reading past midnight.

7. GOLD MOUNTAIN

In 1992, when race riots and then record wildfires scorched Southern California, I hardened myself to the daily grind. Meanwhile, Will made my mother go soft. Joanne was a whole other kind of person in his flirtatious company.

"Jo-Jo!" Will would call out from the car when we picked my mom up for dinner. "Are you still drinking? You've *got* to control yourself around me!" He would tease her mercilessly while she scowled and tried to recover as her God-fearing, church-going Chinese self before predictably melting into a girlish coed.

"Don't be so silly, Will! Stop!" she would giggle. Who was this woman? I only knew the Joanne who pursed her lips when I shared my day and she rewarded me with commentary on how I could do better. A detail as mundane as where I grabbed a sandwich between stories was an opportunity to chastise me.

"Aiya, too much salt in those American places. Why you eat out so much? You should bring food from home!" she would say, pinching her eyes closed. But food was how she wooed Will. Sundays had become our regular family dinner night if breaking news didn't interrupt.

One night, my mom took us to her favorite local Chinese restaurant, where a fog of sweet and sour garlic and ginger wafted from under heat lamps. The owners piled their stainless-steel trays with white rice, garlic rice, and fried rice, a mystery fish, sauteed beef, Kung Pao chicken, and over-cooked vegetables in a generous banquet for an all-you-can-eat price.

I sat across the table, watched my tightly wound mother beam at my boyfriend, and wished I could make her smile like that. Will was so unspooled and free, with his arm slung around my mom's delicate shoulders. He squeezed her and she giggled again. He loved my mother with an openness and abandon that she embraced even as she nudged away my hugs as me being needy. With Will, her worry lines faded, and her cheeks turned pink. She looked happy.

I wasn't jealous. Instead, Will's presence took the pressure off me being alone with my mom when she was most likely to unleash her untethered opinions about me. When Will was with us, I experienced the secret, magical parts of her. I heard her unexpected laughter, saw her at ease, and discovered her wicked sense of humor. This is how I had my mother's love. Perhaps, through Will, she felt mine. Like a loving trinity, Will bridged the distance between us and made us a family.

But my mother wanted to make it official. "When will you marry my Carol?" she asked him shamelessly.

"Soon, Jo-Jo, soon." Will gave her his usual wink.

The LA Riots postponed our first wedding plan. The Northridge earthquake delayed our second attempt. After the U.S. Air jet crash at Los Angeles International Airport, I was sure we were destined for a quick Las Vegas ceremony. I never saw myself as a bride anyway. I was not the girl who thumbed through magazines, dreaming of My Big Day. I bristled at the idea of walking down an aisle to be given away.

My mom, however, deserved to see her daughter in the floral puff of a white wedding. A year after that Sunday dinner, and five years after Will and I met, we took a leap of faith and put down a deposit to marry in California's Napa Valley and set the date for April 10. The day before the wedding, twelve federal jurors adjourned to deliberate the verdict in the second Rodney King trial—the civil one against the LAPD officers who had been acquitted in their criminal case a year before. The LAPD declared a curfew and devised an emergency plan for officers to patrol in seventy-two-hour shifts should another riot break out. We stuck to our wedding plan. Thanks to the generous optimism of at least two LA news directors, our guests attended with the guarantee of a one-hour flight back if all hell broke loose.

Our wedding day arrived with a blue-sky promise. The woody scent of centuries-old oak trees was intoxicating. Jasmine bloomed. The grapevines, still bare as they awaited warmer days, were stunningly beautiful in their thorny, sculptural state.

My brother Stan took my arm and walked me down the garden path to the sounds of Pachelbel's *Canon in D Major*, its classical violins melding together like the marriage of two souls meant to be. I knew Will was my person because we'd become each other's better half over the last five years. My body curved into his. My head nested perfectly on his shoulder. We just fit. He was my safe place. I knew I was his.

Every step down the aisle, I thought about my father and what he would have thought had he lived long enough to be here to place my hand on Will's. Five years had passed since he died, but the wound still felt fresh. I imagined my dad scanning the guest list, quietly calculating the social status of each name. Would he have been pleased? His eyes would've glistened as he wrapped my hand around his arm and walked me down the aisle, proud of me. Proud to be my father.

A bee nested on my skirt. Buddhists believe our loved ones returned to us in different forms. He was here. I knew it. My heart ached, even as it sang. Stan gently tugged me out of what might have been and on to the future I could make my own.

After the ceremony and traditional wedding party photos, Will asked for one more. He lined up his best men and whispered to them. My mom gazed with pride at her new son-in-law, who had finally made me an honest, married woman.

"Three, two, one!" the photographer shouted. Before an aghast wedding planner and my mother, the men dropped their pants, bent over, and mooned the camera. *Click!* In a flash, Will broke tradition because where's the fun if you care what people think?

It didn't matter to Will that our friends saw the mismatch when we had met, and so it didn't matter to me. He, the hectic, hard-drinking life of the party, who fell for practical, tea-toddling, stoic little me. Our friends joked I was a German Shepherd, and he was a Golden Retriever—all bounce, light, and belly rubs. But now, my dark moods and his blond dazzle were inextricably wedded together.

After a short honeymoon, I returned to work and found the newsroom buzzing about new changes. Jose wanted to make KTTV, now called Fox-11, the go-to news channel for exclusive content and hired a mysterious man who looked like a lost sea captain to lead the new investigative journalism unit.

I first met Dan Leighton, fiddling with his faded baseball cap to hide his wispy white hair, at the station loading dock.

"Hi," I said. "Are you lost? Can I help?"

He looked at me, birdlike, through wire-rim spectacles, and waved absentmindedly, before he returned to the storage room he had turned into his office. I followed him, curious.

"Hello?" I repeated. "Are you looking for the newsroom?"

Dan stood by a long table covered with strange-looking gear, wrestling with the strap of a black messenger bag. "You're Carol, right?"

"Uh, yeah. Who are you?"

Dan continued as if we'd already met. "There's a house around the corner that I'm pretty sure is a brothel run by the Russian mafia. We should go check it out," he said as he yanked the strap to shorten it. That's when I noted the small glassy lens of a hidden camera in the side of the bag.

"Yeah? Okay. But again, who are you?" I looked closer at the bag but Dan pulled it away. "Is that a. . .?"

"It's not ready yet. I'm Dan. So, are you coming?" He slung the bag across his faded black T-shirt and shuffled toward the exit like just another drugged-out Hollywood character. He expected me to trot after him.

"Hey, wait a minute. I didn't say I was going! What's your name again?" But Dan already knew the assignment desk had planned boring live shots for me about the recent rains. He heard the click of my heels behind him, and kept going in his own loping gait, the remnant of a childhood brush with polio.

He stopped again. "Keep up! Different shoes next time, 'k?"

One day not long after that, Dan asked the assignment desk to free me from daily assignments permanently. "The Coast Guard just seized a small boat loaded with a bunch of Chinese immigrants on board," he said to me. "Don't you find that strange?"

"Maybe," I replied. It was Los Angeles, the city where strangeness finds a home. But Dan drummed his fingers, lost in thought. He sensed something big, so I took his lead. "Okay. Let's go!"

I didn't know I was walking into a story that was so close to my own.

The passengers on the boat came from the Fukien province in Mainland China, my family's ancestral home. The men looked like my father: tanned, worn, anxious, and, in their situation, scared. They spoke the clipped southern Chinese dialect of my parents. A dozen were dressed in filthy gray cotton pants and shirts, sweaty from their arduous journey to America. They had stood, jammed together and locked below deck by their captors, and traveled like that for weeks.

"Jie-Jie!" they cried out to me. *Big sister*. When Dan and I arrived at the Port of Long Beach, the men were in immigration lockup. They saw my Chinese face and American suit, and their body language pleaded for my help. I noted their dark almond-shaped eyes and felt the dreams my parents once had but I could not do anything for them except report their story.

They told a translator their smugglers had instructed them that a bus would come, and people would help them board a flight to New York, where they would work in shops and laundries. When border patrol agents asked about the smugglers, they went silent.

That night, my mom and I sat at our old Formica kitchen table, the same setting as my childhood dinners, with mounds of steaming white rice, stir-fried meat and vegetables, and fresh potstickers. We each had a cup of hot Jasmine tea, a traditional dinner drink. I described the boat, the men, and the mysterious smuggling operation and saw her eyes flicker with recognition. She had grown up with men like them.

"In our village, we chose one person to leave," she said. "All the families pooled their money to pay the smugglers, who had no names. They were known as the Snakes or Snake Heads."

I focused on my rice bowl, pretending to be ravenous. My mother sat next to me and because she drew closer, I didn't want to break the spell.

"How much did it cost to bring them to the U.S.?" I said.

"A fortune." My mom nudged potstickers around until she found a crispy one and took a juicy bite. "Maybe thirty thousand U.S. dollars? Usually, the families raised a down payment. The smugglers loaned the rest, but the workers had to pay off the debt. It might take many years."

"Mmm," I said, hiding my excitement, "this is delicious, Mom. So, why didn't you tell me about this before?"

She held her small ceramic bowl, pushing a little rice into mine, and placed a sprig of Chinese greens on my dish. "Our village is made up of sailors and migrants. We are used to seeing our people leave. Better opportunity." She looked at me. "They are not educated and only have their backs to support their families, so they do any work."

I twitched defensively but knew she was right to compare my privilege to their plight. By the grace of God, go I.

She continued, "That's why America is called Gold Mountain. They hoped for gold. But they are lucky to send even a few dollars home to China."

I covered her hand with mine; it felt soft and warm. I looked at her for a sign that my touch comforted her. She pretended to be riveted by the birds nesting in the orange tree outside our kitchen window, and then she abruptly stirred with productivity. "Ah! Getting so late!" She stood up, cleared our dishes, and scraped leftovers into a Tupperware for me to take home. Just like that, she was lost to me again.

Two months later, at 2:00 a.m. on June 6, 1993, a large cargo ship, the Golden Venture, ran aground in Queens and ended up on the shores of the media capital of America. The Golden Venture had sailed from Bangkok, Thailand, on a perilous four-month journey. Nearly three hundred undocumented Chinese immigrants were on board. A dozen drowned as they attempted to escape arrest. None of the networks covered it beyond the official statements by federal officials, who themselves did not know who these migrants or their human traffickers were.

In the meantime, Dan and I were well ahead of the breaking news. He had taught me how to use the undercover bag camera, and all three major networks received my resume tape with our Fox-11 undercover investigation. ABC became serious about making me a job offer that would put me among the less than one-percent of local reporters who ever make it to one of the Big Three networks in any given year.

Working for ABC meant stories like the Golden Venture would be the norm. I sensed the unmistakable pull toward the big life I always wanted. When I was nominated for a local Emmy for the three-part series we had put together, I felt like I had finally made it as a journalist, reporting a story that was meaningful to me and made a difference. As a result, local immigration officials began hiring Fukienese translators and law enforcement listened more closely to Chinese American officers who had first-hand knowledge of these boat people. Social service agencies looked at response plans and outreach in Chinese communities, understanding if there was one boat full of Chinese immigrants, there were probably more to come.

At the awards ceremony, I publicly thanked Will, the love of my life, my biggest cheerleader, and the man who believed I had talent from the beginning. He was among the first to believe in me, the man who orchestrated my first big reporting career break. He was my everything. How could I have known that, three months later, Will would become the target of a high-profile ABC News investigation?

8. AMERICA'S CUP

Disasters don't announce themselves. Even when all predictions say a community is in the eye of a killer storm, people still rationalize the storm will pass. It is only in the aftermath that we wonder why, how. In Los Angeles, 1994 began with sunny blue skies, but halfway through January, it rained non-stop for six weeks. A rare phenom of atmospheric high pressure near Oregon had smashed into tropical moisture from the southern jet stream. Southern California's streets became waterways; highways became rivers. Los Angeles was drowning.

My husband was dry in his newsroom but fuming. He had always been the popular ringmaster in a circus of anchor and reporter personalities, the guy who dropped F-bombs and used cursing as a form of punctuation; getting shit-faced at office parties was the way he networked. But KCBS had new management, and the latest news director was on Will's case.

As phrases like "hostile work environment" became more prevalent, the people who used to laugh the loudest at Will's jokes were, suddenly, nowhere to be found.

One night, I came home to find Will sitting in the dark. I dropped my canvas work bag, heavy with reporter notebooks, by our front door.

"Hey sweets, are you okay?" I turned on a light and rubbed his shoulders. His dark mood made our white slipcovered chairs artificially bright and our artsy concrete brick look grimmer.

Will absently touched his day-old stubble. "I don't want to do this anymore," he said.

A prickly panic crept up my neck. We had married, bought a house, and settled down. "Do what? What's going on?"

A human resource manager had told Will he needed to tone it down. His profane sense of humor had rubbed some people the wrong way, and HR had started a file on him because of a complaint. And yet, Will was mild compared to other men who ran newsrooms throughout the 80s and 90s. Some of the biggest names had set trash cans on fire or pushed people into walls, and they were called "legendary." But, by then, HR had grown in power as big media mergers formalized the unconventional break-the-rules culture of local newsrooms.

Will slouched and slowly chewed the tip of a ballpoint pen. He turned toward the lamplight. He was only forty-three, but for the first time, he looked much older than me. He rubbed his face again and ran his fingers through his hair. "Am I crazy? When did everything change?"

Will had just won his eighth Emmy Award for his documentary advocating for Congress to honor black dock workers who'd toiled in unsafe working conditions at California's Port Chicago in 1944. Still, in-depth journalism was expensive and time-consuming. Esoteric topics didn't attract viewers. The most recent news director clarified that he expected the staff to go in a new direction and wanted Will to work on a sweep series about online dating.

Will had made a hard admission to himself and to me that his latest Emmy was probably his last. "I had a good run—the best," he had said but his jaw had tightened. "I can't take it anymore. I'm on my third news director in less than five years. This one. . . this one told me to chop off the backs of the studio anchor chairs because he didn't like the shot. What the fuck. I'm the goddam managing editor!"

"Language, Will. Remember? Management wants you to work on language." I had smiled and reached across the kitchen table to playfully squeeze his hand.

"Fuck 'em," he had replied, as he leaned back and rubbed his eyes. "I am getting the fuck outta there." Will had decided to resign before he suffered the humiliation of getting fired. He felt in his gut that, while he was leaving the news, the news business had already left him.

Now the ring on my finger itched. "Will, shouldn't we talk about this? I mean, we just got married and. . ." My train of thought ended here, on a track that led to an unseen destination. True, I didn't marry for the picket fence and two-point-four children; I had wedded to fit my mother's world view, not my own. But I was with this man because I loved him, and I loved the journalist in him, the common language we spoke and daily headlines we shared and now, frankly, our combined income. "Well, who's going to help me pay for everything?"

That's when he told me about the year-long job in San Diego where he'd join a billionaire's ambition to win the America's Cup. My husband, who lived and breathed the news like me, wanted to join a sailing team.

The man who sponsored the team was the chemical titan Bill Koch, an MIT-trained engineer and heir to an enormous Kansas oil fortune. He had already won the America's Cup in 1992 and was now spending whatever it took to win the sport's most prestigious race again with the first all-women's team. He offered Will the marketing and media director job. Bill also happened to be Will's first cousin, although they were not close, so when Bill paid Will $250,000 for a year of work, Will saw it as a rich man's folly, not nepotism or a favor.

Will moved to San Diego. I kept to my side of our bed. *Nothing to worry about*, I told myself. Just one year apart. Four seasons. We were two peas in a pod temporarily split in two. Without him in Los Angeles, my days felt longer, and the weekends with him were too brief, but our invisible string had turned into an irrefutable bond.

Rick Kaplan, the executive producer of *ABC World News Tonight* with Peter Jennings, was in LA on business and had carved out time to meet me. At ABC, potential correspondent candidates had to be approved by five top executives. Rick was ABC's star executive producer who boosted the ratings for *Nightline* with Ted Koppel and, most recently, *Prime Time Live* with Diane Sawyer. At six-foot-seven, he was a head above his peers, a legendary creative man. I knew I had his blessing.

On a beautiful, crisp Friday night, I raced down the San Diego freeway to Will's beachside apartment. I opened the car door and grabbed my bag, taking in the pink-purple sky that peeked through a grove of fragrant Eucalyptus trees. I loved the sunsets in San Diego. The salty air tasted sweet as I ran up the wooden stairs, their worn white treads squeaking with each step, and pulled open the old-fashioned metal screen door. I tossed my duffel on the floor and ran to Will.

"Hugs! Kiss me; I miss you so much." I wrapped my arms around his neck and pulled him to the rug to share my good news, but Will pulled me up and steered me to a chair. A different gravity took hold, and I had to regain my balance.

"What's wrong?" I said. I felt the soft release of the chair cushion.

"I have something I need to tell you." Will sat in front of me and bowed his head. Were we praying?

"What *happened*?" Surely, whatever this was, it couldn't be that bad. And I still had my own big, breaking news. "What's wrong, Will?"

The America's Cup was a beauty pageant of sleek boats and tanned, athletic bodies, and Bill Koch was a generous sponsor. While his wife and son remained comfortably far in the family's Fifth Avenue home, Bill and his twenty-something-year-old mistress lived in a San Diego statement piece. The waterfront house had massive ocean views and expanses of white walls for Bill's art collection that had traveled from his Boston estate, along with his assistants, private chefs, and house managers. The bar was always open, and alcohol ran as swiftly as the racing yachts in San Diego's wide-open waters.

Will's voice was low and hoarse, as if he'd practiced for hours what he was about to say. There had been a late-night party. A drink. Maybe two. Or four. He couldn't remember much. A cute girl. Well, a woman. A young woman, he said. She'd wanted a ride home. *Can we stop and see Bill's place?* she had asked him sweetly. Everyone wanted to see Bill's place. *Was it on the way? Just for a few minutes. Please?*

"We got there, and inside, she pushed me against the wall. She kissed me, I didn't kiss her. But then. . . then one thing led to another. . . I didn't mean to. . . I wanted to stop. . . She wanted me. . . She was young. And. . . I. . . was drunk. . . It didn't mean *anything*."

It meant plenty to me. I wanted to slap him. And then, what Will said next torched all the love I had for him in that moment. His sex with a stranger was the news hook for an ABC investigation on the debauched lifestyles of the rich and sailing that was to air on the network's new magazine show, *Day One*. Will told me this woman had shopped her story about the behind-the-scenes at the America's Cup. ABC News had already been lurking around the Cup's compound, sniffing out a story about underwater spies stealing intelligence on the proprietary designs of the boat hulls. But sex, parties, and mistresses were much glitzier angles for primetime.

According to Will, the young woman claimed she had enough dirt on the Koch inner sanctum to make news. The ABC crew chased Will up a driveway for the iconic ambush-style video of a man running from the camera because he had something to hide. All this had happened in the last two weeks, while our long-distance phone chats had been regular, without a waiver in his voice.

"Maybe they'll just pass on the story. . .? Bill's lawyers are on it," he said.

I screamed, "Don't be an idiot. The visuals are great. The premise is juicy and tease-able. And everyone on video is good-looking. It's the goddam America's Cup, Will!" When did my husband become the news?

My deal with ABC News was not signed yet. My marriage and my career were two pressure systems colliding and leaving me soaked. Will thought the story was scheduled to air in a matter of days. Would ABC's management connect Will's indiscretion with me, their future correspondent? Would they care?

I stormed away and slammed the bedroom door. He was wise to stay in the living room. The thunder inside my heart had me shaking. I couldn't get enough air and sank to the floor— two breaths in, one breath out. I recalled an article about tricking your brain to stop a panic attack and grabbed for something soft to press to my face, a T-shirt. I inhaled, and Will's earthy scent flooded me and sent my mind reeling with memories of our first kiss, the way his hands felt on my body. I knelt and cried into his shirt and had a new understanding of what caged animals felt. I wanted to run, anywhere, for however long, however far. I needed to exhaust myself but all I did was stare at the ceiling, a blank canvas for my dark thoughts. How could this be happening? I rose from the floor and threw myself on the bed's rumpled blankets.

Sit up, Carol, I said to myself. *Sit* up. *You're not taking this lying down.*

I wiped my face with my sleeve, looked around and saw Will everywhere: the twisted sheets, his socks, shirts, and shorts strewn by the bed or tossed in corners, casually waiting for attention. I scanned the room for a way to turn my chaos into straight lines and squares. I scooped up the piles of Will's dirty laundry and began to sort, first separating the whites. Then I moved on to all the dangerous shades my mom warned me about that threatened to ruin everything you mix with them. Never, ever mix colors with whites.

I pulled the deep blues, earthy reds, browns, and blacks and set them aside. The whites were so filthy that I doubted they would ever come clean. I flipped Will's crew socks into dirty balls and fantasized about stuffing them down his throat.

I remembered how my mom would wag her finger at little-girl me in Sears's children's section when I would zoom over to the white dresses. They reminded me of fresh snow or vanilla ice cream. "Too hard to keep clean!" she would caution. "Not practical because you have to replace them every year!"

Satisfied that I had formed neat piles out of a mess, I yanked at Will's sheets and blankets and turned them back with knife-edge precision and then shook away the familiar indentation from the downy pillow on Will's side of the bed. As a couple, we always loved the smell of warm sheets straight from the dryer, our hands meeting in making the bed, the intimate ritual of him on one side, me on the other, pulling and tucking in unbroken symmetry to make a place for love, reading, and rest. I looked at my handiwork with clearer vision. The tears had dried. I felt Rick Kaplan's business card poke in my pocket. I carried it for good luck. *Rick Kaplan, Executive Producer,* World News Tonight *with Peter Jennings.*

My eyes burned again as I sat on the floor. Even with years of making difficult calls behind me—asking people for their time and tears, for the camera—I didn't know how to do this. I'd do anything to not call the man who had the power to change my career, and also to save my marriage. But I dialed Rick's number anyway, and I scolded myself to sound steady. With everything I had to say, I could not say it like a blubbering fool. He picked up right away.

"Hi. What's happened?" It's as if he knew. Did he know my cell phone number? He must have programmed it in, a good omen.

"Rick," I said. "I need your help."

I barely knew him. We had lunch and, yes, spoke for hours. Our connection was intense, but as editorial advocates. We had shaken hands at the airport curb before he bent to give me a bear hug. "We'll talk soon, Carol," he had said.

That was weeks ago. Now, it was two hours before his show. He sounded friendly but distracted. I quickly explained what I knew and that I *didn't know* if ABC even completed the story or had plans to air it.

"All I'm asking for is a heads up," I said. "Is there any way you can find out if *Day One* is airing the story?"

He was silent. Then, he thanked me for the call.

"You won't hear back from me, but don't read too much into it," Rick explained. "I can't discuss internal editorial decisions with you. I *can* tell you that ABC has an office specializing in news standards and practices, an internal neutral party that determines if a story meets the network's standards of credibility. That's all I can say."

I thanked him, hung up, and wondered what his impression of me was now. Was his subsequent call to the network's recruiter to recommend they pass on hiring me? All the years of building my professional reputation felt wasted if ABC's lasting impression of me was as a jilted wife. Why wasn't I smart enough to avoid this situation in the first place?

Three days later, the minutes ticked down to seconds as Will and I watched *Day One's* opening video, promoting the stories featured on that night's program. No mention of the America's Cup, no footage of Will running past the cameras with a furtive "no comment." He was in the clear. I worried the young woman would try to pitch her story to a different network, but the America's Cup race was over, Bill's all-women's team had lost, and the woman disappeared along with the headlines. Will had told me her name, and I cried. It was one of my favorites if I ever had a daughter.

I never knew why the story didn't air on ABC. Networks often shot footage and never used it. Networks shoot stories all the time, only to shelve them when the daily grind of competing stories made a hot angle grow cold.

All the while, our beachside apartment's once charming white clapboard siding and painted windows felt like a prison. My natural instinct to pull Will closer evaporated as new reflexes developed. We were no longer the teacher and student. He was no longer the more worldly one. He was the child who needed a babysitter, a grown man who needed parenting. Was that supposed to be me? I didn't know anything about parenting. I could barely take care of myself.

"Forgive me, Carol. Please forgive me," Will begged as I stormed back to the second bedroom and slammed the door after the show aired.

An hour later, Will knocked. "Carol?"

Shut up! I silently screamed. He should be worried. Very, very worried. I balled my fists. What was I going to do?

I told myself, *Grab the car keys and go.*

But I didn't.

You'll be in LA in two hours, Carol. Go.

But I stayed.

Every part of me wanted to leave. Dammit. Every part except my heart. I had waited to marry. I had wanted to be sure. We had dated for five years so that I could see Will for all he was, that time invested to be the social x-ray of his character. But we had had too many highs and not enough lows to test us. In every other aspect of my life now, I had agency, I thought, because I earned a paycheck. But all the money in the bank could not rewind how tied up my identity was with his or the sacred promise I'd made my mom. He was the one. For better or worse. In sickness and in health. Until death do us part. But now?

Will knocked again. "Carol, what can I do? What can I do to make this right?"

And I thought, *You can die, Will. You can just go away and die.*

9. ABC

I fought to see the reflection of Will and me in a single glass that was now only half-full. I hated him but loved him, too. These consuming emotions co-existed, like conjoined twins doomed to share the same body. Before, when I curled into him, I felt funnier, prettier, more lovable because he loved me. His gaze had defined me for so long, I didn't believe I'd recognize myself without him. I was the queen to his king, but as in the game of chess, a queen was powerful in her own way, responsible for attacking and defending her territory. Stupidly, I assumed I had nothing to fear. Will loved me. He said so all the time, all these years. But as my mother once told me, words can lie. Judge someone by their actions. When a woman gives, she needs to think hard about what she gets in return.

In her own way, my mother showed that love was transactional, even when I only wanted a hug. "Go brush your teeth, and *then* we can cuddle," she had insisted when I was a child. Love was currency in our home, for your labor, time, or something more material.

In college, sex was love for the minutes it lasted. Sometimes, what I thought was love could last for a few months, depending on the guy. But work was the love that lasted the longest. I loved my agent, Henry. I thought Henry loved me, too. We spoke every day, and he made me feel special. Of course, flattery could be an unspoken deal point in exchange for his ten percent commission of my gross, but still, Henry ensured a television station and I were hitched for a respectable duration. My contracts were almost always guaranteed three-year deals without "outs" or "windows," negotiation slang for when management could fire me.

Even though I thought Will was different, he had let me go that terrible night, without cause. I returned to Los Angeles, back to the work that was my therapy. Amid heartbreak, I was my best, most collected self when reporting someone else's story. ABC eventually hired me as a national correspondent. I signed a three-year contract that defined who I was. That goddam piece of paper said what I was worth. At thirty-four, I was a national correspondent for *World News Tonight* and *Good Morning America*. Will was unemployed. The disparity was my new power paradigm and bittersweet revenge. My new identity would take me far away from my old life, the one I had shared daily with Will.

I started my network career at ABC News' Los Angeles bureau but within months, *Good Morning America* moved me to New York. Will stayed behind in LA to pursue freelance documentary work. And I admit, it was easier to love Will in the minutes before I left him. Curbside at LAX, with the bustle of crowds and my urgency to catch a flight, the old pang of goodbye flickered with a quick kiss, followed by an embrace that lingered but only for a beat. Feeling the lift of first class and flying at thirty-thousand feet allowed me a fantasy that I had a quick-witted husband at home who waited faithfully for me with seven roses.

Any therapist would prescribe more time together, not less, to work through what had happened, to understand the warning signs, and to prevent another breach. But I just wanted to move on. I leaned in like a 1950s housewife and considered my options, which included the lie that "it never happened." It was foolish of me to think something so toxic would disappear, that Will's betrayal had no radioactive half-life.

After the America's Cup ended, Will returned to our Manhattan Beach, California cottage, the house we bought only eight months before to be our forever home. Forever felt elusive now. Returning to a house with so much history was what we needed. Its old wood-framed windows practically begged us to look past the rotted frames and take in the best the house had to offer: the view of the vast Pacific Ocean.

For Will, the 1940s house had been love at first sight. He had run his hands along the old tiles of the kitchen counter and circled back to admire the rough red brick fireplace. The home's age was her true beauty. The shingled roof, stained glass Dutch door, and wear-and-tear showing on the old pine floors boasted of family life and kids. We wanted that house and so did multiple suitors who engaged in a ferocious bidding war, even during the 1994 housing recession that cast a pall over Southern California.

Will had written a letter to the sellers that expressed how much their home reminded him of his childhood in Wichita, right down to the large copper stove hood and terracotta floor tiles and how his mother had recently passed away from a stroke and his father, in his eighties, had grieved himself into a steep decline.

The sellers were anxious to sell. "How do we know this is a solid offer?" they asked our realtor, Lorie.

Without hesitating, she responded, "Because Will loves Carol. And Carol loves the house." I did love its stormy history and salty resilience. Its weathered stucco was hand-troweled by the first owner, who doted on the place. He gave the architectural plans to his neighbor so he could have a view of its twin across the street.

The previous owners had cherished this house, too. It was more than just shelter, a tender word that conjured a safe harbor with more than four walls and a roof. Shelter is where you ward off danger. "Shelter in place" is the universal emergency management term directing people to stay inside when there are threats like an active shooter, tornado, or chemical attack. Does the door lock? Are the windows covered? Think of what you might need. Whatever you do, do not leave.

But that's exactly what I did when my marriage threatened to collapse. I left my house, my husband, our friends, and our life as often as possible. As a network correspondent, I took planes like people in New York hailed taxis. In my first year with ABC, I flew over a hundred thousand miles.

My gold wedding band gleamed in the New York winter of 1994, but my colleagues at ABC News couldn't care less if I was married. They just wanted me available. When producers needed me, they paged. These precursors to cell phones buzzed with tiny text on a narrow screen: *Call the assignment desk*, and I'd go from a pay phone straight to the airport. I kept a duffel bag packed in my trunk and another one in my office because there was no driving home first when New York told you to hop on a flight.

I woke, worked, ate, and slept in New York time. If the story was in California, and *Good Morning America* wanted me on air at 7:00 a.m. Eastern Standard Time, I woke at 3:00 a.m. on the West Coast and chatted on-air with hosts Joan Lunden and Charlie Gibson an hour later. I lived in hotels and existed on late-night pasta and pizza and covered the floods of North Dakota, then a Montana stand-off between the FBI and political anarchists, and then redirected to the Unabomber's arrest. Then, there were the months I'll never get back when I lived in

Boulder, Colorado after someone murdered a six-year-old pageant queen named JonBenet Ramsey.

I quickly learned the five senses the New York executives used to judge talent. Did I look the part? Could they smell my fear? When it came to taste, it was a question of whether I had the right look. My shoes already telegraphed that my heels clicking on the network's linoleum were manmade material and not Italian leather. One time a female executive producer greeted me in the hallway with a hug, and her hand traveled to my jacket sleeve, where she rubbed the poly-blend fabric between her fingers.

"Nice suit," she said. I knew she didn't mean it.

Keeping my job at ABC News came down to the right people seeing me on the air. But getting on the air was a moving target. As the newest hire, my future was in the manicured hands of one man, Peter Jennings, the star anchor and managing editor of the network's most influential broadcast, *World News Tonight*. Every correspondent got onto his program only with his approval.

Management expected each of us to meet an on-air quota, but with more than eighty of us stationed around the world vying for three coveted spots on the half-hour broadcast, being chosen was a weekly pageant of story pitches. Peter and his "Rim," the program's five editors, reviewed our story ideas every Monday. One typo and your chance for airtime that week ended up in the trash. If they didn't take my pitch, I had to wait another week and hope that breaking news in our geographic region forced the show to put me on the air.

During my first six months at ABC, while at the Los Angeles bureau, I worked with two senior correspondents who were Peter's top choices for West Coast stories. After months of Peter and the producers rejecting my story pitches, my bureau chief finally got a phone call for me to step up. The Ford

Motor Company was announcing the first all-electric car, a technological revolution. The EV-1 was debuting at the annual Car and Auto Show at the LA Convention Center.

"Have Carol package the EV-1 story. Peter's going to do script approval," the Rim editor told our bureau chief. This sent chills through everyone at the LA bureau, where it had been years since Peter hazed a new correspondent.

It was already ten in the morning in LA and 1:00 p.m. in New York. I had five hours to gather all my interviews, visuals, and on-camera standup. The LA producers scrambled for Ford's corporate footage of the EV-1 and pulled b-roll of generic freeway traffic to fill out the story. We made a few phone calls to vet the wire copy about the EV-1 and drove down to the car show to get soundbites. We had only two hours to edit the video and uplink the story to New York. All that delayed us was Peter approving my script.

When I called the Rim, the editor said Peter had left the office for a quick steam bath at his nearby club. He deserved the accolades and the high standards he'd set for his program and maybe even this steam bath, but he also needed to approve the top story for his evening program. Our bureau chief called New York again. Peter was still out.

It was 2:00 p.m. Pacific, only ninety minutes before *World News Tonight* aired on the East Coast when the phone rang.

"It's Peter," my desk editor said, motioning for me to pick up on the extension. I had been restlessly fanning myself with a paper copy of my script but, palms sweating, positioned it for my handwritten edits on the desk before me.

"Hi, Peter." I tried to sound casual, as if we spoke all the time.

"Carol. How are you?" His voice was smooth. My head ached, and my skin felt prickly.

"I'm good, Peter, thanks." I tried not to think that this was the Peter Jennings I'd watched and admired all these years, as if I had a schoolgirl crush. I had to make the right impression. I was smart, good enough. They picked me, hired me, warned me about Peter to prepare me for this very moment. Yes, I was ready. Or was I? Suddenly, my thoughts wound in reverse. What if ABC News hired me because their first choice had said no? What if they knew about Will and the America's Cup but my contract was already with the lawyers? No one looked like me at the network. Why did I think I could fit in?

Peter interrupted my spiral. "Let's see now. . ."

I listened closely to intuit his mood. Producers warned me it was a make-or-break rite of passage, the editorial version of fraternity initiation but without the booze. Peter asked me pointed questions about my word and video choices, poked and prodded for weakness in my facts. He asked me if I knew Leslie Stahl from CBS' *60 Minutes*. Was I supposed to know Leslie? Never mind, Peter said, and digressed into a conversation about how he and Leslie had discussed what made good news writing. Did this mean he found my script lacking?

I worried I was on the brink of exile, and then I heard Peter humming. He sang an unfamiliar tune, and under his breath, he read through my script again. He decided to steal my first graph for his anchor lead-in. Maybe "steal" is inaccurate since Peter practically owned *World News Tonight* and I was but one player in a cast. He ended our call without formalities. No welcome to *World News*. No reassurances about my story. Just goodbye. Dial tone.

We had forty-five minutes to edit, half the time necessary, and I was the lead story. The editors had to split the edit between two teams, each finishing half the story and then piecing the two videos together. My hands curled and uncurled. Open. Close. Open. Close. The heartbeat of panic. My chest heaved with the same elephant-sized anxiety I had when Will told me about his betrayal.

It was five minutes to air, and the editors were still not done. I was going to miss my deadline, but my role as correspondent was complete. My fate was in the hands of this team of producers, editors, and the New York control room. I could not control the passage of time. Being a mere mortal filled me with a specific dread. My God, I could get fired. But our bureau chief wasn't going to have his team miss our time slot. He called New York and offered up an electronic Mission Impossible stunt: hot roll the story into the live broadcast.

"Let's do it," the control room producer replied.

Pressing play to air two halves of a story into a live broadcast was called a double hot roll, which required producers in LA and New York to perfectly time when each video dovetails into the other with a fractional second for a margin of error.

Elaine, the producer responsible for supervising the edit of the second video, had curled into a fetal position under the editing console while her editor furiously laid down the final shots.

When two halves became whole on live TV, a roar rose from the newsroom. We hugged, whooped, and congratulated ourselves. I exhaled with a breath of life. Elaine picked herself up and left the newsroom. I found her in the parking lot, lying on the hood of a car, cigarette lit and staring at the sky. She let out white smoke that dissipated in the afternoon breeze.

"Shit," she said. "That was wild! Don't ever fucking make me do that again." She gave me a weary side-eye and then returned to stare at the heavens. Three thousand miles away at ABC News headquarters, no one cared what the LA bureau had pulled off.

I had yet to hear back from Peter Jennings, which was a good sign by some accounts. He never hesitated to let producers know when a correspondent disappointed him, so no news was good news, but it could be another month before I returned to his program. In local news, I was on every weeknight, and the slow pace of network news made me uneasy when it was all about being seen.

Then, one day there was a big Los Angeles story in the midst of the country's latest war on drugs. Actor Carroll O'Connor agreed to give *Good Morning America* an exclusive interview after his son died from a drug overdose. The two other LA bureau correspondents were out of town on assignment. It was just me available for a high-profile, two-camera, celebrity-style interview.

My interview with the actor caught the attention of the network's president, Roone Arledge, the wunderkind creator of the wildly successful *ABC's Wide World of Sports* who wanted *Good Morning America* to mix hard news with home-spun charm. After the interview aired, Roone wanted to move me to New York to see if I could add a newsy edge to *GMA* without alienating the audience, who expected cooking segments and soft-pedaled celebrity interviews. I wondered if Roone was having his Connie moment with me. This was 1994, and Connie had made history by being named Dan Rather's co-anchor for the CBS Evening News. I had gotten so used to churning through my career in Connie's wake that I didn't even consider that ABC might actually see me as an individual.

Different from *World News Tonight*, *Good Morning America* had only three national correspondents, and producers expected us to cover all the same big stories featured on *World News Tonight*. The morning show also wanted to personalize hard news for a morning audience. My assignments ranged from magazine show-style interviews to longer, more in-depth feature stories to round out the network's coverage on a topic. Suddenly, *World News Tonight's* drought became a torrential downpour of work for *GMA*. I appeared daily, often from different cities. I could be shooting in Tampa, get rerouted to Denver, stay up all night putting a story together, go live first thing in the morning, and then head to the airport for the next assignment.

Sometimes, I routed my flights through Los Angeles to occasionally sleep in my bed and check on Will, who had settled into our new/old house. Our neighbor, a house painter named Jim, was busy turning our brown wood paneling into a bright, beachy shade of white. Our fat slipcovered sofas twinned by the original red brick fireplace opposite a narrow galley-style kitchen where our new neighbors liked to perch on tile countertops, dangle their feet over the wood-stained pine cabinets, and wait for Will to pour another serving of whatever he was mixing up. Just as I had turned to work, Will had turned to our new community for comfort.

Riding in late from the airport one night, I heard the Rolling Stones' "Satisfaction" a block away. The beat was vibrating and soulful as it poured out our front door. I walked into a dancing crowd in my house.

"Carol!" Will roared from the bottom of a shot glass. He bobbed with the bodies circling in a conga line through our kitchen and down the hallway. I saw my friend, Adele, dancing with Jim, the house painter. This was the family Will chose, the people who watched over him when I was away and would comfort us more than I knew in the times ahead when we needed them the most.

10. FLYING

Dear Cast Member was how Disney, the corporate owner of ABC News, began emails. To the entertainment conglomerate, we were characters no different from Mickey, Minnie, or the Princess franchises. Internally at ABC News, *Good Morning America* was also a "family." Viewers loved to wake up to Joan Lunden and Charlie Gibson, who exuded the vibe of an old married couple. The affable meteorologist, Spencer Christian, was the humorous uncle, and Kevin, the newsreader, was the favorite son.

It was a dream and a thrill that terrified me when the producers asked me to substitute for Joan on Thanksgiving morning in 1995. The Thanksgiving Day show closed with our TV family sitting at a long dining table stocked with all the holiday fixings: a giant roasted turkey, dozens of colorful side dishes, salads, and candied pies and cakes. The red-and-white floral centerpieces surrounded a ceramic cornucopia bursting with real apples, pears, and oranges. Off camera, the producers motioned for us to take our seats, as one might imagine happy families around the country would also do, except we were digging into a turkey at 8:55 a.m. in a New York City television studio.

I was curious if I was supposed to eat the food for real. It certainly looked that way as everyone went through the motions of passing trays and scooping turkey and mashed potatoes onto fine China plates during the show's last few minutes. I sat across from Charlie, who asked me to pass the gravy, and so I did, and grinned back at him. Everyone cheerfully talked all at once, like siblings after a long time apart, grateful to catch up. My childhood Thanksgivings were never this abundant. My parents didn't like leftovers or the possibility of food going to waste.

When we all had big plates of food, the show's theme music broke through, and we lifted our glasses in a toast. Before we took a single sip, the producer counted us down, "Three, two, one. . . aaand you're clear!" The music stopped, and so did our Thanksgiving celebration. Like Cinderella at the stroke of midnight, Charlie, Spencer, Kevin, and a few of the show's interview guests set down their wine glasses and fled the studio with a wave and a *Happy Thanksgiving!* They were anxious to wipe off the thick TV makeup and get to their own families, who were probably just waking up. The floor crew pulled the dining table and food away, and just like that, the TV family I'd left my own family for returned to their real lives.

I had pretended that I, too, had somewhere to be, but instead I walked alone across Central Park. It was so cold the grass crunched under my boots, and I kept saying to myself, *That was great! Right?*

I bought a can of soup and a bag of donuts from the grumpy cashier at a corner mart and returned to my corporate apartment, where I sat on the floor, popped the top off my ready-to-serve meal, and dug in sloppily, straight from the can. The solitude was stark, almost enough to distract me from Will's one terrible mistake, now three years behind us. My cell phone rang.

"Hi, Stinks!" It was Will. I could hear my mom fussing in the background, pans clanging, her muttering about too much food. She was getting ready to cook. "You were great! We all just watched. I don't think our table will look as good as yours. How was it?"

I had told Will and my mother that staying in New York and co-hosting *Good Morning America* was a once-in-a-lifetime opportunity, but now I wondered if that was true. I listened to the laughter in my own kitchen three thousand miles away. We caught up, and Will passed the phone around so my mom could say hi and friends could wish me a happy Thanksgiving. And then it struck me that spending two hours on television before seven million people was the loneliest I'd ever been.

After three years at ABC News, my dream of becoming a network correspondent had exhausted me. Something was off. I had been flying non-stop for a week, with tornadoes in Tampa, more JonBenet "revelations" in Boulder, and a feature story about a town fighting hate crimes in Bloomfield Hills, Illinois. A familiar brain fog had set in. I had to leave notes to myself on my hotel bedside table stating where I was and what I was doing—*You're in Chicago. Your story is X*—because I had started having midnight panic attacks. I tossed and turned in bed and then fell asleep at work, including once, in front of the camera, seconds before my live shot.

"Carol. Carol! Caarrolll!!" The control room producer had shouted when she saw my eyes closed.

I was someone who once couldn't sleep on planes but now faded to black minutes after takeoff. One time, I kid not, I woke up to the meal service and found O.J. Simpson seated beside me. A jury had acquitted him of murdering his wife, Nicole, but he had just lost a civil lawsuit after a judge found him responsible for the death of her companion, Ron Goldman.

Grateful I had slumped toward the window and not toward him, I touched my cheek where drool had dried and wiped it with the napkin the flight attendant left on my tray. I hyper-focused on the stainless-steel cutlery, especially the serrated edge of the steak knife, since I believed O.J. killed his wife. Any correspondent at ABC would give anything to be in this position, but no, I was the one trapped on a flight with the most famous celebrity murder suspect of the twentieth century, and I wanted nothing to do with him. I unfolded a newspaper between us and pretended to study its two-page spread for the rest of the flight. This was *not* how a network correspondent should think, nor was I living the dream I thought was the life of a national correspondent. The constant travel and overnight deadlines of working *Good Morning America* made me anxious. Yes, a million other people would trade places with me. I told myself how lucky I was, so blessed, but anyone suffering from anxiety knows that telling yourself this stuff only makes the feelings worse. *Everyone else wants this; I should too. What's wrong with me?*

Typically avoiding annual check-ups under the guise of having so little time, I made a doctor's appointment. Even so, I had waited six months to do so. I felt like a specimen in the sterile exam room, such a foreign place for me. The doctor looked mildly disturbed at the near-empty pages in my health record, but at least I had made time for the blood test.

She studied the results and suspected I was developing an auto-immune disorder, theorizing that stress, long hours, and sleep deprivation may be contributing to an irregular heartbeat. "Let's try deepening your sleep to see if regulating your cortisol levels helps first. This means not traveling for a month. Got it? Meantime, I'll order more tests." She handed me a prescription for sleep meds, warning, "We want to be extra vigilant, Carol, given your father's history with heart attack and stroke."

I did have my father's heart alright, all his optimism and ambitions for our better life. His interrupted American story was mine to finish, the reason I'd even made it this far in my career. What if, as the Taoists believed, he lived through me, dancing in my dreams, believing we could be anything we wanted, despite the price of having it all? Perhaps in reality, we were two hearts joined as one but still broken.

At ABC News, airtime was the oxygen that kept careers alive, the necessary proof of life. You didn't just stop flying, something I had learned when I was four and my father showed me what it meant to take flight. His hands gently grasping my tiny wrists, he had spun me around in our backyard with its plum tree, orange blossoms, and a rugged patch of rose bushes surrounded by a silver chain link fence—our American symbol of "mine." The garden, however much it struggled, was my father's little haven, an escape where he grew fruit and flowers, if not his own ambitions.

It was a trip to heaven to feel the wind under my little girl belly and my short legs twist in the breeze, his grip rooted in my psyche that a man's hold on me was behind my momentum. I could hardly imagine my mother's delicate wrists giving me this much pleasure.

"More, Daddy, higher! I'm flying!"

He lived for this moment, to make me screech with delight; his smile was a trophy I collected on a tiny shelf at the center of my heart. But our spinning games also taught me about the pain of hard landings, like the afternoon when the garden suddenly no longer felt like an Eden. Daddy's hands, the ones that gently stroked my hair, spun me faster and faster and I grew frightened.

"Daddy, enough," I cried. "Daddy, stop. Stop!"

But he wouldn't let go.

"STOP!"

The more I cried, the tighter he held on and the harder he spun, until my tears were rolling thick and wet. I braced to fly headfirst into the thorny patch of bushes growing wild down the hill behind our house. He thought I was just playing, or worse, trying to trick him into surrendering. He wanted control.

"Put me down!" I screamed.

When he finally did, his treasured smile was replaced with disappointment.

"We're just playing. Your American friends have made you soft, Lo-Sen," he said, spitting out my Chinese name like a swear word. "Don't be a baby."

I felt a burning shame. Being flung into the thorn bush would have felt less painful. I wished too late that I had the courage to close my eyes and just swallow my fear. I watched him turn his back on me and head to his big chair in front of the television to select a better, more aspirational version of life.

All alone, my small hands balled into fists, my feet had landed in a dry patch of grass where the sprinkler always fell short. I wiped my tear-stained face, smearing perspiration and dirt across my cheeks, and swore I'd be braver next time.

Naturally, when my doctor grounded me, I told myself I just needed to be stronger. I needed to keep moving toward a more ambitious role, perhaps at one of the evening news magazine shows where I'd work on fewer but longer format stories and need to travel less. But making it onto a prime-time evening program was like asking to live among the Gods where the silky brilliance of Diane Sawyer set an impossible bar for both brains and beauty.

"They're never going to pick you. You will be disappointed, Carol." My mom shook her head earnestly when I came home for Christmas that year. "You are not Connie Chung. What makes you think you're different?"

Connie, again. I already doubted my news instincts after letting O.J. walk off that plane without giving him my business card.

"You, Mom. You made me think I was different," I said, my sarcasm light. "You always remind me that I am."

As the years had passed, her boasts about my globe-trotting life held less status with her friends whose children had children and visited their parents. Why couldn't I submit to becoming the dutiful daughter who cared for her as she aged? But she was right about one thing: My destiny was to be different.

At the same time my body was putting me on notice, my mentor at ABC News was giving his notice. Rick Kaplan was leaving the network to become president of CNN.

Rick hired several ABC News correspondents and a five-time Emmy award-winning executive producer, Jodi Fleisig, from New York's local CBS station, to run his new morning show, *Early Edition*. He wanted me to be an anchor, co-anchoring with CNN's beloved Leon Harris. Together, as an African American and Asian American team, we would kick off the weekday mornings of a new CNN. It was my chance to be seen in the context of something greater than a career move, to represent in a publicity photo that CNN valued diversity.

Being an anchor was less physical but more mental. I would cover the world from the anchor chair, until the biggest stories broke—war, presidential impeachment, historic hurricanes, deep floods—and then I could still report in the field. Rick promised I'd keep my journalism chops. It was a substantial job that offered a real life outside of it: making plans, developing hobbies, reading books for pleasure. There was only one problem. After three years of living on planes and in hotels, I knew how to reunite with my husband, but I didn't know how to live with him.

During those first few weeks, Will and I circled each other at our rental house. I kept bumping into him as if my body didn't know how to make space for my husband. Suddenly, my life called for grocery shopping, homecooked meals, and being the other half of nightly chats about the workday. My friends said this was marriage.

The CNN Center was everything I imagined an international network to be, with television monitors circling the newsroom with video from around the world and the daily hum of exotic names and places. But once I stepped outside, I was in Atlanta, a leafy southern city where there were more golf courses than museums and locals proudly asked newcomers if they'd seen the famous landmark, The Big Chicken, off Interstate 75. One day, I was exploring the city and asked a friendly stranger where Buckhead was. The famous Atlanta neighborhood has a strong history, distinctive antebellum architecture, and a sense of place—a place you just couldn't miss. He politely twanged, "You're standing in it, darlin'. This here is Peachtree Road."

CNN, a family-oriented company, grew fast in 1999 in response to competition from Fox News and MSNBC. The company offered Will a job as a documentary unit producer so we could transition to Georgia together. The America's Cup was five years behind us, recent enough for me to still feel the hurt but an eternity for Will, a guilty optimist who believed our marriage had weathered that passing storm. He hoped Atlanta, far from the temptations of California or New York, would be the right place to start a family, but I didn't trust he could carry half or more of the responsibility of a child. Will wanted a baby, but I needed a real partner. As the outlier wife who made more than my husband, my salary paid the bills. As long as my age teetered from thirty-eight to thirty-nine, I was still in my thirties—young, I thought—and had time to think about children. So, when the war in the former Yugoslavia ended just as I was hired by the world's most trusted name in news, I left for my first assignment overseas, not knowing that more than the war would end for me in Kosovo.

11. THEATER OF WAR

It was four o'clock in the afternoon, and my brain was heavy with jet lag from the last twenty-seven hours of air travel. Atlanta to New York. New York to London. London to Frankfurt. Frankfurt to Macedonia. The dress of the passengers on each flight reflected where they were headed. First, there were the tourists in fashion sweats juggling mixed drinks heading to the Big Apple, followed by a flight filled with businesspeople in dark suits on the red eye to London. It was the leg from Frankfurt to Macedonia where things started to get real for me. There wasn't the usual American-style chattiness of the Atlanta to NYC flight, only the severe reserve of passengers returning to their war-torn homes, traveling with chickens. Yes, there were chickens on board, in wooden crates with rope plaited into a braid for a handle, tied through the wooden slats, making the birds easier to carry. The airplane cabin wreaked of fowl and human sweat. I looked like a woman who boarded the wrong flight dressed in a black, stretchy top and black wash-and-wear slacks.

I nursed my jetlag with bottled water at baggage claim at Macedonia's Skopje International Airport, which turned out to be a small outdoor affair with a rickety conveyor belt grinding away in an oval roundabout. Macedonia's regional airport was the only one with a runway that hadn't been bombed to bits during the war. Assuming my ride showed up, I still had another two-hour drive to get to CNN's operations inside neighboring Kosovo.

More than thirteen thousand Kosovars died during the two-year war that displaced nearly 1.5 million Kosovar Albanians after Yugoslavia and the Serbian minority began a bloody campaign of violence and political repression against local Albanians fighting for autonomy from Belgrade's iron grip control. I could see the war etched on my flight's passengers' grim faces, husbands and wives with hollow expressions, holding tight their small children. For some, this flight began their journey home. Others were returning to investigate what happened to relatives during the war or properly bury the dead. I saw the human toll in their wary looks, how they stared back at me and my black duffel bag with the signature red "CNN" visible on my leather luggage tag. I felt like they saw right through me—someone who didn't know their hardship yet.

The crowd dispersed and thinned to a few who perched on a concrete ledge, smoking. The acrid scent of cheap cigarettes hung heavy. A twenty-three-year-old named Jason Bellini was assigned to pick me up, but I didn't see anyone resembling an American news producer, and I didn't have a cell phone to confirm he'd gotten the message. I didn't even have a phone number for the CNN bureau in Pristina's Grand Hotel where I would be stationed for the next six weeks.

Outside a quaint stucco building next to the baggage claim was a Visa credit card sign hanging on a metal shingle. How American of me to spot a symbol that signaled I could buy my way out of trouble. I was not a war correspondent by any definition yet, but I knew how to check into a hotel for a night and figure out how to get myself from one recovering warzone to another. Soldiers with different colored uniform patches, helmets, and hats milled about, including people wearing the United Nation's blue insignia. Maybe I could hitch a ride. My cheeks reddened at the fact that I'd arrived unprepared for my first solo international assignment.

Kosovo was a tiny autonomous province within Yugoslavia until 1989, when Serbia controlled it. More than half the province was agricultural. From the photos in research books I'd read for this assignment, Kosovo looked a lot like central California, with beautiful open fields bordered by vistas of the rugged Accursed Mountains that stretched to the Montenegrin border where I waited for a recent college grad to pick me up. I was starting to worry.

Suddenly, I saw Jason waving me over. Even from across the way, he exuded the bright-eyed earnestness of an up-and-comer. By the length of his wavy brown hair, I guessed he'd been in-country for a couple months already and I envied the freedom that youth gives us to just up and go, stay as long as we'd like, without question.

"I've been here," he explained, noting my impatience. His sweet, nervous gaze never left mine while he pointed vaguely to the other side of the luggage carousel. Not so long ago, I was like Jason—the newcomer. I relaxed, we shook hands, and I grabbed my bag to climb into a CNN SUV, crusty with mud. "I hope you don't need a bathroom," he hesitated, briefly turning pink, "or food. We have to stay on the highway. The military hasn't swept the fields for landmines."

Soon we arrived at Pristina's Grand Hotel, which was not very grand after the war but very gray: gray walls, dirty gray carpeting, and a dark-paneled front desk. But the hotel was bustling anew with journalists checking in, milling about, bumming cigarettes, and sipping espresso from tiny white ceramic cups while they pored over paper maps. CNN had set up a news bureau in a ballroom with portable edit bays, desktop computers, and all manner of camera gear sitting in heavy silver cases. Maria, who usually worked as the Rome bureau chief, headed up the Pristina operation. She handed me my room key and curtly explained that pizza and spaghetti were the safest things to eat since the local cows and chickens still grazed on grass laced with bomb residue.

"The eggs are probably fine, too," said Maria. "Eggs and bread for breakfast. Spaghetti for dinner. Don't shower with, or drink, the tap water." She handed me two giant jugs of water. "Shower with these. Sparingly." She paused. "Welcome to Kosovo."

The following day, I woke to the August sun baking me through the open window of my hotel room. Rousing myself from a dreamless fog, I heard the roar of a helicopter overhead. NATO allies coordinated responsibilities for security and rebuilding the city's war-torn infrastructure.

My first assignment was to cover an ethnic Albanian student rally at the University of Pristina. Before the war, the Serb minority had banned Albanians from attending college, but now the city buzzed with new beginnings. Thousands of students flooded the university campus, and my crew set up for a reporter stand-up where I walked across the university's central square to highlight the huge crowd. We sent my stand-up and narration back to Atlanta via satellite, and I returned to the hotel news bureau to an angry Maria.

"Atlanta is very upset," she said.

"Why?"

"You're in a Muslim country but wore shorts on camera. It's disrespectful. They killed your stand-up, but your story will still air. We can't waste the crew's time."

I was baffled and embarrassed that long khaki shorts that hit just above my knee were offensive. I knew Kosovars had a liberal interpretation of Islam, unlike say, Saudi Arabia. Meanwhile,

Maria tried to control her tone, given I was among the new CNN president's first hires. I hated that being in someone's shadow protected me when I should be able to do that for myself.

"Got it. No shorts. My apologies. Won't happen again," I reassured her, and then bit my tongue. This assignment was too important to pick a fight. Plus, there was someone new in our workspace.

Margaret Moth, CNN's legendary news photographer and one of Christiane Amanpour's favorites, had arrived. Margaret was funny as hell and famously fearless for getting the key shot. She, a lean tower of black in cotton capris and braless with a black camisole strap hanging off her shoulder, put her gear case down and took a seat. This was her fourth tour of duty in Pristina because she had covered the actual fighting, too. Post-war must have felt like a vacation.

"Well, hello there," Margaret lisped slightly. Half of her face was severely scarred from a sniper attack that had shattered her jaw seven years ago in Sarajevo. Yet, she was still a great beauty, with shoulder length, raven black hair, and piercing violet-blue eyes rimmed with kohl liner for full effect. Margaret vibrated with life and mischief. And she didn't treat me any differently than the celebrated international reporters she worked with regularly. But Margaret was about trouble: causing it, getting deep into it, and covering it as a photojournalist. She reminded me of Will.

It was Margaret, a gifted storyteller, who first introduced me to the extraordinary life on the road, decidedly free of family bonds and expectations. Other people buy rugs and ethnic marketplace tokens while on assignment. Margaret collected life experiences. Based in Paris but mainly traveling for CNN, she embodied why "what happens in. . . stays in. . ." is a saying. Not that Margaret had cared what others thought when she had seduced a young Buddhist priest, chaste no more after sex with her at the top of a mountain in Bhutan. She just didn't want to be alone drinking in life's pleasures. Margaret's cat eyes flicked toward the British press officer who arrived to escort us to a weapons cache.

"Margaret, I told you, I'm married," I whispered.

"Carol, darling, that's exactly my point!" she replied, louder than I hoped.

Margaret described the officer as *darling*, like a doll she wanted to dress. Indeed, Callum was gorgeous, unlike the PR flacks I had encountered over the years. Six years younger than me at thirty-two years old, he was tall and lean with big blue eyes and short, dark brown hair combed back neatly. He walked through our workspace in casual British Army fatigues with another soldier who was also young but paled by every other comparison.

"Hello, Carol," he said. "Captain Baird. Very nice to meet you." Callum's voice was like butter; his accent curled gently over my name and made him more like a Scottish poet than a military man. His thick eyebrows framed a softly angled face, and his aquiline nose cast him as more beautiful than ruggedly handsome. I usually did not notice such things about men. These were the intimate observations I made about Will.

"Hello," I said, hyper aware of my hand in Callum's as he shook mine. He was respectful as we stood only a few feet apart—professional as could be.

When Callum arrived to deliver the press release about a newfound cache of weapons, something about him felt intimate, as if I had known this army captain before. When our eyes met, I was a willow struck by lightning. Was it the jetlag? The foreignness of the assignment? It had to be. Perhaps it was the multi-car pile-up of domestic wife and daughterly expectations that waited for me at home.

Off to the side, Margaret slouched in a desk chair and petted us with her kohl-rimmed eyes. She telegraphed that Callum was my mouse who didn't have a chance.

To say I recognized what was happening would be to admit I was not the person I'd worked so diligently to become. I had been exquisitely mindful of my reputation and the burden of being a female journalist who wanted to be taken seriously in a male-dominated profession. I made sure my skirts were below the knee and held high expectations for my show team. I was never the subject of salacious gossip or party to some trope-y newsroom affair. Nor would anyone suspect it. I was the strait-laced, narc-y, goodie two shoes, married to the only conquest I ever had while "on the road." Besides, press officers and spokespeople were the enemy of impartial journalism, not to be trusted, and yet, never quite this gorgeous.

Callum was not the enemy but entirely something else. He was the primal drink I didn't know I thirsted for when no one else looked. What did I want from him? What did he want from me? Callum had arrived only expecting good press for the British army's capture of Kosovo Liberation Army weapons and then perhaps to enjoy my professional company. Unlike the men in my life, he didn't want me to have his child, or to take credit for my work, or confuse me with another well-known Chinese American female journalist. Callum didn't even know who Connie Chung was, nor did he care. He was my escape from the people imposing on me their opinions and their world of needs.

And when we met, all I felt was pure physical desire. I knew I wanted something to happen with this man, and worse, that I would make it happen, to escape my now predictable life and be my own character in a Brontë novel. He'd think he made the first move by asking me to dinner to talk about work and story ideas, remembering the coy way I had asked about local restaurants and my concern that I might get lost which, of course, was total bullshit. He'd insist he didn't mean to lean in so closely at dinner or again in his jeep, not realizing it was I who pointed the waiter to the smallest table outside to sit candlelit under the stars. I was the one who spoke in a low whisper that forced him nearer after sensing his propensity for impeccable manners. He was my mouse, just as Margaret had cast him to be, and it was pure pleasure and ego for me to act as bait and pull the strings. Did he remember how I brushed my hand over his collar to pick off a piece of lint that wasn't even there? Did he notice the sheer fabric of my blouse? When he turned toward me and our faces were so close, only our breath between us, there was no turning back.

Temptation was in full bloom before me, but more than chemistry was at play. I'd call it revenge. In the five years since Will put his lips on another woman, I had convinced myself that our marriage was mine to make or break. But now, I wanted to know what it felt like. What was so urgent and primal that made Will lose his mind?

I also thought I deserved this, like Callum was a reward, and not a person. I was in my element, far from home, drunk like a child fed wine or whisky, and so gluttonously full of myself. I was a CNN correspondent, co-anchor of CNN's morning show, and soon to return home to host a new magazine show. Both CNN U.S. and CNN International praised my stories (minus the shorts incident). The celebrated executive producer of CBS' *60 Minutes* had called the Atlanta International desk to compliment my reporting. I mean, I worked for CNN, the international standard for credible journalism, and people saw my stories, remembered them, remembered me. CNN International influenced the decision-makers, and for the first time, I saw my reporting in the context of a global conversation. All of this was reflected in the eyes of a handsome stranger in a place where oppression had given way to the cathartic release of unabashed freedom.

The adrenaline that flowed in Pristina was contagious. Every night in this war-torn city, young ethnic Albanians sang and danced in the main street, casting off the years under Serbian discrimination. At dusk, the square before the Grand Hotel transformed into a sunset promenade of revelers with festive lights strewn across the reopened storefronts. When the sound of gunfire rang through the hills, no one flinched. The war was over.

One night, Callum and I walked and swayed between holding a respectful distance and allowing our hands to brush lightly. The Backstreet Boys' "I Want It That Way" played loudly from a food market's boom box, and I threw my head back and laughed. Yes, I do. I want it exactly my way. I pulled him around the corner, and he laughed, too, those beautiful hands reaching for me. What came next was written in the summer stars.

12. RETURN

After a month of reporting duty, I didn't want to come home. I booked myself into a small hotel along Paris' Left Bank and hoped the City of Light would cast away the last four weeks of living in the shadows.

As I packed up in Pristina, I chatted with Will who happily said we should meet up in London. "It's still a nine-hour flight from Atlanta, but it'd be worth it. What do you think, Carol?"

I stuttered and said something about a girl's weekend in Paris with Margaret. "We planned this. . . a while ago. Just a quick stop. A couple more days. She's my photographer. . ." I mumbled something about manicures.

"But you've been gone for so long. I don't understand. I miss you, Stinks. We. . ."

I interrupted him with a harsh, "No!"

"What's going on?" Will asked more seriously, then softened his pitch. "I booked something special. Time together. Doesn't that sound good? Then we could see Tony and Sue. . ."

Any other time it would have been perfect to meet in our favorite city, warm ourselves in pubs, walk cobbled streets, and see family. But I said no, and Will was stunned. Then, rightfully, he was suspicious.

"I already booked my tickets through Paris," I stuttered. "Just a few more days and I'll be home. Then we can plan a better trip to London. Later. Not now."

I couldn't bear to see him. I needed a buffer, a no-fly zone where conversations about our future and motherhood were banned. We fought. He apologized for not being sensitive that, after the dirty job of covering a post-war city, I wanted to treat myself and get back to our Atlanta home sooner. Will's empathy made me feel worse.

I checked in to a boutique hotel within walking distance to Margaret's Left Bank apartment. "Key for one," I responded to the desk clerk, wondering how that number registered with him, but he was politely focused on my credit card and passport information. I took the narrow elevator up two floors and tossed my duffel on a chair, my brass room key clanging on the coffee table glass, and threw myself down on the soft queen bed. I longed for neither Will nor Callum. No, I wanted the woman I used to be who was so sure of what she wanted and how to get there. Be a journalist and reach the network. Check. House, by the beach no less. Double check. A partner, a man, his steady gaze on the best version of us. I closed my eyes with a mental TBD. A part of me thought twin affairs, Will's and now mine, balanced the scales of justice. Instead, my wound only re-opened and doubled in size. Hurting Will hurt me. Besides, who was I, if not the aggrieved wife, the righteous white knight against my husband's sea of black?

Margaret said to call when I wanted to get together, but that meant putting a face on all this and I wasn't ready to greet anyone with a smile. I craved the company of strangers to whom I would be a nameless tourist and headed downstairs for a long solitary walk along the Seine.

Margaret got straight to it over coffee the next day. "So how was he?"

"How was who? Callum? He was. . . nice. Interesting." I tried to leave it at that.

Margaret smirked, her violet eyes crinkling. "Carol, darling, you're a fool if you didn't sleep with that man."

"I'm a fool alright, Margaret." I sipped my latte and flinched when it burned my lips. "I'm a total idiot."

I insisted on taking a yellow cab home from Atlanta Hartsfield Airport and Will, surprisingly, didn't argue. The taxi headed toward my house and turned a thirty-minute drive through airport traffic into a swift fifteen-minute ride through town. I realized that soon, I'd be home, far from my marital crime scene. I'd just leave it where it belonged, in the past. I looked out the taxi windows at the high canopy of trees along Lenox Road. A quick right turn, and I was home. There was our white two-story cottage at the top of a long driveway. Nothing had changed.

I expected Will to open the front door at the sound of the taxi rolling up, but the house remained strangely quiet. When I unlocked the backdoor to the kitchen, I found Will standing at the bar counter, his back to me. Then he walked into the living room with a stack of paper, without even a glance in my direction.

"Will," I said. "Honey?"

"What the hell, Carol!" He stood before our fireplace and threw a stack of emails onto our hardwood floor. The printed sheets fluttered and curled in the air, dovetailed and landed between us. I didn't have to read them to know what they were.

"Did you see him in Paris? Is that what that was about?" Will held out his hands as if I had something meaningful to give him in this what-the-fuck moment.

I dropped my bag and froze. I wanted to turn and catch the taxi to drive away, hit rewind and rewrite the script, laugh at Margaret's warzone flirtations about Callum and then stick to the assignment. I could hold the moral high ground.

"Do you want him?!" Will screamed.

"It's just words. Those are just words. I'm so sorry!" How did Will find the emails? I thought I was so cool, opening an email account while in Paris. We will stay in touch, we said. He, across the Atlantic Ocean, couldn't be a threat but I had gotten in over my head with Callum. The mess on the floor was not just words. They were the aches and pains of longing.

"Who is he!" Will demanded. He crouched over the paper trail and began to cry.

The sight of him, kneeling, was like kryptonite. I went weak.

Afraid of what we'd say next, I tried to put on a poker face and play a liar's hand. "He's nobody, Will. Nobody. I'm so sorry. This is not what you think, not really."

I wanted to say what Will wanted to hear, anything to take his hurt away. But what happened with Callum meant more to me than just a fling in a dingy wartime hotel. On our last night together in Pristina, Callum and I had laid in my hotel room, arms entangled and mirrored each other in the dark. He and I were two sparks that came in a box of bullets. Nothing good would ever come from that. I was not leaving Will. I loved Will. Callum was not leaving his wife. Our relationship would be as brief as the peace in Kosovo before the province descended into chaos again. It had felt like love. It had felt real. But then again, all fantasies do.

Will thought he read emails of love and longing, but it was all make-believe dialogue. The messages read like two writers playing with different scenes, a little plot twist here and a little foreshadowing there. I was just some version of Julia Roberts from *Notting Hill*, standing in a doorway in a strange city and asking Hugh Grant to love her. Our words were for pleasure and a show. Callum said I was like smoke: there and gone. We both were.

The Pentagon refers to the theater of war as the setting for a strategic battle plan. Kosovo was my stage for climactic reinvention. With Callum, I cast myself as I had wanted to be seen, not as an on-air talent getting picked on by the international desk about her clothes or the old guard at CNN who saw me as a cold wind blowing in from New York. I wasn't the wife expected to give birth to a family or the daughter whose success was a constant surprise to her mother. There was no spouse waiving to-do lists, piles of laundry to be done, or, in my case, babies to be conceived and born; I was merely the witty American news anchor of a global network, a woman far from home. And I had never felt so free.

Will stood and turned his back. I couldn't see his expression, but he was a body of opinions; back hunched, arms crossed, his leading character energy exuded anger. I knew he was on the verge of saying it out loud, so I leapt first.

"No. No, no! Will, don't." Now I was the one who dropped to the floor. "Don't. . . don't leave. Please." I couldn't breathe. A force sucked the air out of a room filled with our family photos displayed on hard surfaces under soft lights. We had surrounded ourselves with textures that made this house a home: the smooth stucco walls, the melted wax in the crevices of our old pine dining table, the bowl of crushed dried roses whose scent had faded long ago. These were the remains of daily life.

Will pulled me up off the floor, and I buried my face in his shirt, clutching his back and sobbing, "Don't leave me. Please don't leave." After all that I had achieved in my career, and all that had happened between us, I still believed that Will was the best part of me.

13. GOING TO THE DOGS

Our home in the leafy Buckhead/Lenox neighborhood, once a cozy retreat of slipcovered furniture and wood-beamed ceilings, now housed our weighty comparisons. Who wronged who more, and did it even matter? Professionally, Will and I distilled complex stories into ten-second soundbites, thirty-second voiceovers, or ninety-second reporter packages—miserly timekeeping that producers considered generous. But our hearts would need more than time to heal.

One day, a few weeks after I returned from Paris, we thumbed through our health insurer's paper directory for a therapist. We selected a marriage and family counselor who worked out of her home close to our neighborhood and made an appointment for the following week. Neither of us had been in therapy before, and finding someone was like throwing darts. A therapist named Abigail sounded comforting; her home "office" was located at the bottom of a long curving gravel driveway off a busy road. The crunch of our tires alerted her dogs, who barked as we made our way to a charming house styled like a wood cabin with a bright blue front door.

"Hello! Welcome!" Abigail greeted us with a big pink lipstick smile and jangle of bracelets as she swung open the door. A colorful caftan swallowed her small frame in soothing shades of green and blue.

Yip! Yip! Four miniature terriers alternately jumped on us and then ran in circles. *Yip!* Abigail shooed them but didn't do much more to keep them away.

"Take your shoes off! Get comfortable!' She motioned to the pile of slippers by her front door. Frankly, I worried what the dogs would do with the shoes we left behind, but we complied and followed Abigail to a large sunny room off her kitchen, the sink full of dishes and the countertops covered with cookie tins, dog treats, and six-packs of soda. The room smelled of incense and musty, wet dog. A coffee pot quietly sputtered and dripped a steady dark brew.

"Coffee? Tea, anyone?" she asked.

"No, thank you," I said.

"Make yourselves at home." Abigail gestured toward two long sofas covered in mismatched blankets. I tried to make small talk, noting Will assessing the surroundings with skepticism. Abigail asked, "Will? Coffee?"

"No thanks," Will said as he stepped carefully over the dogs. The terriers running in circles at our feet broke away and leapt on the couches and gave an expectant stare at Will and me. We instinctively held hands, like we were about to get bit.

Abigail poured herself a cup of coffee, grabbed a notepad and pen, and sank into an oversized easy chair also covered in blankets but with its threadbare arms exposed. "So! Will. Carol. Tell me why we are here today." Abigail leaned back and crossed her legs.

Will and I glanced at each other. How do we put into words what we are going through?

I began, "I think we are trying to figure out if we should. . . stay married." Will winced. "To put things bluntly. Two months ago, I had an affair. Five years ago, Will cheated on me." I told Abigail the general details about the night of the America's Cup and how I thought it might damage my career. When I began to talk about Callum, the room suddenly erupted in snarls and shrieks.

"Carl! Siggy! Stop that," Abigail hollered. Two terriers had lunged across Will's lap and tumbled off the sofa; tiny teeth bared as they rolled onto the rug in a furry death match. Abigail leapt up to wave them off. "I'm so sorry. Sometimes they get this way but usually not with clients!"

This was not reassuring. Abigail left the dogs panting under the coffee table to work out their differences.

Will was irritated. "Are the dogs *staying* during our session?"

Abigail looked startled. "But of course! They're therapy dogs, trained to stimulate a more open dialogue."

"You gotta be kidding me," Will muttered as two other Yorkies stayed on the sofa, sniffing him and tentatively licking his sleeve. I squeezed his hand to signal we should make the most of being here, weird as it was getting. The clock was already ticking on our $190-an-hour session.

Abigail suddenly brightened. "You may not know that men cheat out of opportunity. Women cheat out of resentment. Carol, do you think you had an affair because you were angry at Will?"

"I don't know?" I said. "His. . . was three years ago." I couldn't even say the word *affair*. It sounded silly in this setting. "Can resentment last that long?"

Abigail became more animated. "I think we should try an exercise. Will, have you ever told Carol the most intimate details of that night? I mean *everything*. Sexual acts, escalation, how you felt. . . Sometimes the mystery is what hurts the partner. . ."

"What the hell? Of course not!" Will turned bright red.

"Well, I think you should. What she doesn't know can do irrevocable damage."

As Abigail said this, I vehemently shook my head. "No way. I don't need to know the gritty details."

"Oh, but I think you *do*, and Carol, you need to tell Will all the details of you and Callum. Everything."

"I'm not doing that," I replied. "I don't think this is necessary."

"Secrets are what kill a relationship, Carol. Don't you want to *heal*?"

"Ow!" Suddenly, Will jumped to his feet. "Your dog just *bit* me!"

"What? Sophie! Bad dog!" But Sophie didn't listen. Instead, she latched on to Will's backpack. Her little body wagged back and forth as she snarled at the pocket. "Sophie! Stop!" Will grabbed Sophie's collar and pulled her off. She yelped, more out of surprise, and then scampered under the table to join the other two.

"Let's go." Will stood and pulled me to my feet. "This is not going to work."

Abigail finally stood up. "Oh no! Please. I'm sorry about the dogs. Honestly, they're such good pups. And the trainer said to keep to voice commands because physically removing them can cause trauma."

"Abigail, that's all well and good, but this situation is not for us." Will was firm.

"Um. Okay, but I still have to charge you for a full session."

"Fine! Go ahead!" Will tugged me toward the front door.

"Bye, Abigail!" I called behind me.

When we got into the car, Will turned the key, revved, and peeled out of the driveway, gravel flying. Once on the main road, he pulled over and turned off the engine. I peered at him quietly, not knowing the right thing to say. Then, he burst out laughing.

"What was *that*? A fucking porn show?!" He laughed so hard, he had to unbuckle his seat belt to double over the steering wheel. "A fucking peep show!" He ran his hands through his hair, golden strands now flecked with gray, and cupped his face as if he'd just woken up from a nightmare. "She wanted all the dirty details, man. Sick, man, just sick!" Then, Will stopped laughing.

We sat in silence with just the sound of the traffic whooshing by. Our breath warmed the air between us. Just for this moment, we were back in 1988. I was the willful, starry-eyed young producer in Des Moines, Iowa, and Will was the seasoned journalist, the blonde missile about to blow up my world. I realized I had grown from a young aspiring journalist to a forty-year-old woman with this man. Where did it all go wrong? Or maybe this was what "right" looked like.

Will covered his face with his hands, then rubbed his eyes. His palms were wet. A deep sob welled up from his chest, and he leaned his forehead on the wheel.

I grabbed his hand and pulled it to my cheek and then I cried too. "I'm so sorry, Will. I'm so sorry it's come to this." Then, the image of our caftan-swathed counselor with hungry eyes broke through. "But seriously, Will. What the hell *was* that?" A stranger goading us for details about sex with strangers? We journalists had heard weirder things. I tried to meet Will's gaze, but he stared at the car floorboards. "I mean, what's the lead to that story? 'Sex-Starved Therapist Arrested for Malpractice'? Followed by 'Dogs Impounded, Available for Rescue!'" I smiled at my own joke but sensed he waited for more than a cheap laugh. "I love you, Will. I really do."

Our eyes met, uncertain. We embraced awkwardly in the car to the sound of traffic whisking by and tires crunching loose rocks that skittered across the road. We started to chuckle, then snickered, then laughed so loud, we snorted and then laughed even harder. Tears flowed as we pressed our foreheads together.

"We've made it this far, Will," I said, setting aside questions about who was right or wrong, for better or worse. Our history was the enduring truth. Will and I clung to each other on the side of a busy road, letting go, but still together.

Two months later, we rang in the new year. It was the turn of the century, 2000. We made the promises people made when one year folds into the next. To the sound of glass clinking, we swore we would be better people, wiser, and more grateful for the time ahead. A new century had to mean something. Something big. We felt this in our bones.

14. 9/11

September 11, 2001 did not begin as a sexy star-making day but a lot was at stake for our morning show. Our top story was whether basketball great Michael Jordan should return to the NBA (which I would end up saying, inexplicably and on air, was a terrible idea), followed by renovation plans for the nation's Capitol building.

I had caught sight of myself in the CNN makeup room's large mirrors, and regretted my olive-brown suit, an unflattering color for my Asian skin tone. Why was I wearing this when executives were paying close attention? CNN was auditioning anchors for a revamped morning show, *CNN Live at Daybreak* and I faced fresh cable TV competition from *Fox and Friends* and MSNBC's *Morning Joe*. No longer being guaranteed the morning anchor chair put me on edge.

It was too late to return home to change, even though it was only four o'clock in the morning. I needed the next three hours to prep, get makeup, review updates on the wire services, and re-write scripts.

Anyway, I already concluded it was a long shot that Vince Cellini, a handsome golf anchor with an easy-going smile and on-air repartee, and I, a hard news reporter who sometimes had to be reminded to smile, would be the future A-Team. But today, Vince and I would be judged as the traditional pair at the main anchor desk, with Kyra Phillips anchoring headlines from a spot in the newsroom.

It was 8:45 a.m. and CNN was in a commercial break right before my satellite interview with Amy Tan, author of my hero book, *The Joy Luck Club*, who was in a San Francisco studio to promote her new cartoon series, *SaGwa* on PBS. The control room director instructed me to move from the main set to the spot where executives had added studio lighting for anchors to make viewers feel they were part of newsgathering along with the CNN producers and writers. Leaving the main anchor desk was also a visual cue that we were transitioning from the hard news hour to the last fifteen minutes of human-interest feature stories.

"Mic check, one, two, three," I said. "Hi Amy, can you hear me? Good morning! I'm Carol. I'll be doing the interview straight after the commercial. SaGwa! So *cute*!"

"Hi, Carol! Yes, I can hear you. Thanks for having me," she replied graciously. It was only 5:45 a.m. in California, bless her heart.

SaGwa meant "silly" or "naughty" in Mandarin and was exactly how I felt pretending to be CNN's version of a chipper morning news anchor.

By then, the executives already had an hour and forty-five minutes with fifteen minutes left in the show to judge Vince, Kyra, and me as the face of CNN morning news. I was quietly resigned that whatever I did in the next few minutes would not make a difference in their decision. I turned and saw Kyra going over her scripts for her next hit of news headlines.

"Hey, Kyra, baby," I said. No matter who the executives named to the main anchor chair, Kyra was that versatile team player; whether she was the main anchor or in the field, there was no ego. She winked at me and mouthed, "Hey." We both wondered how a three-anchor show was going to work but liked how the new format could tap the energy of a working newsroom.

The tick of a clock and everything changed.

One minute I'm. . . and then. . .

Sixty seconds later, precisely at 8:46 a.m., American Airlines Flight 11 plowed into the North Tower of the World Trade Center in New York City. Initially, all we knew was what we saw on the small screen.

At 8:47 a.m., a CNN news executive ran behind my live position in the newsroom.

"What's going on?" I asked. CNN was so battle-tested, no one ran in the newsroom.

"Reports of a small plane flying into the World Trade Center," she responded, breathless, a human missile headed for the control room.

A small plane. Of course.

"Carol, get to the set. Get to the set. We're going into rolling coverage." Jodi's voice, usually Long Island warm, was cold. This wasn't good. Kyra and I quickly glanced at each other and then she motioned me to get going. It was 8:48 a.m.

'Rolling coverage' meant we stayed 'live' on the air without a break. It was the high-wire, fly-by-the-seat-of-our-pants kind of news coverage that makes or breaks an anchor. I ran the twenty feet from my live shot position to the anchor chair. Vince was on set. His morning show audition was all but over. I had the steady presence of Jodi in my ear, but also a familiar team of control room producers running the live coverage: Jen, Chandra, Sonya, Liz, and Dee, ballsy women who never broke under pressure, who kept me, their anchor, steady with quick, calm, and concise directions.

At 8:49 a.m., Jodi got in my ear again. "Get ready to adlib. Coming out of commercial with the breaking news animation. Full screen." That meant viewers would see only a shot of the North Tower with black smoke billowing out against a bright blue New York City sky.

People ask me all the time if I was nervous, overwhelmed by the magnitude of the story. It would sound more human to say I was, but truthfully, I was trained by the years of breaking news to shut down my emotions and focus, and I did, on the small screen embedded in the anchor desk. I waited for directions from the control room. Facts. We needed facts to fill the live coverage. How many people worked in the World Trade Center? What businesses are based there? What subway fed south Manhattan? Each World Trade Center tower was massive: 110 stories, providing office space for about thirty-five thousand people. Each floor was an acre in size.

The live feed from one of the local news affiliates in Midtown Manhattan showed the North Tower on fire. I searched the internet for credible background information as CNN's New York bureau dispatched camera crews, correspondents, and live trucks to lower Manhattan and the control room was still working on getting live interviews. Do we go to John King at the White House? Barbara Starr at the Pentagon? Candy Crowley on Capitol Hill, or would the Washington, DC studio bigfoot us and steal the live coverage?

At 8:49 a.m., three minutes after the first attack, I was live: "This just in to the CNN Center. You are looking at the World Trade Center and we have unconfirmed reports that a plane has crashed into one of the towers of the World Trade Center. CNN Center right now is just beginning the work on this story, obviously calling our sources and trying to figure out exactly what happened, but clearly, something relatively devastating happening this morning there. . ."

Relatively? I didn't consider this my finest moment. But the opening phrase, 'this just in,' fit the image of the iconic breaking news anchor and made this the go-to video clip of the 9/11 attacks in Hollywood films, documentaries and later, the Newseum of News. It was quoted in multiple national newspapers and magazines, the iconic moment when America entered a new era, the War on Terror.

Vince's sports adlib skills kicked in. Both towers were still intact.

The anchor desk was intentionally situated in the middle of CNN's world headquarters; the International Desk editors were to my right. The National Desk was behind me, with CNN's different daytime programming show teams scattered in desk pods filling up the background. All the editors and producers were standing now, with phones pressed to their ears. The International Desk was on with producers and correspondents in critical locations: London, Saudi Arabia, Beijing. International Correspondent Nic Robertson was ready to do phone reports from inside Afghanistan. The National Desk lined up Turner Broadcasting Vice President Shaun Murtagh on the phone, our first eyewitness to confirm this was no small plane accident. The control room switched his call to live television where the shot of the burning North Tower remained full screen.

"This is Sean Murtagh. I just witnessed a plane that appeared to be cruising slightly lower than normal altitude over the city, and it appears to have crashed into the—I don't know which tower it is—but it hit directly in the middle of one of the World Trade Center Towers."

"Sean, what kind of plane was it?" I asked. "Was it a small plane? A jet?"

"It was a. . . it was a. . . it looked like a two-engine jet, maybe a 737?"

"You're talking about a large passenger commercial jet."

"A large passenger commercial jet."

"And where were you when you saw this?"

"I'm on the twenty-first floor of 5 Penn Plaza."

During the minutes after America came under attack, unsubstantiated information rolled into the CNN Center of such magnitude, we decided to wait for confirmation about a car bomb outside the State Department, a plane heading for the White House, and the mayor's office sending ten thousand body bags to what would become known as Ground Zero. My historic moment on the anchor desk lasted less than twenty minutes before CNN switched to the live coverage of a New York local affiliate WNYW while the next shift of anchors, Daryn Kagan and Leon Harris, swapped places with Vince and me. I walked over to my show team's pod where rows of desktop televisions echoed the burning North Tower with a hall of mirrors effect. My God, a passenger jet flying into the World Trade Center. Unimaginable and yet, there it was. And then, two minutes later, at 9:03 a.m., a second plane, United Airlines Flight 175, slammed into the second tower and the newsroom roared. This confirmed terrorism. Editors and the national and international desks yelled even louder into their phones, dispatching crews. That moment, unforgettable, horrifying, haunting to this day.

One of our news photographers approached me, worried. "Hey, the control room asked if I would shoot bump shots of the newsroom they could use to lead to commercial breaks, but I started rolling right after the plane hit. Do you think I should keep shooting?"

"Of course! Why?"

"Because Walter Isaacson just told me to get the fuck out of his face." Walter Isaacson was the chairman of the news division. The poor photographer looked crushed. He was just doing his job.

"Keep shooting. They're going to want this," I reassured him.

His footage became the only documentation of CNN's real-time response to the terror attack. By 9/11, CNN had long superseded industry expectations with more correspondents based worldwide than any other news organization except for the BBC. In the weeks that followed the attacks, there was no escape from the visual carnage rolling into the newsroom from New York, Washington, DC, and Shanksville, Pennsylvania. Black plumes of death rolled down the streets of lower Manhattan as people ran for their lives. Bodies fell from the towers as people chose to jump rather than burn to death. First responders still arrived in droves and entered the building—too many police and firefighters never to be seen alive again.

Fresh off the anchor desk but with adrenaline still pumping, I fidgeted and watched the television monitors. The Pentagon was on fire, people were evacuating the State Department, and our nation's leaders poured out of the Capitol Building.

Will. I had to call Will. He probably hadn't left yet for his office at the CNN Center where he produced for the documentary unit.

"Hi. Are you seeing this?" I asked when he picked up. In the twenty minutes since I was on the air, a third plane, American Airlines Flight 77, had crashed into the Pentagon.

"Shit. This is unreal," he said. "Are you okay?"

"Yes. Yes, of course." Finally, I set aside the anchor persona. "I love you, Will. You know I do." It was important I said this, that Will heard me.

"I love you too, Carol." Whatever healing and heartbreak we still had ahead paled in comparison to the grief and loss we all felt on 9/11.

For three weeks, I anchored six-hour shifts, as did the other CNN anchors, to cover non-stop 9/11 breaking news. We simulcast across CNN US and CNN International, the combination giving us arguably the biggest live audience in television news. Off-air, I begged CNN's international operation to send me overseas to wherever this story was breaking, in countries across Central Asia and the Middle East like Saudi Arabia, once home to the Bin Laden family, Yemen, Pakistan, and, of course, Afghanistan, the training ground for the 9/11 terrorists.

But first, I'd have to go through the warzone training required for every CNN journalist. Typically, former British Special Forces trained journalists at a base outside of London where they tested our survival skills in an open field, but after 9/11, real experience came without this much rehearsal.

A month after the attacks, I was certified and vaccinated, and CNN relieved me from the anchor desk. I was headed to Islamabad but was told to make my way south to Quetta, Pakistan's gateway city to the Taliban stronghold in southern Afghanistan. As I packed my bags, the news played in the background of our bedroom and Will walked in, eyes taking in all my stuff spread across our bed.

"Hey Stinks, I'm going to be gone for six weeks. Maybe longer," I said, absently counting out travel-sized toothpaste and shampoo.

"I thought the usual rotation was three weeks to a month," Will said, trying to make his suspicion sound like innocent curiosity.

I called his bluff. "We're okay, Will. I think we're good."

Thought? Or hoped? CNN script approval editors would have loved to wordsmith this one: Carol, what do you *really* mean?

"Better than good, we're *better* than good," I repeated. Besides, one week here, two weeks there. I didn't want to fight with Will about the minutiae of time. I took him in my arms and breathed in his scent, then held his face to meet his eyes.

"No one but you," I said. "Will, your turn. Say it."

Will paused and pulled back. "No one but you."

This was our vow. *No one but you*, we promised each other, God, and Heaven.

I turned and took stock of my clothing, shoes, cosmetics, and toiletries, now separated into piles. Then, Will relaxed and laid down and stretched out his legs, absorbed by the rewind and repeat on the TV airing the 9/11 attacks. He didn't notice as I took in the endearing sight of him: eyes crinkled, shirt rumpled, collar turned in, hair mussed. At fifty, he possessed a rugged handsomeness. Then, we both stared at the plane, the fireball, and the towers on loop. *By God's grace*, I quietly thought; that could have been any of us. And then the next morning, I left him, again.

15. MORE

When I arrived in southern Pakistan one evening in October 2001, America had declared its War on Terror, but it was still a war of words. Without actual troop movements and bullets flying in Afghanistan, my assignment took on a cinematic quality. I joined a cast of characters, international journalists who looked like actors rehearsing for the next James Bond movie. Dozens lurked in the hotel lobby, dressed in more khaki and cargo pants than stocked at an army surplus. Alongside the tanned cotton crews were the local "businessmen" with the twitchiness of international drug runners and spies. They lingered in the corners, smoked and eyed me suspiciously. A woman traveling alone was synonymous with being a prostitute. I had to move with the confidence of someone who belonged, especially as dusk turned to dark. I made long, quick strides toward the hotel desk, and said my name and title a little louder than usual: "Carol Lin with CNN."

The Hotel Serena was hardly serenity situated in a dense ghetto of make-shift storefronts. Pedestrians stepped into diesel-fueled traffic, off the main public transport of wildly painted buses nicknamed jingle trucks for their décor of tinsel and bells. Inside, the smooth stucco walls and thick local carpets dimmed the noise outside. A walled-in courtyard and Porte Cochere made for a grand entrance and gave the Hotel Serena a misplaced Mediterranean flair.

Off the record, journalists said the hotel was the urban pitstop for drug traffickers making deals along the Silk Road. This was typical of the two-shots-of-tequila gossip among journalists but plausible because why else would investors plunk a luxury hotel in the middle of Quetta, more renowned for its murder rate than relaxation? In fact, Quetta was so violent, the Pakistani government had tried to ban journalists from staging news operations there. But Quetta was the last major city within two hundred miles of Afghanistan, so journalists came anyway. Should NATO forces eventually invade Afghanistan and succeed in defeating the Taliban, having an operation in Quetta put news agencies in the best position to move quickly into southern Afghanistan to cover the breaking news. I had heard the government had tried locking the reporters behind the hotel's giant iron gate, ostensibly to "protect" them. That did not go over well. Reporters rammed the tall gate with their SUVs or scaled the walls, which only stirred up the chaotic street scene outside the hotel. The government backed off and the journalists stayed.

Strangers assigned by far-flung news organizations abided by an unwritten code of conduct. We learned to trade essential information and watch each other's backs. Are the hotel phones tapped? Is the food drugged or foul? Is the Afghanistan border open? Who got arrested? But after the initial rush of arriving in Quetta, the hotel bar soon filled with frustrated, and often inebriated, chain-smoking men, getting high on past glories. When would the war start in Afghanistan? If it did, how long was it before NATO forces reached Kabul to the north, and Kandahar, the Taliban stronghold, to the south? They lived for dodging fire and taking cover. Now, with no option but to wait for the war, they were sullen and left to pitch their editors feature stories that rarely made the newscasts or landed on the front pages.

CNN had set up its Quetta workspace in a conference room off the lobby with high ceilings, white walls, and patterned wool carpets suggesting a tacky elegance, but beyond CNN's double doors, it looked like a TV engineers' frat house. Trash cans overflowed with paper wadded up from games of toss. The burnt stench of old coffee and cigarettes oozed from the mismatched upholstery of the sofas and chairs that haphazardly surrounded long folding tables jammed together in the center of the room. The crew set up desktop computers between tangled wires and video-editing gear. About a half dozen rumpled men dressed in dark jeans and old T-shirts sprawled on the sofas like man-boys, some with baseball caps that covered their faces as they snored quietly.

"Hey Kieran, good to see you," I said, smiling tentatively at the only person who was awake. I quickly felt a chilliness that had nothing to do with it being October.

Kieran was an Atlanta-based CNN International producer, but we had never worked together. He sat in the Atlanta newsroom, tied up on calls, like the other editors, with correspondents around the world, not needing to deal with Atlanta-based anchors who worked on domestic news.

I tried to make small talk, but Kieran clearly wanted to dispense with courtesies. He greeted me with a sneer that telegraphed his disdain, like I was the so-called 'talent' he was supposed to babysit through a tough assignment.

"I know why you're here, Carol," he said. "You don't fool me with your 'I'm a CNN anchor' bullshit." He puffed up his chest and bore into me with glassy eyes that gave him an angry-drunk look. He had just spent several weeks working with CNN International Correspondent Nic Robertson, who had made news as the only western journalist reporting from inside Afghanistan immediately after the 9/11 attack. Nic's status at CNN and his work reflected well on whoever was his field producer. By the way Kieran looked at me, he saw he had more to lose than gain from my arrival. "Don't play hero. You're *only* here because your contract is up." (More sneering, because there's no better word for this moment, seriously.) "I heard they were going to let you go." (Ouch.) "So, this is your chance to redeem yourself."

I dropped my duffel bag and ran my hand through my hair, a cornered animal trying to look bigger.

"First of all, that's not true," I replied. I had just renewed my contract and what the hell difference did my contract make when we were all here for the story? And who's this mysterious *they*?

"Just stay the hell out of my way." Kieran tossed his notepad on the desk. Its pages slapped the edge of the table before it landed with a soft thud on the dirty carpet. I thought he might spit at me if I gave him a reason. My senses alerted, the beginnings of my fight-or-flight response. My second instinct was to fetch Kieran's notepad and hand it back as a peace offering. Sometimes that old nice-girl thing still pinged in me. But I wasn't the one making war. I went quiet. Jodi always said if they think you're a fool, don't assure them that you are.

The rest of the crew stopped snoring. No one moved. I didn't know the whole CNN team, but I needed to work hand-in-hand with them for the next couple of months. Personal chemistry with my crew determined whether I got the shot and if my cameraman framed me in a flattering way. I learned that from a local reporter who told me that, one time, her photographer had neglected to mention that her long necklace had looped around one of her breasts and that's how she appeared in her live shot. When she viewed the recording later, he just shrugged and mumbled something about being more focused on what she was saying.

I hoped the boys would return to napping while I ducked into the hallway and called one of the most senior editors on the international desk. He wasn't fazed by Kieran's disrespect. "Just forget about it," he said. "He's under a lot of stress."

Stress? Like I'm not stressed? This was the courtesy men gifted each other for poor behavior. If I took it further up the management chain, I'd get the familiar "Maybe you're just being sensitive" response. I had only so many fights to pick. I just never knew how many I had left.

Kieran had stepped outside to smoke. He was returning tomorrow for Atlanta since his tour of duty was over. Still, the exchange made me nervous. Being treated like a bimbo was harder to ignore than it should've been. Happens every day, Kyra had told me. Right about then, a Navy public affairs officer was telling her all the reasons why he would deny her request to report on the U.S. Navy Air Wing which was preparing for war against the Taliban. It was a woman, Torie Clarke, Assistant Secretary of Defense who pushed Kyra's request forward and gave her exclusive access to shoot the Navy's elite training operations. The decision set the standard for journalist military embeds going forward, including the 2003 war with Iraq.

Later, a female editor with CNN International explained to me that Kieran equated anchors to teleprompter queens—news readers, not journalists. I didn't expect Kieran had read the CNN press release that told of my background as a national correspondent for ABC's *World News Tonight* and *Good Morning America*, but I had more reporting years than he had as an editor. Still, at some point, he had decided I didn't belong.

I awoke the next morning to the popping sound of distant gunfire and men laughing in the hotel hallway. My room smelled of stale cloves and dust. I looked at my digital watch and saw I was already late to meet the crew. Damn! I just gave them reason to wisecrack about "beauty sleep."

I scrambled into my uniform of Levi's and a blue shirt and threw a scarf around my neck. My satchel was preloaded with notebooks and pens by the door. Grab and go. That's the rule. Little did I know about the winding road ahead, or the pending death stare of a Taliban fighter at the Afghanistan border that afternoon.

After I made it out of the sniper's crosshairs, my world became bigger. The higher the stakes, the bigger my profile, and my confidence grew with each assignment.

The Taliban showdown had scored points for great video and earned me a certain respect that gave me agency to pursue original stories. The less I focused on what the notoriously selective CNN International producers thought of my work, the bolder my ideas became. Like when I heard that Pakistan claimed it had successfully outlawed gun ownership to prove the government's control over a notoriously armed society. If convicted, buyers could get a life sentence. To put the law to the test, I asked Ahmed, the fixer, to use his contacts and set up a gun buy. And in TV, no video means no story. The promise of $500 US dollars got the Pakistani gun dealer to meet in a dark field and show us a brand new .45 caliber handgun, wrapped in a kitchen towel and stuffed in a paper sack. He promised more weapons if we needed, cash only. The CNN producers went nuts, angry that it appeared I had broken Pakistani law (I hadn't; the dealer drove away disappointed), but our story aired multiple times across CNN US, International, and Headline News.

The crew and I watched from our hotel workspace and high-fived after the international desk called to congratulate us, but a correspondent is only as good as her last assignment, so I reached for a fresh notebook from my satchel.

Then I saw my husband's familiar scribble on the cover: *Think about it*. Seeing his words jarred me out of my happy haze. He'd whispered the same at the airport curb and I had silently nodded. But no. No, I will not think about it. This was not the natural place to contemplate bringing a tiny human, with oversized needs, into our life.

Tomorrow, I'd leave for the tribal territory between Pakistan and Afghanistan as the guest of a warlord, a tribal chief with a reputation and taste for violence. It turned out our fixer, Ahmed, had a personal connection with this powerful man, who was amused by the possibility of hosting a CNN correspondent. Being a warlord's invited guest should keep me protected, but I'm not in a place that comes with moneyback guarantees. Two months later, a *Wall Street Journal* reporter, Daniel Pearl, would be kidnapped and killed in Lahore, Pakistan. He would be a guest in the country, too.

16. TRIBE

Ahmed sat at our small workspace table and spread out a map of the Baluchistan Province, Pakistan's mineral-rich and largest land mass. The territory bordered Iran and Afghanistan to the north and stretched to the Arabian Sea to the south. Baluchistan was Pakistan's second major supplier of natural gas and, as such, became disputed territory for the local tribes and Pakistan's government who battled on and off for control.

The map's faded sepia tones outlined the faint borders of Baluchistan's Dera Bugti district, ruled by Nawab Akbar Khan Bugti, the chief of Pakistan's second largest ethnic tribe, the Bugtis. He and his army of over 200,000 men controlled four thousand square miles that bordered Afghanistan and gave the Nawab, which means "chief," an eagle-eye view of cross-border terrorist activities. The area was so remote, we had to apply for the Nawab's permission to visit him. While he had jurisdiction inside his district, it was against Pakistan's law for foreigners to travel there. Ahmed had a plan to smuggle us to a small airport in Baluchistan where our covert road trip would begin.

"His men will meet us on the airport tarmac. We must be ready as soon as our plane lands," Ahmed explained.

"How do his guards have access to the airport tarmac? What about security?" I asked, worried I was getting in over my head.

"No one will stop them," Ahmed replied.

"What happens if airport security tries?"

"They will be shot. They know this."

"Shot. The chief's guards will shoot airport security. C'mon, Ahmed!" I jostled my leg under the table to burn off my anxiety, but I couldn't afford to offend Ahmed, who had gone to great lengths to arrange this meeting.

I was resigned about where I was and *what* I was—completely dependent on the men in this violent, patriarchal society. While Ahmed worked for me as my translator, as far as Pakistani society was concerned, I, as a female, belonged to him. Once I arrived in the tribal territories, social ownership of me would transfer to the warlord who proffered the privilege of being his guest. Ahmed only occasionally hinted that, while I worked in his country, I was merely a bird nesting under the wing of men. He was paid per diem, whether I took flight or not.

"The drive to Dera Bugti?" I said. "What's that like?"

Ahmed perked up. "We have to pass through several army checkpoints. You will need to hide when the truck stops."

"Hide? From whom?"

"The Pakistani Army."

"What happens if the army sees us? What happens if they don't let the chief's men through the checkpoint?"

"They will shoot them."

"Again?! Oh my God, shoot *who*?"

"Nawab's men will shoot the soldiers." His tone was calm, lightly considered, the voice most people used when ordering lunch and deciding between an appetizer or a salad.

"Oh God, Ahmed! Do they have any other options other than starting World War Three?!"

I imagined that phone call to CNN's international desk would be alarming, with a representative from the Pakistani Army apparatus stating that their correspondent illegally traveled into tribal territories without government permission.

"They have the chief's orders to bring CNN back. That is what they will do, Carol." At least Ahmed acknowledged my worries. "Likely, things will go fine but it is up to you if we go."

I turned to Scott McWhinnie, my cheerful London-based photographer. "Sounds dangerous. Should we go, Scottie?" But I knew that Scottie loved a warzone, which made him, in this case, an unreliable source.

He slouched and smiled his wide, toothy grin and said in his South London accent, "C'mon. S'alright. I'm good."

Order a beer? Scottie would say the same. Cross-border human smuggling operation? Still the same. But I trusted his experiences in Kosovo, Northern Africa, and the Middle East.

"It'll be fun. We'll get knackered and get a good story." Scottie tugged on the strings of his dark hoodie sweatshirt and leaned back for a snooze. He knew thinking too hard about any situation caused well-adjusted people to do nothing.

We each packed a small duffel for the week with the Bugti tribe. I stuffed into my bag long scarves, three traditional shalwar chemise, and a pair of handmade leather sandals with the Balochi tribe pattern woven onto the straps. Only my toes and half my face would be exposed, which was still too much skin for the tribesmen of Baluchistan who surely expected me, a woman, to stay home.

"Where are the local women?" I had asked Ahmed when we first met two weeks ago while I was checking into CNN's Quetta operation.

"Inside the home. It is not appropriate to be out in public." Ahmed had explained the Pashtun code of conduct. A measure of a woman's virtue is *purdah*, or seclusion. She stayed socially invisible to honor her male relatives. I wondered what Ahmed thought of me, on day one, with my short, dark brown hair worn uncovered, dressed in jeans and a T-shirt. Ahmed had mentioned that satellite television made European programming available in Pakistan but with limited choices. Some shows were already controversial.

"Such as. . .?" I asked.

"Fashion TV." He blushed.

"Fashion? Video of Paris runways?"

"It is considered pornography in my country." A smile had danced around Ahmed's dark mustache. "Sometimes the models do not wear under. . ." He gestured toward his chest and looked bashful. Ahmed was twenty-seven. His family wanted him to marry, but he hoped to travel the world with the money he had made from CNN. One hundred US dollars per day, seven days a week; there was no legal job in Pakistan that paid that much.

But the story in Dera Bugti was worth whatever risk we had to take. We boarded a flight which was smooth until we landed in Sukkur with a bump. Ahmed motioned to be quick. "Push to the front. Do not stop. I see them on the tarmac."

I peeked out the small airplane's window and spotted three red Toyota pick-up trucks parked on the dark asphalt. The chilling scene below instantly made the abstract vividly real. Six men dressed in long black tunics, armed with AK-47s and dark eyes darting back and forth, stood alert. I wore my long scarf like a hood and wrapped it around my face as a traditional sign of respect. Only my eyes peered out, which robbed me of my peripheral sight. I felt around, grabbed my bag, pushed and climbed past the other passengers, and quickly stepped down the metal staircase, gripping the rail and trying not to trip.

The tallest among the Black Turbans waved and shouted in Pashtu, then pointed for us to quickly get in the backseat. We threw our bags and then our bodies into the truck. I landed on my side, half on Scottie's legs, half on the dirty floorboards, my scarf blinding me with layers of fabric. Scottie let out a playful yelp as the truck sped off toward the gate, tires squealing. Two other trucks peeled up, then stayed behind us.

"Is everybody in? Everyone okay?" Ahmed shouted.

Scottie laughed so hard he could barely speak. "Damn!"

I squirmed upright and felt the early suffocating wave of a panic attack. I yanked my scarf off and tossed it aside like a snake that tried to strangle me. The truck's dark interior smelled of old sweat and dust and matched our black-turbaned escort. Gold charms jingled from the driver's rear-view mirror. His partner propped his automatic weapon on his knee and stared out the window.

"Scottie, want to get your camera out? Just in case there's something to shoot?" I whispered.

Ahmed interrupted, "We should stay down. There are at least three army checkpoints ahead." He pulled a blanket off the floor in case we needed to hide but then decided it was better to slouch. Then, we wouldn't look like we had something to hide.

After our initial rush, the desert landscape outside the truck's dusty windows had a hypnotic, calming effect. The textures and colors were infinite as they shifted from browns to creams to shades of pink, even hints of blue in the low-lying shrubs that spread like a soft carpet.

We arrived sweaty and covered in dust after crouching in a hot truck with the airless wheezing noise of a broken air conditioner, but safely. I had forgotten to ask Ahmed if Dera Bugti had plumbing. I longed for a shower and food as we crept along in the truck and I watched skeletal cattle roam unpaved roads. Low-rise white stucco bungalows with flat roofs and rusty satellite dishes anchored to their sidewalls lined the main street. Clusters of armed men stood around. We pulled up to the only two-story building, a grander affair with tall windows and iron gates. Scottie and I untangled ourselves from the cramped backseat. Ahmed and the Black Turbans motioned us into a covered courtyard where at least twenty gray, bearded men sat

in a circle. Welcome to Dera Bugti. We had arrived at Nawab
Akbar Khan Bugti's compound.

Nawab Bugti sat elevated on a small platform covered with
a rug. Pakistan considered him the governor of Dera Bugti and
the Tumandar, or head of the Bugti tribe of the Baloch people.
However, the government had also accused him of leading a
guerilla war for autonomy from Pakistan. He exuded the quiet,
intense authority of a man accustomed to having the last word.
He stood to greet me, but clearly, I was to walk to him while the
all-male tribal council glared with quiet outrage that I had
interrupted their proceedings.

I placed my right hand over my heart, bowed my head, and
offered the traditional Muslim salutation, "*As-salaam alaykum.*"
Peace be with you, an ironic salutation when meeting a known
killer.

The deep lines in the warlord's face were a map of his
violent past. Nawab Akbar Khan Bugti reputedly was five years
old when he fired his first rifle and twelve when he first killed a
man. By the time he was twenty-one, he'd killed so many men
he'd lost count. Now, somewhere in his early seventies, he still
looked robust. His long, combed-back hair and closely trimmed
beard were snow-white. Barrel-chested, he stood over six feet
tall and had the calculating mystique of a strongman rumored
to have grasped a man's throat and strangled the life out of him.

"*Wa alaikum assalaam*," Nawab Bugti replied. "We can use
English now."

"I am grateful, sir. It's the only language I know."

His eyes twinkled like a Santa Claus who worked as a serial
killer in the off-season. The chief's English still had the trill of
his years at Oxford University. Nawab's father, the ruling chief
in the 1950s, allowed his son to spend his youth mingling with
European elites. Nawab Bugti had attended Queen Elizabeth's

coronation and developed a penchant for German lap dancers. He found the West, he said, stimulating.

When his father was murdered, the tribe had called Nawab Bugti home. He traveled through time, from a twentieth-century life of privilege to the tribe's seventh-century ways, to fulfill his filial duty.

Now, dressed in long white flowing robes, the chief rested his manicured hands on a polished walking stick. He gestured for me to sit next to him and join the elders. These men sat in a circle, upright and cross-legged on small carpets and low pillows. Their heads wrapped tight in traditional black or white turbans with patterns that showed their status. One wore a pair of Ray-Bans. None looked my way, as if the only way they could withstand the indignity of my being there, was to pretend I was invisible.

"I've never had a woman sit with me at the Jirga," Nawab mused. I sat within his arms-length in case one of his tribe members sprang towards me; Scottie shot video from the perimeter for a better angle. "We are meeting now to decide on wrongdoing to our people. A rival tribe kidnapped a girl from our tribe. We are deciding whether to go after her."

Of course, they should go after the girl, but I kept this to myself.

"But that will mean some of our men will be killed in the rescue," he continued. "It might be wiser to bargain for her release."

My feminist sensibilities prickled at a man talking about a young girl's price. "What do you think she's worth?" I said.

The chief, lost in thought, counted on his fingers. "Perhaps a goat," he concluded, then watched with delight as my eyes flared. "But the girl is not why I would send my men. You cannot allow another tribe to take what is yours. If you do, you have nothing. Nothing," he repeated for effect. "But you are here for more important matters. What is it that you want to see?"

"As requested, I'd like to see your justice system at work." I turned to a less volatile topic. "Pakistan's president assures the United States that Pakistan controls its borders. Your province, your tribe, operates on a quarter of the national border with Afghanistan. Who rules here? You or Pakistan?"

Nawab laughs. "Not Pakistan—and not Osama bin Laden. Your government has it wrong. Why do they think *that* man could survive here?" The chief referred to news reports that Bin Laden also used the self-governing tribal territories as cover.

"What would you do if you saw Osama bin Laden in Dera Bugti?" I asked as I pulled my notebook out and double-checked to see that Scottie was still rolling.

"Nothing," he replied. "He is nothing to me, *if* he does nothing to us. Your war is not our war."

I pressed on and poked the bear. "*I* am not at war, sir. America is at war with the terrorists who attacked my country. If you see Bin Laden and do nothing, doesn't that make you complicit in hiding a terrorist?"

"That is a silly question." The chief seemed bored and changed topics. "You said you want to see our justice system." He pointed me to an open field a few steps away from the pavilion where the Jirga, or tribal council, continued its debate about the kidnapped girl.

"Scottie, ready to roll?" I saw he still had his camera on his shoulder.

"Ready, boss!" Scottie was the rare cameraman, happy to please. We followed Nawab Bugti and his guards to a large crowd gathered around a fiery trench, a hellish stripe of red-hot coals a foot deep. In the corner, four men held knives to the throats of two baby goats who screamed, then collapsed in a bloody sacrifice to Allah. The crowd prayed in a rising chorus.

I turned back to the trench where a group held aloft a terrified man in gray pants and a long tunic. His knees were bent like he sat in an invisible chair. His dark eyes were wild with adrenaline. Another man, dressed in a long, black tunic, fanned the coals with large leaves. The chanting grew louder. The crowd pushed forward and then, to the roar of the onlookers, the men tossed the frightened suspect forward. His feet landed on the hot coals, and he screamed and ran the length of the burning trench. One, two, three. . . I counted twelve steps before he reached the end, where two men scooped him up and guided his feet to a large metal bowl of water. The liquid sizzled on contact. They carried the suspect away, a light breeze delivering me the smell of burning flesh.

The chief burst out laughing when he saw me so startled. "The man is accused of plotting to hire someone to kill his neighbor." He let out another gut-splitting belly laugh, and I burned as he took pleasure from something so primitive and inhumane. "With our tribe, you choose your trial. You can pick a jury trial or leave your fate to Allah. He chose Allah. If his feet blister, he will be pronounced guilty."

"But of course his feet will blister," I said. "I saw the coals. They were burning hot."

"Not always, Carol. But it's better to gamble on fire. Our tribal jury trials have a ninety-nine percent conviction rate."

That evening, Ahmed went to visit his brother, while Scottie and I joined Nawab for supper in his grand dining room. We sat beneath a tall white plaster ceiling on fat, downy floor pillows set on an antique Persian rug and ate a sumptuous meal with our hands. Servants laid out a luscious and spicy dinner of lamb, chicken, beef, chickpeas, and long, tender vegetables with warm, buttery bread. Nawab Bugti leaned back against several large cushions and scooped meat and sauce out of a wide bowl.

"I want you to meet my granddaughters," he said, signaling to a servant who scampered away to fetch them. A few moments later, two little girls, dressed in long white linen dresses ran in and threw themselves at their grandfather with such force, it almost knocked him sideways. He playfully grasped the girls by their tiny waists and seated them beside him. Chief Bugti's eyes lit up with affection. He pointed to the first girl, the smallest. "This is Afsana, who is nine years old. And this is Meena, who is ten." He caressed Meena's cheek and then patted her on the head. "Meena is the oldest, but I am saving her."

"For what?" I asked and licked a spicy sauce off my fingers. I found myself sentimental for a moment, watching a grandfather dote on his family.

"For a proper marriage match," the chief replied as if this were light dinner chat. He beamed with pride. "Meena is quite smart. I may even teach her to read a little. But this one," Nawab pointed to the other girl, who giggled, ". . . is a little. . . dim." He playfully pinched Afsana's cheek. "I have already promised Afsana to her second cousin. They will wed next year when she turns ten."

I quickly grabbed a cloth napkin and pressed it to my lips. Scottie looked at me to see if I wanted him to record, but Nawab interrupted, "No recording! This is family business." He whispered to the girls, who skipped cheerfully back to the waiting servant and off to bed. In some other time and place, this would be a sweet goodnight before the girls retreated to bedtime stories. My heart ached that even he, who knew the modern world beyond his tribe, would trade his youngest family members like property. But Nawab Bugti judged his granddaughters to be blessed, and I a fool for not respecting him as their guardian.

"I see I have upset you," he said. "You disapprove." Before I could interrupt, he continued, "I understand your ways, but she is not from the West. Here, girls do not have protections without a man." He wiped his mouth and tossed the napkin aside. "The male I choose for Afsana will preserve and protect her honor, ensuring she is fed and cared for. I will make sure he is kind and waits for her to be of age to have relations with him."

Good, I thought. *She has time.*

"She will marry her second cousin, who is only eleven years old." Nawab Bugti selected a prickly fruit from a bowl and took a bite. "And she will start her new life caring for his family. It is our way for seven hundred years."

"But you are the tribe's leader. You can change the laws. You have the power to make it happen." The reporter in me pressed forward, but then Scottie raised his eyebrows to remind me I was a guest far from the safety of a TV studio.

"I *am* protecting her." Nawab turned from his half-eaten fruit and gave me a withered look. "How unfortunate that you live on hope and optimism for a so-called better life," he lectured. "These are things even *I* cannot change." He tossed the pit of the mystery fruit into a dish, where it dinged and alerted a servant to clear the plate. "And why should I? As it was, so it shall be. I am not a leader if I do not honor our Bugti traditions. We endure because of what we fight for: honor, virtue, and tradition. And despite what you *think* you saw here, we believe in family, above all."

Insist all he wanted, I saw a society that forced girls to marry and a tribal people who believed you didn't get burned when you walked on hot coals.

The double doors opened, interrupting dinner, and two guards entered carrying the criminal suspect from earlier. The guards forced him to lift his burned feet mid-air for Nawab Bugti's judgment. The verdict was "guilty." This time, the chief didn't stop Scottie when he reached for his gear. He issued orders in Pashtu, and the guards backed out, carrying the now sobbing man.

"What did you say?" I asked.

"Allah has deemed this man guilty. Therefore, he faces the death penalty. But I ruled that the family he tried to kill should decide his fate."

Nawab played God.

"They could shoot him dead. Or they could strike a deal in exchange for his life."

"What kind of deal?" I asked.

"He could give them land or animals. Or he could give them a daughter to work as a servant." The chief waved as if this was nothing. "Whatever they like."

Whatever they like sent a chill through me. "But why wouldn't the man leave the tribe and escape into the desert?"

Nawab Bugti explained what was obvious to him. "Carol, you need your tribe. Without your tribe, you are no one." The warlord leaned into his plush pile. "You are the same as dead."

The image of Will unexpectedly popped into my head. What am I without him? *Less*, I thought. *I am less*. Yet, a big part of me judged me weak to need him.

But Nawab's point was that an individual could become something greater than who they could be alone, to live as a community who were each other's ride-or-die. Throughout the week, I saw how they looked with reverence to their chief for wisdom and direction. "As it was, so it shall be," was how he answered my questions that began with "why?" Spending the week with Nawab's tribe had me questioning my own story.

There is an old Chinese saying that having a daughter is like water spilling into a river. Once she is gone, there is no way to get her back. Despite this proverb, my mother had been feverishly hoping that one day, something would turn the tide and send her daughter home to Los Angeles.

"Carol, you've done enough for yourself," she pleaded as she imagined my fertility flowing right off a cliff. "Think about me. Think about Will! Before it's too late!"

But I had spilled myself into a career that took me farther than she ever imagined possible. It was almost Christmas by the time I returned from the Afghanistan border, with more overseas reporting chops plus a team Emmy Award for CNN's 9/11 coverage. This was a historic time to be a journalist. The war on terror would spread from Afghanistan to Iraq. The hunt for Osama bin Laden was still underway. The ever-persistent fear of another terror attack on U.S. soil spun an endless news cycle. Viewership was up.

When I came home, Will met me at Atlanta's Hartsfield International Airport with seven red roses and held me close at baggage claim. He and his CNN documentary unit had been sidelined. War coverage was expensive, and now the network had to cover two fronts. Will said there were rumors about another round of layoffs.

"Are you worried, Stinks?" I said as I settled into the passenger seat of our beat-up Volvo.

"I dunno," Will sighed. "First-world problems. Technically, I have a job. For now. Hey, you probably saw the domestic coverage on CNNI, but it was pretty intense here, especially those early weeks. Reporters going live from Saint Paul's in south Manhattan were just bawling. I'd never seen anything like it."

While I was in Pakistan, international news coverage homed in on the geopolitical factors around 9/11, but Will described how the American networks focused on the missing and the dead. Families taped rows of photos to New York's chain link fences outside the rescue and recovery operation around Ground Zero. People held up pictures to the TV cameras and asked viewers if anyone had seen their missing loved ones alive. In reporter-packaged stories, voicemails aired of those onboard the hijacked planes saying their final goodbyes, their voices edited over video of the ill-fated plane's final impact.

Will and I arrived home from the airport and switched on the news. CNN played a story about mothers who sat vigil near Ground Zero holding photos of sons and daughters who worked in the World Trade Center. I wondered if I knew how to love like *this*, to be joined in collective tears that flowed into a river with no end, no husband or child to return home, and what would that make me? These women and their children would be forever remembered as victims of the worst terror attack on U.S. soil. I watched Will, seated now in his favorite chair, elbows on knees, hands clasped, eyes riveted to the small screen, and my heart was full. How could it not be? We were living our second chance at getting love right—you know, the ride-or-die kind. The kind that lasted forever.

Nearly a year later, a nurse called and chirped with good news: "The test is positive!" I was in the middle of my show team's weekly editorial meeting, discussing whether we needed to lead the show again with the war in Iraq.

"You're pregnant!" the nurse repeated as I stepped into the hall. Going from the Middle East to my middle section was a monumental mental leap. "Hello?"

"Wow," I blurted. "Thank you. Um. That's great news!"

A year of trying to get pregnant was like entering a science fair as a long shot. I had about a forty-five percent chance of conceiving at age forty-two, but Jodi already had one child, a boy, and another baby on the way at age forty-three.

"Geriatric" pregnancies were not ideal, but I didn't feel old because later-life pregnancies were more common in my world. Or maybe I just knew a lot of women like me—baby procrastinators. Before the nurse called, I had lulled myself with an "A" for effort and settled for a free-wheeling, childless life. Apparently, all the blood tests, follicle tickling, egg retrieving, and stirring of Petri had worked, despite delays when CNN sent me to Israel and the West Bank for a month to cover the latest intifada and the siege of the Church of Nativity, followed by the 2002 Winter Olympics in Salt Lake City.

Being pregnant was not the best time to realize I'd never changed a diaper—not even one—or spent any time alone with a child. What would we talk about? I called Will and whispered the news.

"Oh my God, Carol," he said. "That's great, Stinks. We're going to have a baby!"

"Aren't they loud? Dirty? Very selfish?"

"Well, yeah. They're babies." I heard Will tapping on a keyboard.

"Oh no! You can't tell anyone yet. I'm only four weeks along. You can't tell anyone for another two months!" I tried to focus on how life would change. "Don't babies pee on people?

What are you going to do when it runs around naked in front of total strangers!"

Passersby in the CNN hallway turned at the word "naked." I smiled and rolled my eyes like I was in the middle of a bad joke.

"Carol, that's what diapers and clothes are for," Will laughed. "Why are you so worried?"

I leaned against the wall. The idea of getting pregnant felt right. But I went about this with the same mindset of shopping for the right dress. I thought I needed one, but no rush. Now, I had a little one baking inside me. And I had heard it gets worse as they grow. They stole your heart and then your credit cards. They wanted soccer and dance lessons, cool accessories and sporty outfits. And then your car—to drive it, dent it, destroy the beautiful things you've worked so hard to buy.

When I had said I was ready to try, Will had exclaimed, "You're going to be a great mother. And I'm going to be right by your side. Fifty-fifty." Yeah, that was the first co-parenting lie. Mothers looked depleted for a reason. Speaking of, I called my own mother next.

"A baby!" she whispered. " Aiya! Carol, when is the baby due?"

"Uh. . ." I quickly did the math. "March next year. 2003."

"A spring baby! That's good luck!"

"Mom, everything for Chinese is good luck when it's something you want."

"Ah, Carol, don't sound so bad. You are lucky, too! I will come out and stay with you to help!"

Yes. Lucky me.

I ducked back into the producers' meeting, feeling strange that I had this secret. I nodded at one producer's suggestions for live guest interviews and possible lead stories, but my senses were on high alert. Did I always feel this full? Was my skirt this tight before the nurse called with the news?

I drove home and found Will in overdrive by the refrigerator.

"What do you want to eat, Carol? We've got strawberries. I can make quesadillas. . ." Will held the door open to show me all the options. The sight of all that food was alarming, but the cold air felt nice on my hormonal face. Mac and cheese. I could eat mac and cheese. But as soon as I said the words, I knew I never wanted to eat mac and cheese for the rest of my life. I wanted white bread and sardines.

Speed had been a natural part of my life. The hours covering, say, a wildfire wound down to sixty minutes to write a script. Then, I had fifteen minutes for script approval to tell the whole story in a minute and thirty seconds. The countdown to my baby was a nine-month entanglement of oohs, ahhs, and assumptions about how I'd spend my career with a child. Will had taken a buy-out package from CNN and was trying his hand at writing, something he'd always wanted to have time to do. He would be the stay-at-home dad. No doubt, I was having this baby for him. I would continue to work. Plus, I hadn't forgotten what happened the last time Will left journalism. But this time he was accountable to both me and a baby.

Three months later, I still had not told CNN I was pregnant, but my profile clearly had changed, and CNN did not think it was for the better. The email from the vice president of talent management went like this: *Carol, Great news! We've booked an appointment with a wardrobe consultant for you. You'll love her. A quick note. Ask her about V-necks.* The shape of things was important to him. True, my belly curved like the moon's dark edge during a solar eclipse, and I wore silky work blouses a size too big, untucked over a wardrobe of polyester black skirts—so many black skirts. Everyday. Made with wide stretchy waistbands that itched like an artificial torment. The maternity shop swore these were their best seller, a style you could wear "even after the baby's born."

My morning sickness passed just as the United States accused Saddam Hussein of building weapons of mass destruction. I wanted a piece of this huge story. CNN was sending me to Northern Iraq, no wardrobe consultant required. I, along with journalists from around the world, would join the United States, British, Australian, and Polish military forces preparing to invade Baghdad. The CNN International desk already told me, if I agreed to go, I should expect to be overseas for at least two months. I did the math. I could deploy and return before I was six months along.

And hell yes, I was going. I wouldn't miss this assignment for the world, or apparently for my baby, who was doing just fine. Early pregnancy had been as simple as watering a plant; it was just a matter of following the instructions. I stopped by my obstetrician's office to find out if we could schedule my weekly check-ups via CNN's satellite phone. I thought he'd be excited for me, as most people usually are, because they like to hear the behind-the-scenes stories. Instead, my doctor pursed his lips and reminded me, *again*, that I'm a "geriatric mother" and have a high-risk pregnancy.

I wasn't asking for his permission. I was going to Iraq. He sensed me digging in and folded his arms in that fatherly way.

"You waited this long to have a baby. . . " He trailed off and left his medical judgment hanging heavy in the exam room. "Your choice. Trust your gut." *No pun intended*, I thought.

I decided to do the right thing and tell Teya Ryan, the general manager of CNN, that I wanted to go to Iraq, *but she might* be interested to know that I was three-and-a-half months pregnant. Teya had recently adopted a baby girl. *An ally*, I thought to myself—*a girl's girl*. As a hardcore producer with decades of breaking news experience, surely Teya understood a baby didn't stop a journalist from doing her job. The baby was my body's responsibility. My brain was free to cover a big story.

"Just focus on taking care of this baby, Carol," Teya said, her gaze soft. She rose and circled her desk, signaling our meeting was over. On the way out, she patted me on the arm, which felt a little patronizing, and told her secretary to send in her next appointment. Later, CNN assigned one of the morning anchors in my place, someone good but with less experience and not pregnant.

It was frustrating that everyone assumed not going to a warzone was good news. "Aren't you relieved?" they would ask.

No, I'm not relieved. I'm pissed.

Jodi and I met for lunch at the CNN Center one day.

"You know you're going to have to give up these overseas assignments," Jodi said as she ordered the pasta.

"Nanny. We will have a full-time nanny, and Will wants to be a stay-at-home dad," I replied, still thinking all I had to do was gestate, give birth, and reward myself with some modern restorative measures.

I had arrived for lunch in a foul mood and questioning why morning sickness made me both starving and hideously freaked out by food. I was jealous that Jodi could eat.

"But you're the mother, Carol. You have to be the mother." I felt Jodi judging me over her pasta. I eyed her with envy and a touch of nausea. Jodi was mother-splaining to me how much I would love this kid and how much my life would change and *for the better*.

"You'll see! And you *can't* just go off for six weeks to God knows where and leave the baby!" This was coldly ironic, considering Jodi was the beneficiary in the control room, filling her show with my live reports and managing me from the other side of the long-distance phone line.

"Yes, I can. Just watch me. I can do whatever I want. I'm birthing this baby and expect other people to do their part. Isn't it enough that I'm giving my body to this project?" I baited Jodi into a fight, although I didn't think we were arguing about the baby anymore.

"Carol, this is not a 'project.' It's not like you got an assignment. It's a baby. You're having a baby!" Jodi repeated as if I hadn't heard her the first three times.

"Everyone acts like it's okay to touch me and give me advice I didn't ask for. I can smell everything. Everything!" I was on a tear about all the ways my body betrayed me. "Do you know what it's like to smell the meat section from the *entrance* of a grocery store?"

Never mind Jodi's pasta. I had grossed myself out now.

"Yes, Jodi. I know I'm having a baby," I repeated, my voice now a low hiss so I didn't attract attention from the lunchtime crowd.

Jodi took a hearty mouthful of rotini. The red sauce made me anxious. I crushed small packets of saltine crackers in my palms, making plastic-wrapped cracker dust.

Three weeks later, I was still stewing. I looked like an angry egg, hard-boiled and slouched in a swivel chair, when the newsroom computers pinged. Anonymous killers were on the loose in the Washington, DC area. A terrifying shooting spree had gripped the nation. Snipers were shooting and killing innocent people who were going about their business pumping gas or leaving Home Depot. Ten people had died, and several more were wounded. Law enforcement was stumped.

"Forget that I'm pregnant. I'm a journalist. Let me cover this story!" I stood at the national desk and stared down the editors and weaponized 'pregnant' to conjure every stereotype of a volatile, hormonally charged, expectant mother that CNN management could imagine. Don't mess with me. Avoid an ugly (possibly damp) scene and just say yes.

In a matter of days, I was in DC getting ready for the morning show outside the police command post. I got mic'd up at my live shot position and put my earpiece on to hear Jenny Wilburn in the Atlanta control room yelling at me, as only a good friend was allowed to do.

"You've lost your mind, Carol!" she said so that everyone in the control room and the live shot crew could hear. "Um. You *do* know you're pregnant." Again, reminded! "And that random people are getting shot and killed on the street?" Her sarcasm oozed through the open line. She watched me on the control room monitor minutes before the morning show began.

"Well aware. On both counts. Thanks, Jenny." I puckered my lips and reflexively tugged the edge of my bright red coat over my belly. The bold shade, more saturated than a bullseye, looked great on camera. How do I tell Jenny and everyone listening that I needed to be here because I still felt the burn of Teya's sympathetic pat on my arm? I was the same person, the same reporter, the same woman, only twenty pregnant pounds more, but still devoted to the job. To be otherwise was to lose myself to this small being growing inside of me. I lived in the world of eat-or-be-eaten. My career consumed me by a lot, but I feared this baby was already swallowing me whole.

"And stop *walking* to the live shot position. Take a cab. A caaab." Jenny snapped me back into live shot mode, then clicked off her mic and gave herself the last word. No way was I taking a taxi the one-block distance from my hotel. If the crew saw me arrive in a car, it would only further highlight the pregnancy that already cost me the most significant wartime assignment since 9/11. But I understood what Jenny was saying without her saying it. I should think about the baby. To everyone, my life was worth more because I was pregnant. But there was no escaping my round belly and flushed face that introduced me as "Expectant Mother" before I said a word. The baby was the reason I kept hearing 'no.' No more covering war zones, no more waistline, coffee, eating raw sushi, or eight hours of sleep.

But there was one bonus. People brought me food all the time. Snacks: the fastest way to any pregnant woman's heart.

"Jenny Wilburn told me to make sure you ate," Michael Heard, my live shot producer, said and held out some candy bars and a vending machine sandwich. "This is all they had inside the cop shop." He gave me a sheepish look.

"Aww, thank you, Michael," I said and reached for the chocolate peanuts while he self-consciously flipped through his notebook.

"So, Jenny tells me you're, like, halfway through the pregnancy?" Michael looked up. "She said I should get you milk." He reached a slender hand into his pocket for another roll of quarters to pump into the vending machine. "Want milk?" Milk was probably not the usual drink he'd offer a gal, but I saw empathy in his dark eyes and sensed that Michael, as the rare African American network producer, understood why both of us willingly stood outside under bright lights to do the job while a sniper was on the loose.

"Ah. That's okay, Michael, but thanks!"

"Because what Jenny wants, Jenny gets." Michael laughed and then cleared his throat. He returned to his list of scheduled live shots, a menu he was more comfortable with.

"Yeah, I know. A little bossy, that one." I grinned, thinking of pint-sized Jenny back in Atlanta, producing my story and my baby's needs from afar. She knew losing the Iraq assignment was hard for me and that the sniper story was a big deal but a consolation prize. Jenny didn't have children yet, but she loved them. To her, babies were nothing but fantastic.

A month later, the baby became more than a blurry photo with a steady heartbeat. I was having a girl. Knowing her gender made her more real to me, more than a flutter or a wave of nausea or another chapter in *What to Expect When You're Expecting*. While anchoring, I flinched at her tiny punches to my lower ribs. She *was* just like me. And she was Will, and she was life itself. For the first time, I thought, *Maybe I can do this mother thing*. Yet, after years of covering breaking news, I should know that the story I thought was mine could change instantly and always without warning.

"What time will you be back from the dentist?" I hollered at Will from the shower, the steam warming me. At six months pregnant, I had gone from subtle curves to the shadowed outline of Alfred Hitchcock.

"I don't know. My appointment's at eleven? Damn!" Will's toothbrush hit the tender spot in his mouth near his molar, and he spat into the sink. "I'm so sick of this." He looked in the mirror, where his swollen jaw had turned pink, a toothache that, for a month, the dentist hadn't been able to diagnose. I wrapped an extra-large bath towel around me and kissed him quickly before reaching for another towel to dry my hair.

"I'm sure it'll be fine. Didn't the dentist do an x-ray?"

Will lightly touched his jaw and ran his finger over a bump. "Inconclusive. We're doing another scan today. A more detailed one."

I thought it was probably just an infected gum. Antibiotics should knock it out. Will was such a baby; the pun was not lost on me. I pulled on a stretchy black top and dark blue maternity jeans, and slid into sandals, the only shoes that fit my swollen feet. Some days, I barely fit into my own skin, but this week before Thanksgiving, I was grateful. As I became rounder, so did my sharper edges.

"I'm having lunch with Lesley today. It's a new burger place. Call me when you're done?" I gave him a quick kiss. "Don't worry. You'll be fine!" And then I headed out, already thinking about what to order for lunch.

I wish I could have bottled up the next two hours to savor the crisp November air, that shower of golden leaves that danced with the autumn breeze along West Paces Ferry Road, and my friend's smile.

After lunch, I was stopped at a light when my cell phone rang. "Hey, honey! How's it going?" I rattled off the juicy details of lunch but then realized I hadn't let Will say a word. "Oh! What's up? What'd the doctor say?" Someone honked. I jerked the steering wheel to the curb and parked. Even the running engine sounded impatient. My hands instinctively drifted to my belly, and I felt the baby kick. "What did he say?" I repeated, and I heard Will take a breath.

"It's cancer. I have cancer."

And there it was: the split second when everything changed. As television journalists, Will and I managed moments like this in our careers during countless video editing sessions, when we spliced the fractional freezeframes between life and death, the public unaware of the impersonal toggling that moved action forward and back as we decide where to start the shot. One click forward: a fireball. One click back: the last millisecond people were still alive. The difference was a thirtieth of a second.

Engine running, the whoosh of traffic. Hazards blinking. These visuals were my story now, heartbreaking and real, as an imaginary clock wound in reverse, and I found myself amid a different kind of day. My grip tightened on the steering wheel.

"No. No!" I repeated with a scream. I didn't believe Will had said cancer. "It's just a *toothache*! What did he say?"

"There's a tumor in my sinus that's spread to my gums. It's why my tooth can't heal." Will sounded calmer now that he leaned on the dentist's words. "They can't tell how bad it is. Not yet."

I found hope in this air gap of information. "If the dentist can't tell how bad it is, then maybe it's not that bad!"

Will sighed. "I don't think so. I think it's bad."

I breezed by his negativity. "We are going to beat this, Will. You are going to be fine." I'd ignore this first test result. Who was this doctor anyway? He's a *dentist*, not a cancer *specialist*. If it's cancer, Will's cancer was surely treatable. We were CNN. We knew people! Ah, early-stage denial. I equated curing Will's cancer to snagging an impossible-to-get dinner reservation or a last-minute airline upgrade, the privileges a network anchor could gently twist out of someone. Will just needed the right doctor. So, we were going to get the best care possible, beat this thing, and then, dammit, we were going to raise our baby.

"Where are you?" I shifted from park to drive and merged back into traffic.

"I'm home."

"I'm ten minutes away. Stay right there. I'm coming home, too."

I pulled into our driveway and, for the first time, noticed how steep it was, as were the stairs to the front porch and the charming, paneled front door with its decorative iron grill. More steps rose toward the backyard that leveled out to a patio where Will pensively looked up at the tall pine trees that bordered the house. He turned, his eyes pale blue and wet. We embraced, our baby girl between us, and I whispered, "We're going to get through this together. It's going to be okay."

His hair tickled my nose. I kissed his ear, then his cheek, brushed my lips on his morning stubble, and kissed him softly again before guiding him inside. Will slumped into a chair. I called Sanjay Gupta, CNN's Chief Medical Correspondent and a neurosurgeon at Atlanta's Emory University Hospital.

Sanjay answered on the second ring. I was embarrassed that we barely knew each other despite working together at CNN. Now that I needed his help, I wasn't sure I had the right to ask for a favor. We were congenial with hallway hellos and appeared to be best friends on the air. But here in my living room, I phoned him with the fever of a desperate colleague.

"Sanjay, I need your help. What do we do?" He listened carefully and asked if he could call me back. When he did, he gave us the number of an Emory Hospital oncologist who could see us in the next few days. First, Will needed tests. Tests felt hopeful. Maybe this was all a terrible mistake.

A week later, the Tuesday before Thanksgiving, a nurse guided us to a room. "The doctor will be with you shortly," she said. The space was devoid of color, metallic and glassy.

Will and I sat patiently and held hands in a comfortable silence. After twenty minutes, the room's lighting began to feel ghostly. Why were exam rooms so cold?

We heard his voice before we saw his white coat of authority, and the door finally swung open. "Good morning. I'm Dr. James Marcus."

Is it? Is it really a good morning? I offered a quiet hello and thought, *Let's just dispense with the pleasantries, shall we?* Will was quiet but his eyes tracked Dr. Marcus as he crossed the room.

The doctor sat on a stool and rolled toward him with Will's record in a dark green folder.

"Hello, Will," the doctor said. He focused on the patient while I, the wife, was to remain quiet. Good luck with that. Over the years, I'd learned to get louder.

"Dr. Marcus, I'm Carol Lin. Sanjay Gupta's colleague at CNN? Thank you for seeing us on such short notice," I said as I wedged my presence into Will's exam. The doctor nodded and offered a pale hand, then quickly turned back to Will.

"I've looked at the scans and consulted with my colleagues. We also received the biopsy report from your dentist. After careful review, we concur with the dentist's initial concerns." Dr. Marcus paused. "I'm sorry to inform you that you have a rare sinus cancer called Squamous Cell Carcinoma of the Maxillary Sinus." The doctor spoke slowly, as if to a child who might miss the point, this probability of dying. "It is usually diagnosed when the tumor is at an advanced stage—when it has spread into other areas of the body. This is true in your case, Will." He set aside Will's folder; he'd seen all he needed to about his case and leaned forward to rest his forearms on his knees and interlace his long fingers. He looked more relaxed than I thought appropriate. Give me the survival rate, doc. What are his odds?

As if he read my mind, Dr. Marcus continued, "The five-year survival rate is fifty-two percent." I brightened and clung to that extra two percent. More than half the patients with Will's cancer will live at least another five years. That's a good sign, right? In the bell curve of cancer statistics, researchers were only beginning to understand what hereditary or environmental stressors determined which patients lived or died.

"In your case, the tumor has spread," Dr. Marcus continued. "We don't know to what extent. It may already be in your brain, your lymph nodes, or, at this point, your spine."

"Oh God," Will moaned. He let go of my hand to cover his face and quietly cried with small gulps of air before he wiped his tears with his sleeve. His left cheek, where his tumor manifested, swelled red. I shifted awkwardly and tried to wrap my arm around Will's shoulders. My other hand reflexively rested on my belly, and I felt her kick. At six months developmentally, the baby could hear us. She and I thought Dr. Marcus was holding back.

"Dr. Marcus, what's the treatment plan? What's the next step?" I redirected the conversation and considered why this doctor seemed to ignore me. Perhaps to see me was to see double—woman plus child on the way—and raised the stakes. Or maybe he thought this dry-eyed woman was pushy. Wives and mothers should cry. I'd cry him a river if it meant a cure for Will. Perhaps I should be what he expected: a woman to be pitied, then rescued. Yes. Rescue me, doctor. Rescue us.

He explained that Will's cancer was an orphan cancer with little research and few treatment options. According to the National Cancer Institute, orphan cancers are those that fewer than 200,000 people a year are diagnosed with, too small a cohort compared to, say, the one million annual cases of breast cancer.

"Doctor, what are our options?" I repeated.

"If you want to try treatment, Will, know it will be aggressive. We're talking about eight to ten weeks of high doses of targeted radiation combined with the highest doses of chemotherapy, as much as we think you can tolerate. There will be side effects. They will be brutal. There's no guarantee it will work."

Neither the doctor nor I could tell what Will thought. He was folded in his chair, rolled into a silent ball.

I interrupted, "How long does he. . . do we have without any treatment, doctor?"

"The data indicates six months. So, maybe six months."

There are reporters who love the slam of breaking news, the mind-bending challenge of a seamless live shot under pressure. My live shot prep trick was to work backwards. How I ended my live shot determined how I began. Knowing where I was headed meant the middle would take care of itself. With Will's type of cancer, the likely end was too much to bear, so we began in the unknown.

My father's last words to me sprung to mind: "Lo-Sen, sometimes things don't work out."

I reluctantly did the math. It was the end of November. The baby was due in March. A little over four months. He'd make it for the birth, wouldn't he? I looked his way. Will was physically present but mentally far away.

"He'll do it. We'll do it. When do we start?" I spoke for Will, for us and our baby, who still kept kicking. Our baby will have her father. We reject death. No matter how painful, no matter what the cost. How high would I jump to save Will's life? I would leap to Heaven if I thought my mother's God would have me.

While the nurse went over a treatment plan with Will, I ducked into the hospital chapel. Wasn't this so cliche, this sudden, conveniently earnest search for the Almighty when I drowned in a sea of desperation. I knelt at the alter in the low light, put my hands together, and looked up at the stained-glass depiction of Mary and her baby Jesus. "Please dear Lord, have mercy on me," I prayed.

Silence.

If God was present, this was the awkward pause of a first date.

All the reasons why I didn't deserve divine intervention scrolled through my head. As a child, I whined and huffed when my mother dragged me to worship at her Chinese evangelical church where the pastor equated volume with salvation.

"By the grace of Jesus Christ, the Son of God, we are saved!" He would raise his arms and look toward Heaven. "Believe!" Even as a five-year-old with a vivid imagination, I only saw the drab ceiling of an old church. Later, I was the god to my career, not God with all his rules. I assumed it took being almighty to do the work. And now cancer laughed. I, so mortal, did TV. Big deal. Will needed a real miracle.

"Have mercy on Will and save his life," I tried again. The chapel air conditioning hummed quietly as light and shadows danced from the small votive candles lit by other desperate souls. I considered what I had to offer and prayed again. "Take me. Take me after our baby is born, not him. Let him live."

Chin down, I wept. I felt wholly unworthy of my life that seemed so one-dimensional. God and I hadn't shared enough holidays, birthday parties, or even the newsy miracle of my pregnancy. And here I was, bargaining with Him in my hour of need.

If He decided I would live, I promised that, going forward, I would be whatever He wanted me to be: a devoted wife, attend church every Sunday, and host Bible study even after the baby is born. I would turn down reporting assignments and stay home to care for my family. Please, dear Lord, punish me, but don't punish Will. I stared at the stained-glass Mary and her baby and was reminded that the Bible taught that salvation came at a high price, even for God, who surrendered Jesus, His beloved and only son.

19. SOMEONE TO LIVE FOR

UCLA basketball coach John Wooden famously said never to mistake activity for achievement. He believed that the best results came from methodical planning and close attention to detail, but Will's cancer made me jumpy and impatient. I became a devilish whirl of activity, nervously cleaning, folding, driving to the drug store for any off-the-shelf remedy to ease Will's symptoms from chemo and radiation. He was on a ten-week course of Cisplatin, a chemotherapy drug so toxic that Will had to sign forms acknowledging the Food and Drug Administration's black box warnings of such.

I would regularly drop off Will curbside at Emory Hospital, saying "Wait right here! Don't move!" and then quickly park, run back, hands supporting my bouncing pregnant belly, to walk Will to chemotherapy. Then, I would dash and duck into the hallway to answer a call from Sloane Kettering in New York or MD Anderson in Dallas for alternative treatment options. There was also a new radiotherapy at Loma Linda in California. My reporter's brain wanted to know it all. My phone would buzz repeatedly, and I would pace from the waiting room to the hallway, waiting for the callbacks. Then, one treatment day, Will caught me by my hand.

"Wait. Just come sit with me," he said.

"Just a sec. This is the doctor from Cleveland Clinic."

"Leave it. Send it to voicemail. Come sit with me." He gave me a plaintive look. "Please."

The phone went silent. What if. . . what if. . . But I forced myself to sit still. Will rested his hand on my stomach. "Was that her? I think she moved."

"Yup. She's pretty feisty lately." I smiled and squeezed Will's hand, which warmed mine. "I think she's ready to meet her dad."

Two months later, my water broke as I rifled through Will's clothes to find him something to wear to his radiology appointment.

"Come on over!" the maternity nurse had said cheerfully when I called, expecting I'd dash to the car and immediately drive directly to the hospital like every expectant mother-to-be in active labor.

"Can I take my husband to his 10:00 a.m. doctor's appointment? I have time, right?" I didn't say it was for cancer treatment.

"Ma'am, I don't understand. Technically, you're going into labor. I mean, I can't tell you *not* to come. I can only say that you should arrive as soon as possible. . .?" The nurse's voice trailed off, befuddled.

"Got it. I hear you. I'll be there as soon as possible," I replied and hung up the phone. I turned to Will "We can keep your radiology appointment."

"Are you sure?" Will looked for any excuse to miss the appointment. He wanted to save his energy.

"Yes! Yes. I'm sure I'll be fine. I don't feel anything yet. Not really." Actually, how would I know? I had no idea what labor contractions felt like. Only the night before, I had finished the last chapter of *What to Expect When You're Expecting*, not expecting the chapter about needing to breastfeed every two hours. When would I sleep?

Six hours later, we arrived at the maternity ward, and minor cramps pinged. The nurses quickly put me in a wheelchair and rolled me down a long hallway to a delivery room.

"Nurse, can you please slow down so my husband can see where we're going?" She hadn't even noticed Will, a frail man trying to keep up.

"He's in cancer treatment," I explained. Ah. There it is. Her surprised look but then also a dose of pity. I sighed, "It's okay. Let's go slower. Baby's not going anywhere yet."

Eight hours later, my blue hospital gown fell around me like a crop top, and the monitor's pitch tone alerted it was time again to push. *Push!* everyone screamed. Two nurses, the doctor, Will, and Jodi, who had brought me sandwiches, even me.

"Yes! Yes!"

"Harder!"

"Now again. PUSH!"

"I'm trying!" I shouted and stared at my feet, dressed in shapeless fuzzy socks. I was buck-naked under a white sheet that barely clung to my knees, and I was on the brink of falling, surrounded by a cheering squad. The obstetrician peeked at my (no-longer) private parts and looked mildly concerned. I would have batted him away with a "Stop that!" if I wasn't in so much pain.

He noted my grunting. "We don't want to prescribe too much anesthetic. At your age, Carol, we need you to feel the process and the baby."

I felt her alright. She was stuck in the middle of my vagina, which was where Will pointed the video camera.

"Hey! Hey! Hey! Watch what you're recording!" I shouted.

Will sidestepped to a different position. "Okay, give me a sec."

Who exactly was going to see this video anyway? There wasn't an audience, not even my family, who'd want to watch a gooey baby slide out of that place. Thirteen hours into labor and more shouts of "Okay, okay, here we go!" and the contractions started coming faster.

"PUSH!!" I took a deep inhale and pushed. Nothing.

"That's okay, sweetheart," Will reassured me. He teetered to the big chair in the corner of the room by a window overlooking the hospital parking lot and collapsed into the vinyl cushions with a sigh; the video camera paused beside him.

Jodi tenderly asked, "Will, do you want me to take over?" She gestured toward the camera. "I don't mind."

"Nah. I'm good." Jodi picked up the camera anyway when Will closed his eyes. The next round of contractions will be it. I just know.

"Okay! Again!" I looked at Will as he rose out of the chair.

"Push!!" the nurses screamed.

"Carol. It's time," the doctor urged me to make the extra effort.

Will stumbled toward me. When I had spoken for him and agreed to the most aggressive therapy, was that what he really wanted? Would he have said yes if we weren't pregnant? He reached my bedside.

"She's coming, Will," I said. "She's coming." I took another big breath in and squeezed his hand.

"Push!"

"Let go, Carol, let go!"

Everyone said I wouldn't remember the pain.

Chloe arrived in the middle of a thunderstorm shortly after four in the morning. She weighed seven pounds, eight ounces and looked like a tiny Chairman Mao. Her chubby cheeks and pinched eyes gave her the "What the f___" attitude of a small, ruthless dictator. Even with her startled, angry demeanor,

Chloe was breathtakingly beautiful, a miracle. I was a hot mess but so practiced at a solid game face, I was surprised to see my newborn's skeptical look. I was terrified, and she knew it.

She screamed while the nurses bathed her and gently placed her on my chest. But Chloe was hungry, and the room was cold. She and I were pragmatists. I pulled her to my breast the way the book said I should, and she suckled tentatively at first, and then with more commitment.

We were off to a good start, if not a completely tender one. I wrapped the hospital blanket around her, felt her buttery, warm skin on mine, and fell into her dark, expressive eyes. Just hours into Chloe's life, I could see she had my eye color, Will's square face and half-moon chin dimple, but also the deeply furrowed brow of an old soul, the worried expression of my mother.

A couple weeks later, my mom flew to Atlanta to help.

"Who are you? Ch-ch-ch!" She dropped her suitcases in the front hall and reached for Chloe to kiss and tease her cheeks. "She needs changing!" I knew Chloe's diaper was dry, but my mom swept her off to the changing pad on the kitchen counter, where I had set up a stack of diapers and a package of baby wipes. Chloe stomped her left foot on the pad and squirmed indignantly as my mom instructed, "Chloe, stay still. Let me do this! Aiya. Put your leg down." I imagined this same scene forty years ago, but with my mother changing me.

That evening, I found myself hoping that Chloe's feistiness was a good sign. I needed my girl to be strong. But I also felt desperate for her to sleep. You're not missing anything, Chloe. Perhaps, she sensed I was full of it. Perhaps, at only two weeks old, she intuited she'd miss Will most of all. I curled around her round little body in bed to warm her. She squawked.

"It's okay, darling. Are you still hungry?" I pulled up my maternity top, and she found me and latched on. I craved her life force, her nourishing me as I fed her. She fit in the bend of my arm and filled a space I didn't know I had. And I hoped and prayed, with all my heart, this was how it would be for her and me.

"Mommy's here. Daddy's here. You're alright." I started to hum, as I thought a mother would. An old Beach Boys song from my sunny southern California childhood came back to me, like a dream, and I sang the familiar melody. "Don't worry, baby, everything will turn out alright. . . don't worry, baby. . ." Then, the words and tune trailed away—proof to my child that I had never taken the time to learn the entire song.

20. ILLUSIONS

A few weeks later, Will and I returned to Emory Hospital to learn if the treatment had worked. We were concentrating on his unsteady footsteps across the slick and shiny linoleum floors when a voice rang out.

"It's you!" A woman stopped us, and her eyes lit when she recognized me. She was in a floral dress and pretty gold earrings and looked like she was on her way to lunch. She casually draped her coat over her arm and held her dark red purse by its faux bamboo handles in front of her skirt in that poised, lady-like manner that Atlanta mothers had refined through the generations.

"I just *love* watching you on CNN." She tilted her head and smiled. She reached out, and for a split second, I thought she would pinch my cheek. Instead, her polished nails landed lightly on my forearm, and she let out a giddy squeal. "I just knew it was you by your hair! You're Carol Lin!"

"Thank you," I said, trying to be polite and subconsciously smoothing the bangs of my signature short haircut, but I ached a little when her gaze traveled from me to the stroller and on to Will and her smile faded. We looked like characters from a dystopian play; I was the Madonna with an extra fifteen pounds of baby weight, and Will was frail and weak. Her eyes searched for positivity, proof of life.

"Well, um, it's nice to meet you in person, Carol. I can see why I haven't seen you on TV lately." Then she quickly added,

"I mean, the baby. The baby! You had a baby and. . . I should say. . . congratulations!" She clutched her purse and took a small step backward in case whatever was going on with me was contagious.

"Thank you," I called again to the woman, who was already halfway to the parking lot.

Will shook his head, more disappointed than embarrassed. I turned to him. "Just ignore her, Will." I pretended not to care what people thought of us, the odd couple pushing a stroller.

Will took his free hand to pat my arm and smiled for my benefit. "It's okay, Carol. They're just rentals."

'Rentals' was a term Will used to describe people who wafted in and out of our lives without purpose. Rentals bought you drinks so they could get introduced to your boss. Rentals flattered you into inviting them to a free dinner because they knew about your connection to the restaurant's owner. Rentals were the opposite of Keepers, who were more challenging to find when you worked in television. And also, when you were very, very sick.

When we arrived at the clinic, a nurse handed us a clipboard. "Fill this out, please. I'll let the doctor know you're here." She handed me the same white form as last time, on the same blue plastic clipboard with a dirty white string holding hostage a ballpoint pen that bled blue ink.

"I filled this out last time. I fill this form out *every* time. And aren't his prescriptions listed in his medical record?" The nurse ignored me, which was difficult considering how much space I and the stroller occupied at her counter. She gestured for Will to get on the scale and returned to her paperwork on the counter as Will gingerly stepped up to keep his balance. He kept his heavy jacket on, hoping to weigh more for any reason.

"One-hundred-forty pounds," the nurse said as she jotted down the pittance of the number.

Sanjay Gupta knew Will had continued to lose weight. "Sometimes the chemo attacks the muscle, Carol. Just stay with the treatment plan. Take it one day at a time," he had reassured.

I wheeled Chloe over to the side and then returned to Will to guide him to the plastic-molded chair next to us. I kissed his reddened cheek to lighten the moment, but his face swelled from the steroids that were supposed to relieve pressure where the tumor pressed on the delicate areas around his eyes.

"Stud!" I whispered, and Will grinned in that way that made him so charming.

We waited in a separate room where the immune-compromised chemotherapy patients were less exposed to others in the waiting room. I rocked Chloe in her stroller and wondered why the black hands on the wall clock didn't seem to move.

When the nurse signaled it was our turn, I lightly jostled Will, who had dozed off. She led us down a vanilla-colored hallway into a brightly lit office, asked us to sit, and then closed the door behind her. Dr. Marcus, bent over his notes, closed the green folder on his desk. Our entire future was in those clinical pages. He removed his reading glasses and rubbed his eyes, and in the seconds before he spoke, I thought about the video milliseconds in a dark edit bay of the before shot, and the after.

When we first met Dr. Marcus five months ago, we were grateful to get the appointment. But as time passed, we had felt pawned off to resident doctors in training. We wondered if Dr. Marcus even remembered Will was his patient. Today, there was no hug or high five or reassurances for us. Then again, what did we expect?

Good news. We expected good news.

"How are you, Will?" Dr. Marcus turned Will's face this way and that and lightly touched his swollen jaw.

"I'm okay, doc," Will said, politely waving the doctor's hand away, "I'm ready to hear. Did it work?"

Dr. Marcus sighed and circled around to sit at his desk. "Will, as you know, we put you through the most aggressive therapy available for head and neck cancers. I'm sorry to tell you, that while we thought the tumor was rapidly shrinking, it's actually grown larger and become more aggressive."

"Oh no," Will rasped and covered his face with his hands.

A rush of adrenaline surged through me, and I nervously rocked Chloe's stroller back and forth. At the same time, a brain fog had set in after *larger and more aggressive*. "Dr. Marcus, I don't understand. . ."

The doctor showed us Will's most recent MRI on the light board on his wall, crowded with framed medical degrees, gold seals, and black-and-white certificates meant to assure his patients they were getting the best possible care from the smartest man in the room. He pointed to the constellation of cloudy white tentacles that reached down Will's jawline, indicating the tumor was a "breakthrough cancer."

I asked Dr. Marcus to explain what he meant when I thought medical breakthroughs were positive. He repeated that a breakthrough cancer first appeared to succumb to early rounds of treatment but insidiously adapted and eventually grew stronger.

Will stared at his shoes, but the heat of what the doctor said scorched. I howled like a wild animal caught in a trap. "How can this be?!! He's done everything you've asked of him. Everything!"

Dr. Marcus startled and blinked. "There's nothing more we can do."

"Nothing? What the hell do you mean nothing?" I shouted and abruptly stood. Chloe started to whimper, and Will tried to pull me back into my chair, but I raged on. "You're not giving us options. What about a clinical trial? A second or third opinion? Another round of radiation? You said the tumor is supposed to be extra sensitive to radiation." Then I shrieked, "*You told us at one point the tumor was shrinking!*"

I hung all my hopes on the more than fifty percent of patients with Will's cancer who responded well to treatment. The doctor must be holding out on us. Did he want us to beg for his secret stash of cures? If not for us, then who? Why wasn't he making us feel we were being given every option available, telling us about all the clinical trials underway, all the magic happening in labs nationwide? Where was the hope?

"I'm sorry, Carol. I have to leave it at that. Again, I'm very sorry." Dr. Marcus stood and motioned to the door. "I know this must be difficult to hear. Would you like to meet with one of our social workers?"

Ah. The handoff. We were officially cancer castaways. Orphans. Lost causes. The poorly performing cases that cut into an oncologist's otherwise good statistics built upon all the lives he *could* save. We wouldn't want to lower your average now, would we, doctor? It might cost you that research grant. This was the venomous, hate-filled, enraged me, who blamed the doctor because this wasn't our fault. Will was going to live, you'll see, you fucking bastard. We never liked you anyway.

"Let's get out of here, Will. This is not the place for us." I pulled him to his feet and fought the urge to shake Dr. Marcus, to spit and claw at him and wipe his desk with one sweep of my arm. That's what I thought of his efforts. This was a ridiculous waste of time.

As I drove us home, Chloe's crying broke the silence, and reality sank in like toxic lead heading toward the ocean floor. What were we going to do now?

I was winded carrying sleeping Chloe, still strapped in her car seat, up our front stairs, but I ran back to help Will. With one arm around his shoulders and the other hand gripping his belt, I walked him up the steep steps. We paused to catch our breath at the front door and then found our way inside, inconsolable.

My mother stood in the foyer between the stairs and the living room. She knew. Somehow, she had known all along. She froze with her hands clasped, lips pursed tight, and eyes that stared at the floor. I started to cry.

I thought when my mom saw me cry, she'd instinctively come to me. Come to me, Mommy. Throw your arms around me; tell me it will be alright. But she was bolted in place. My mom was all about doing, not saying things. We Chinese are supposed to show our love with our deeds, not words. She was here to help with the baby and left me to deal with my passions as I saw fit.

Jodi burst through our front door. She was the first call I had made in the car. She immediately threw her arms around Will, almost knocking him off his feet. "Whoa, Jodi, or I might have to beat you off with a stick," Will half-joked but then retreated to the other room.

"Will, it's gonna be alright!" she called after him before she spun around and saw I had dropped to my knees. "Carol, oh my God."

My brave, beautiful girlfriend hadn't even wiped the tears streaming down her face before she tried to dry mine. As the senior executive producer, Jodi had been all business on 9/11— focused, calm, the only way to be when news breaks. But here, she cried for me, tender and protective, as close to me as a sister. My mom watched from a safe distance and greeted Jodi with a slight wave before she retreated to the kitchen to make the tea that no one wanted.

"I don't know what to do, Jodi," I said. "There's got to be something I can do."

"What did the doctor say?" She led me to the living room sofa where we could sit without disturbing Chloe, who slept in the car seat in the foyer. I repeated what the doctor said, and Jodi calmed me with her logical list of options and ideas for cancer specialists elsewhere. What about Sloane Kettering in New York or MD Anderson in Houston, Texas? What about UCLA? We brainstormed like when Jodi put a show together, by itemizing and evaluating who we knew and how to make those connections pay off. I brought my computer over and researched emails to various specialists to start a back-and-forth with different doctors who might have other experimental treatment paths for Will.

What did Will want? I hadn't asked. Of course, he wanted to live at any cost. This was not up for discussion. Journalists beat odds by never taking 'no' as the final answer. There was always a path to 'yes.' My cousin and her husband, both doctors, got a lead at UCLA, a research hospital, and found specialists who thought more broadly when one therapy fails and what others might work.

In a matter of days, I was on the phone with Dr. Fairooz Kabbinavar, a specialist in prostate cancer who had taken a particular interest in the types of head and neck cancer that Will had, as some prostate therapies had shown promise with Squamous Cell tumors. Dr. Kabbinavar was interested in Will's case. "We have a different chemotherapy protocol that might be useful, Carol," he said. "When can you get here?" 'Useful' differed from 'effective,' but I'd take it for now.

Getting from Atlanta to Los Angeles was as realistic as flying to the moon when one passenger was only six weeks old and the other was an immuno-compromised cancer patient. Both were prone to life-threatening infections. We couldn't fly commercially. Driving would take too long and be too arduous for Will. I needed a plane. The company jet. I would offer to reimburse CNN, even though I had no idea how much a private jet cost to rent. Could I even rent CNN's plane?

Working for CNN sounds bougie but the company has always prided itself on being grassroots. The news was the star. If you wanted an upgrade, by all means, pay for it yourself, Carol. The CNN jet was for the most senior executives flying to wherever it was senior executives needed to be. Not my world. Will and I were still people who shopped at Costco, flew economy, clipped coupons, and borrowed Halloween costumes. I took inventory of what I could sell, including the house, cars, and clothes. I'd sell everything I owned if I had to. I had a sick husband, a newborn, an elderly mother, and a large cat, Billy, and I had to get all of us to Los Angeles as quickly as possible.

I knew how to ask difficult questions. And yet, in those moments, I still had to coach myself: *Ask. Just pick up the phone. Like you've done a million times over the years. Just speak. Your words matter, Carol.*

I was about to call CNN's Worldwide President to see if we could buy a ride to Los Angeles. Jim Walton was one of the most influential men in cable television, whose job, when it came to my position at the company, entailed seeing me as no more than a line item on a spreadsheet of salaries. At his level, I was a business decision. He managed up, not down. I had never seen Jim on the newsroom floor. His people had people, and I worked for *their* people. But Jodi always said, *if you don't ask, you don't get.*

"I understand what you're going through, Carol," Jim said. "I lost my sister to lung cancer. It was devastating. Let me help."

Periodically, the CNN jet was scheduled to fly to LA to be serviced. He would arrange for my family to be on one of those maintenance flights.

Cancer, that evil bastard, united us.

Will, Chloe, and I, along with my mom and cat, were able to fly home safely to Hermosa Beach, California and stay with my friend Adele, who by then was living with the house painter, Jim, who had become Will's best friend. They made space in their duplex, which was only a few blocks from our house that was still under renovation. Will and I had started construction because of our long-term plan to return to Southern California. Now all we had was today.

Arriving at Adele's, we rolled out of the taxi like a clown car of luggage, baby gear, and Billy in his carrier. Chloe kicked excitedly in her car seat in the back of the cab. Adele, now officially "Aunt Adele," leaned in, took Chloe's little feet dressed in white socks, and playfully stretched out her chubby legs to make her giggle.

"Yoga baby!" Adele teased. Jim joined us outside, too.

"Hi, Adele! Thank you again for. . . for this," I said. "Hey Jim, good to see you. I think I need help getting Will out of the car." I unbuckled Will's seat belt, braced, and reached under his arms to pull him out of the taxi. Jim offered a hand so Will could steady himself. Adele turned and hugged him, careful not to show her shock at how different he looked.

"You still have your hair!" she teased.

"Yup. Good looking as usual," Will replied with a short chuckle. Adele carried the car seat and Chloe while I got the cat and bags to the downstairs apartment below where Jim and Adele lived and worked. I looked over my shoulder. Jim teased Will who leaned on his cane and brightened at all the old jokes. I smiled for the first time since leaving Atlanta. This was a turning point; I just knew it. The change was already doing us good. Chloe would get to know her Aunt Adele and Uncle Jim, and I'd have babysitters if needed. Will's first new chemotherapy was already scheduled for this week.

"Don't think of the end goal as old age," Dr. Kabbinavar advised. "Think of it as living with cancer and being able to collect memories and experiences."

At our first in-person appointment at UCLA, I immediately liked Dr. Kabbinavar. He reminded me of a sage with warm brown eyes behind thick glasses. "We have to keep Will strong enough to endure a different chemotherapy and buy time for a scientific breakthrough," he said. "We have to hope the body of cancer research already underway worldwide will pay off. Yes, this means praying for a miracle."

That God thing again. I nodded politely but I knew even God didn't offer lifetime guarantees.

"Sounds good, doc," Will replied.

Dr. Kabbinavar repeated that our goal was for further treatment to keep the tumor from growing larger. Eliminating it altogether was not going to happen at this stage. But this strategy meant Will and I had gone from running a marathon of chemo and radiation to playing hopscotch against a cancer with no cure. Three jumps forward to make the right medical connections, but now the hard part was upon us to ensure we didn't go two steps backward.

At least we had a plan, and our clock reset with a new timeline: ten weeks of chemo, once a week at UCLA. And then there was my personal plan: I'd read articles about the psychology of doctor-patient relationships, and statistically, patients who had a positive relationship with their medical team had better outcomes. Every appointment at UCLA became a critical opportunity to make a strong impression and win over the medical team who had fifty other patients to care for. I needed everyone at the hospital rooting for us and to be inextricably invested in our outcome.

Turns out my mother was right: how others saw us determined our destiny. The more the cancer sapped Will's energy and natural charisma, the more Chloe and I had to make up the difference.

I needed my baby with me to bat her eyes at the nurses. It was not beneath me to roll by the nurse's station pushing Chloe in her stroller, a breast pump and diaper bag slung over my shoulder. I'd hold Chloe up like a little human billboard and hope the nurses took the baby bait and asked, "Who's your daddy?"

"Can't wait to see him!" I'd smile and add, "Room 325!"

If I could have, I would have printed Chloe a T-shirt with a 1-800 number to call "for more information. . ." if it guaranteed that Will stayed at the top of their priorities for an extra blanket or faster dose of pain medication.

As it was, I made sure she laid against my breast every two hours and timed her feeding to the doctor's morning and afternoon rounds. Chloe and I set the scene, and thus the stakes, when they checked up on Will. I didn't feel guilty about any of this. Attention-getting was essential for any reporter in competition for an extensive interview. Choose me over my competition. I had to be memorable. Of course, other patients were not competition in the same way as NBC or CBS was for CNN. But five months spent in hospitals since Will's diagnosis had taught me that nurses were pressed for time, and I knew how precious a commodity time was. But never more so than when my husband had so little of it left.

While my mother didn't understand why Chloe had to go to the hospital with me, at least she was pleased to know exactly where I was at all times. I was either sitting with Will at chemo at UCLA or Torrance Hospital's emergency room because he had a complication, or I was at Little Company of Mary because Will's complications required special equipment. Sometimes, I was in the ambulance because Will's complications became urgent. Still, I thought this was progress because we weren't sitting around. We were doing things, important things. We were on the road to the acupuncturist, the radiologist, the oncologist, and all the "'ists'" who would make Will better. I saw what I wanted to see: the possibility that Will was getting better.

Two weeks into his new treatment, my hope almost killed him.

"Will, time for a walk!" I said. I kept Will on an exercise routine because Sanjay said chemotherapy attacked the muscle. I interpreted that to mean Will should bulk up.

"Okay, sweetheart, here I come!" Will winked playfully as he pulled on his leather jacket that now swallowed him whole. I tied his shoelaces, rationalizing that I was better at pulling the leather laces tight, not that he couldn't do this himself. I handed him his cane for better balance on the sloping beach streets. He initially stepped tentatively but tried to speed up when I pulled his sleeve.

It took twenty minutes to reach the flat alley at the bottom of the street.

"Honey, this way. Let's go on the ocean walk." I cheerfully steered Will toward the beach, but he suddenly stopped and lurched out of my grip. The neighbor's iron gate broke his fall.

"Will!" I screamed. He hunched over, breathing hard, with big gulps in and gasping breath out.

"Will, I've got you!" I screamed again, and he pivoted to steady himself on the side of the neighbor's house.

"Carol. . . get Jimmy," Will whispered calmly as he winced. I lunged forward to wrap my arms around him, but I lost my balance as he continued to slide, the rough stucco scratching his jacket.

"Oh God, I'm so sorry. I'm so sorry! Help! HELP! Jimmy!" I caught my foot on the rough alley pavement and grabbed Will's jacket to keep him from falling. His five-foot-ten-inch frame only weighed 138 pounds now, nearly fifty pounds less than when he was diagnosed six months ago.

"Jimmy! Jimmy! Help! Help!" I screamed again. I pressed my entire body against Will to keep him upright against the wall, but I knew we were both going down.

Jim raced around the corner. "I've got him, I've got him. Good God, Carol, where were you taking him?" He scooped up Will like a doll, carried him back to the house, and laid him down on our bed. Will closed his eyes and began to breathe normally, so we decided not to call an ambulance.

"I'm sorry, Will. I'm so sorry," I babbled, teary-eyed, high-pitched, and childish. "Thank you, Jim. I'm sorry. I thought. . . I thought Will wanted to go outside." Chloe began to cry from her bassinet. Babies intuitively knew what was happening, even if they didn't understand it.

I needed to believe Will was getting better (wasn't he?) and that the new cancer treatment was working (wasn't it?). I had already planned that we'd move back to California for good next year when he regained his strength. And Will never disagreed, refused to discuss whether he might die. We were willingly, lovingly complicit in all the lies we told ourselves.

21. ALL OF YOU

Doctors diagnosed Will's sudden weakness as a new infection which sent him back to the UCLA Medical Center for a blood transfusion. His white cell count had dropped to almost zero. It was an ominous sign that only two weeks in, the new chemotherapy we counted on was brutally attacking his healthy cells.

"Carol, Will, it's time to make some decisions," Dr. Kabbinavar said when he stopped by Will's hospital room to see how he felt. "Ultimately, surgery is the standard of treatment to remove a tumor of this size. Chemotherapy and radiation have done all they can."

Surgery? Why hadn't it been recommended before? I sat on Will's bed and held his hand. I bit my lips and thought bitterly about how I had failed as Will's advocate. Why didn't I ask about surgery when he was first diagnosed?

As if Dr. Kabbinavar had read my mind, he said, "Surgery was always the highest risk because the tumor originates so closely to vital functions like the brain, eyes, and nose. Many things can go wrong. We always hope less invasive treatments will be sufficient. But Will, I think you've had all you can take with the chemo. It may just kill you before the cancer does." He flipped through Will's chart and noted the downward spiral of his blood count profile. The numbers depicted Will's body as a warzone, with good and evil battling on a cellular level. Today, his white cells, the good guys, were overwhelmed as the cancer cells claimed more territory. Hadn't I once begged to immerse myself in a warzone, where lives—even the survival of entire populations—were at stake? But now, with a month left on my maternity leave, only two lives mattered to me: my husband's and my baby's.

Dr. Kabbinavar set aside Will's chart, pulled up a chair next to us, and explained that the operation would require seventeen surgeons with different skills to excise the cancer and infected tissue, along with large portions of Will's sinus and sections of his teeth, gums, mouth, and jawbone. A different group of plastic surgeons would try to rebuild Will's face. Dr. Kabbinavar told us a surgery of this magnitude would take twenty-one hours.

I felt Will's hand tighten around mine. Breaking apart Will's face and putting it back together again sounded like science fiction. Of course he was terrified. But why wasn't I? The operation sounded insane, but I had been living my own kind of crazy. Tunnel vision had set in ever since Chloe was born. I only allowed myself to see the light. My brain considered one singular conceivable outcome. Will and I had endured. I was his; he was mine. Will had to live. He just had to. But the doctors warned that the operation was most definitely an eleventh-hour Hail Mary.

Will tightened his grip, but his voice sounded calm when he asked, "Doctor, what do we have to do to make the operation work?"

Dr. Kabbinavar sighed. He wasn't soft selling the complicated approval process, the number of decision-makers, and the possibility that UCLA might still say no. UCLA's Tumor Board and Ethics Committee would have to review Will's case. Each of the seventeen doctors required had to personally sign off and agree that the operation was the most viable next step, and that surgery of this magnitude would do more good than harm for the patient. If a single doctor said "no," it would be the end of the road for us.

I didn't think Will's body could take any more punishment. The nurses had difficulty finding a vein for his regular blood draws. Still, I focused on the future. "When will we know if the board agrees to the operation?" I said.

Dr. Kabbinavar put Will's chart back on the hook at the end of the bed. "By the end of this week or early next week. I'll let you know how the process is going. Hang in there, you two. I know this is hard, but we're still in the game."

While the decision-makers worked on our next play, Will and I remained sidelined. Patients and families were not allowed to attend the Tumor and Ethics Board meetings. I had to imagine what the auditorium would look like, filled with doctors in white coats and a stage with a podium. In my imaginary meeting, a large screen displayed a Power Point about the patient, my husband, with a list of his treatment, poor outcomes, and limited options. On paper, Will sounded average: white male, middle-aged, of medium height but diminishing build. Married. Father of one. I liked thinking that Chloe's presence in his life might spark the doctors' compassion. Might they also mention that the baby was only eight weeks old?

While we waited for the Ethics Board to review Will's case, Chloe and I commuted back and forth between Manhattan Beach and UCLA. We weren't sure, this time, how long Will would be hospitalized. Again and again, I loaded up the car seat, stroller, baby in one hand, breast pump in the other, and finally, a diaper bag on my back, so full it could stand up by itself.

A week after Dr. Kabbinavar submitted Will's case for approval, Chloe and I navigated through rush hour traffic and returned to the hospital as the sun dipped below the horizon. In Will's room, I turned off the harsh overhead light and flicked on the table lamp that cast a warm glow. Chloe quietly sucked on her pacifier and played with the plastic monkey toy I had tied to the car seat handle. The toy's rattle woke Will.

"Hi Stinks," I whispered and kissed him on the forehead.

Groggy from painkillers, Will smiled and watched sleepily as I lifted Chloe, bright-eyed in a pink cotton zip-up, and laid her next to him. "How's our girl?" he asked. I crawled in, the baby between us.

"She wants her daddy," I said as I folded the edges of the hospital blankets into a nest where Chloe gurgled and rolled contentedly side to side. Will tickled her and Chloe smiled and slapped at the tangle of plastic tubes that dangled from his arm.

"She's getting so big," he said. He'd been here for a little more than a week, but he was right. Chloe seemed to change by the hour, grasping at things, furrowing her brow, then dissolving into smiles. She gave Will a happy sigh as her eyes finally grew heavy with sleep.

We heard a soft knock on the door. "Hello? Can I come in?" A doctor I didn't recognize entered.

"Of course. Hi. Oh." I sat up and straightened out the crumpled blankets and brushed my fingers through my hair. "Excuse the mess."

"Good evening, I'm Dr. Jansen, one of the surgeons considering your case. Will and Carol, is it?" He remained in the doorway with one leg casually crossed over the other. His hands rested in the pockets of his long white doctor's coat. "I'll only be a moment. I don't want to disturb you," he said quietly, noting our little family. "I just wanted us to meet."

"How can we help you, Dr. Jansen?" Is this what he expected from meeting us? Did he recognize me from CNN? Did he even care about such things? At the same time, I was very glad he came. It meant they were still considering the operation.

The doctor pursed his lips and then explained, "I want you to know the serious nature of this surgery and ensure you understand the extent of the operation." I had already heard the details from Dr. Kabbinavar and assumed this was just another performative risk management conversation, but I thought twice about interrupting him. My aggressive reporter intuition was a turn-off but still so much of who I had become. I needed Dr. Jansen to like us and take our case, so I listened as if this was the first time hearing the horrific details. "Your husband will be on the operating table for more than twenty hours. We will need to remove the entire section of the left side of his face to remove the tumor and create margins wide enough to feel confident we've gotten as much of the cancer as possible."

Mmhmm. Yes, yes, I know.

"He may be permanently disfigured. There's no guarantee we can rebuild his jaw. And. . . ," he paused, "you realize he may never eat solid food again." Dr. Jansen chose to be specific, more graphic than Dr. Kabbinavar, but I didn't want to think about what family dinner would look like in the future, or what Will could not do, or even how Will would feel about his life. The important thing was he would be with us. That's what this fight was all about. When you are in the fight for your life, why would you ask what is a life truly worth living? Only healthy people can afford to ask such a question, to consider choices like eating more vegetables and less red meat or weighing the virtues of cardio over resistance training.

But Dr. Jansen insisted we think hard about the life ahead. He said the man returning from the operation would look nothing like my Will, and this did frighten me. "This next step is not for everyone, Carol. Some people are ready to let go." Dr. Jansen was saying we could say no, let Will slide away on a cloud of time and painkillers.

I grabbed Will's hand, expecting it to be sweaty, but he felt cool and dry. This time, Will didn't squeeze back.

Dr. Jansen continued, "There is only a four percent chance that the operation will be successful. You may die on the operating table, Will. Is this the risk you really want to take?" Dr. Jansen wanted us to understand we had a choice.

Will watched Chloe at his side, sleeping. His hand rested on her belly which rose and fell with her steady breath. She was every reason to have this conversation. She was the heart of us, so full of life, her scent the honey that offset the sour hospital disinfectant.

I itched to answer Dr. Jansen—yes, this was what Will really wanted. But this doctor needed to hear from Will. Please say yes, darling. Of course you'll say yes. Love us, Will. Be with us. Just say yes.

Will hesitated. Then he said, "Doctor, we could flip the percentage around and say, even with the operation, I have a ninety-six percent chance of dying. Or that I have a four percent chance of surviving. But that four percent is four percent more than I have right now."

I exhaled, relieved, and kissed Will's forehead.

"No truer words, Will." Dr. Jansen remained in the doorway, crossed his arms, and looked at us as if he saw us anew. Perhaps even the doctor didn't know for sure why he was standing in our hospital room. Before meeting us, Will was an easier decision, just a cluster of statistics and outcomes in a case file, a person reduced to numbers on a page. Part of me believed this doctor wanted the story behind the patient.

"If the odds are so minimal, doctor, why would you decide to do the operation?" I asked.

"Frankly. . ." He hesitated and looked around the room littered with baby things. Finally, his eyes landed on our little family again, sandwiched between steel bed rails, and he continued, nodding at Chloe. "I would consider doing the surgery because of you. All of you. You have a lot to live for. I wanted to be sure that you're in it for the fight and understand the risks but are realistic about what life would be like for Will. If he survives the operation."

Dr. Jansen's 'yes' sent a surge of hope through me. Afterall, who were we to him? I had nothing to trade for this favor, no airtime or swag. I was so used to being a friendly pawn in someone's personal strategy that I hardly recognized myself as Dr. Jansen saw me: a wife and mother trying to save her family.

"She's beautiful. How old?" Dr. Jansen nodded to the baby.

"Eight weeks," I said with a sigh.

He smiled. "She looks like her dad."

"I know. I hear that all the time. All of the work, but I get none of the credit," I joked.

Dr. Jansen paused with a smile, then returned to business. "I'm going to recommend the surgery."

For a few seconds, my fear gave way to relief and gratitude. We've got a chance. Will and I grasped one another and grinned like cats. This was the break we'd prayed for.

"However, I have one last criterion," Dr. Jansen added.

One more hurdle. There was always just one more hurdle. "What is it doctor?" Will asked.

"We'll do one more scan of your vertebrae. Will, we want to be realistic. If any area lights up on the scan, it means your cancer has spread to your spine. We would call the surgery off."

I didn't understand. Why this one last test?

"Carol, if the cancer has reached his spine, the cancer is everywhere. And my dear, the surgery will be for naught."

I gulped. Cancer clusters on CT scans looked like fireflies against a black background—small, bright, deadly spots. Just one light the size of a pinhead and it'd be over for Will. For us.

22. JADE

Southern California's winter eased into cool spring nights. I was acutely aware that the world outside Adele's house still hummed along. Dogs barked, then whimpered happily. The sun rose, set, then rose again. I wanted to stuff that fireball below the horizon and keep it there, stop time, but the sun mocked me. I had lived a hurried life: rushed toward deadlines, kept a tight show, and knew how to close out newscasts to a steady countdown. Carol, in thirty. Fifteen. Ten. . . and. . . you're out. In this way, it felt like I controlled the clock, but now the days raced past me to an inevitability I still could not imagine.

President George W. Bush had just declared "Mission Accomplished" in the war against Iraq, but the camera angle that showed my CNN colleagues on the anchor desk was a portal to my past. I had been gone from work less than three months, but it felt like a lifetime since I had stared down the Taliban. All these months, as sick as Will was, I had bet on the steady stream of treatments offered. Even after hospice had set up the bed and morphine drip, I read articles that reported miraculous patient turn arounds. That impossible, irrational, against-all-odds hope got me up in the morning and convinced me we could be that feel-good news story closing out a dark-of-night newscast. I sat by Will's bed, expecting any moment that he'd open his eyes, energized, cured.

My mother came downstairs where Will laid in a hospital bed in Adele's guest room and padded quietly over to me in her stocking feet.

"Not now, Mom," I said.

"You need to eat, Carol." She gently placed her hand on my shoulder, her touch so foreign.

"I'm not hungry. Please. Just let me sit."

"Chloe needs you." She thought Chloe's need would energize me, but being wanted had become exhausting. "I'm worried about you."

"Well, Mom, I can't make you feel any better. I'm worried, too." I rubbed my face, wet with tears I didn't remember shedding. "Speaking of Chloe, where is she?"

"She's upstairs with Adele. They're playing music. I tell Adele we need to keep Chloe downstairs where she won't fall, but she. . ."

"Mom, she's not going to fall," I interrupted. Will stirred at my rising voice. "She's only ten weeks old. Everyone's holding her. She can't even crawl. Stop worrying all the time." I noted the irony and then spiraled. Cancer gave me a hall pass to explode. "Now you're just going to say I'm wrong. Why don't you ever give me more credit? You. . . you. . . never seem to *like* me, Mom."

She gasped, "You're my daughter!"

"You *love* me. I know." I sighed. "But you don't *like* me. Sure, you like what I *do*. You can brag to your friends. But do you even know me? Do you ask how I *feel*, or what I *want*, or whether I'm scared, or. . . *what I need from you*?"

My mom was aghast. "That's not true! That's not true!" she cried. She looked furtively at Will, then me. "I thought you were *happy*! Why should I ask?"

"You win, Mom. You win." I covered my face with my hands. "I lose, okay? You always said bad things happen to good people all the time. I never wanted to believe you meant. . . me."

"Carol, stop." My mom jostled my shoulders.

"I can't, Mom, I can't. I can't stop," I sobbed. "I don't want to stop! I want to be angry! I'm so *angry*! I can't do this anymore!" I wanted to hurt somebody. My mother was in my crosshairs. I was desperate to throw something. Instead, I folded in half and laid my head on Will's lap.

Will and I had been so high with the prospect of surgery that falling into despair this final time, when a tiny green dot on Will's T5 vertebrae glowed ominously on the scan, was painful. There would be no surgery, no more treatment. For Will, peace had already taken hold and allowed him to savor the time he had left. Now he drifted in and out of a morphine slumber. Just days earlier, the hospice nurse had said, "Soon. It will be soon."

"Carol, I don't want to upset you. I came downstairs to show you something." My mom reached into her sweater pocket and unfolded a green silk pouch and gently pulled out a delicate strand of rich green jade, the gift her mother had given to her, that she was now passing on to me. The last time I saw her bracelet, I was a teenager. She had taken me to a safe deposit box at her bank where she stored small treasures collected over the years: a strand of white pearls my father had bought her, a matching pair of earrings, and this bracelet that she loved with a quiet memory all her own.

"Ten pieces," my mother whispered. Her eyes shined as she gently held the strand of jade up to the light where it glowed. "You and Will married for ten years now?" She smiled, sweetly remembering our wedding anniversary had just passed. "I went to the bank and got this for you."

"For me? Why?" I sniffled and blew my nose.

"I'll tell you a story." She pulled up another chair to sit next to me and reminded me of the night she left her mother and childhood home to come to America to marry my father.

"Your grandmother said goodbye to me at her garden gate. She gave me these ten pieces of jade. I told her it was too much and that she should keep it if she needed to barter her way out of trouble. The civil war was happening. But she insisted a young woman's treasure comes first from her own family, which is always the source of her strength." My mother's voice was from another place and time, and her gaze misted over with a faraway look. She pressed her eyes with a wrinkled tissue. My mother wanted me to see her courage, not her tears. "And when she said goodbye to me, Carol, she told me to come back when it's safe. I will tell you, Carol, you will come back, too. You will see." She pressed the jade in my palm, pleased. "Ten pieces of jade, one for each week since Chloe was born. One for each year you and Will married." She closed my hand around it.

"I don't know what to say." I was her little girl needing to be held. "Mom, I. . . I don't know what to do. What will I do without him? You and Daddy had thirty years together. We. . ."

My mom hugged me and rubbed my back. Her physical touch ignited my lifelong craving for her love. "There, there. I know, Carol. I know. There is never enough time. Carol, it will be okay. You will see."

A week later, Will stirred, dazed but awake. I rushed to his bedside from putting Chloe down for a nap.

"Will. Hi baby, I'm here." I reached for his hand. "What am I going to do without you. Tell me. What. . . what am I going to do?" It was the first time I said these words out loud to him.

He could barely whisper his last words to me. "Be happy," he said. "You will be happy. Just try."

23. ORANGE

The gray of May turned to June Gloom—southern California's dirty little secret never mentioned in the come-hither tourist ads. But that summer of 2003 was my darkest season, when both cold and color took on new meaning.

Two years after 9/11, under the purview of the nation's federal threat analysts, green signified the lowest risk of a terror attack. Red warned that an attack was likely, even imminent. Yellow, like a traffic light, told us to brace, that danger swung from "imminent" to less likely. The summer after Will died, Homeland Security's alert was stubbornly stuck at orange. Orange meant there was a "high" probability of another terror strike, and this notion that we could predict when our lives would irreparably change made me a little crazy. I had just turned my beautiful husband into ash.

In June, I moved Chloe and our cat, Billy, out of Adele's home and into our newly renovated beach house just half a mile away. It was beautiful and modern but really just an empty two-story house that had replaced the original 1940s wood and stucco split-level. Toward the end of construction, the contractors hardly made eye contact with me. They had rushed but knew Will was never going to see the finished home. At one point, the painters had asked what color of white I wanted for the interiors. What do you mean? By then, hospital white was the shade I knew best. To discover the infinite shades of white at the paint store required I get dressed, pack up the baby, and fill her diaper bag with all the things babies need for the simplest errand: toys, snacks, diapers, change of clothes. Suffice to say the subtleties of Swiss Coffee, Decorator White, Canvas, and Ballerina remained lost on me. I only existed in shades of gray.

At night, Chloe would nestle against me, feeding and dozing, while I slumped against the cushion of a gliding rocker, one of the few pieces of furniture scattered around the master bedroom that begged for attention. A brand-new crib painted ivory with white cotton sheets sat in the corner, pushed against a plain wall. My un-made king-size bed was covered in the chaos of mismatched blankets tangled up in sheets. A solitary flattened feather down pillow had the imprint of my head. Gifted books with titles like *The Journey Through Grief* sat unread on the floor next to my only light source, an old lamp that once belonged to Will's parents. There used to be two, but one got lost in the move. One light had to be enough in a world that liked people and things in two's.

Night after night, I would feel Chloe suckle and will myself to feel something more than her tug. Anything. But all that ever came was an iron weight around my heart. The heaviness would pull at me as Chloe pulled and pushed at my breast. At least for her, I was functional and existed to feed her and keep her safe. When she cried, I would rise, gather her up from her crib, fall into the rocker. I was capable of little more. The cracked plastic face on the clock could read two or three or four o'clock in the morning. Time no longer mattered. Days and nights now passed without consequence.

"Let's give her space," friends had whispered as they slipped away and closed doors, real and symbolic. I didn't blame them for wanting an escape, like strangers who flinched on a crowded bus when someone let loose with a sneeze. I read that grief was contagious, that our social brains picked up moods like a virus. Besides, what was left to know? I was the story that had lost its arc. A single widowed mother with a newborn. We were not the obvious party invite.

But I was not alone. Will's cancer was still powerfully alive in my mind with a voice that taunted from the grave. *Do you miss me*, it whispered. For the last seven months, since his diagnosis, the cancer and I had been inseparable. But now, my life was empty without its demands and routines.

I had thought about our future, if I'd be returning to CNN; me, more beast than beauty, nursing, crying, nursing again. Eyes, breasts, and body, red and swollen. My, how far I'd fallen in just two years, from the mountaintop of reporting 9/11 to the losing side of the war on cancer at home.

Jim Walton, the president of CNN Worldwide, had called recently. "Come back when you're ready," he had said.

"I don't know what to say, Jim."

"Don't say anything. Not right now. Just know we're here when you're ready."

"Thank you."

"We want you back. Think about what you want to do." Jim hesitated, then said, "Sometimes we really need to get back to what we do best, Carol. You've got more to offer."

Do I? I was the car engine that refused to ignite.

"Eason is coming out to LA. He wants to see you," Jim had said.

Eason Jordan was CNN's president of news gathering, and his poker-faced demeanor made him hard to read. He'd been with CNN since 1982, virtually from its founding by Ted Turner. Eason oversaw CNN's global news bureaus, but since I was an Atlanta-based anchor handling occasional reporting responsibilities, I was not usually under Eason's purview.

Eason often flew to Los Angeles for meetings, but the trip Jim referred to timed well with the end of my maternity leave. Eason took the quick ten-minute cab ride from LAX to

Manhattan Beach to meet me at a family-owned restaurant before the lunch crowd gathered. I wondered if I looked the same, but Eason, of course, recognized me. I kept forgetting I'd only been on maternity leave for four months, though it felt like years. The hostess sat us by a large window that overlooked the main street, normally considered a prime table where diners want to see-and-be-seen. I winced at the sunny gaze of passersby.

Eason gave me a warm hug before we took our seats. "Carol, I'm sorry for your loss. I arrived early and walked to the end of the pier. I thought it was a place you and Will probably spent time at."

"Mm. Yes," I whispered. I looked down at the pretty table-setting in front of me. I didn't want Eason to see me cry, but teardrops fell onto my salad plate anyway.

Eason laid his hand on mine. "You know that I speak for all of us at CNN. We want you to return to work that's meaningful to you, Carol. Have you thought about what you'd like to do?"

What I'd like to do. I hadn't thought about what I liked or didn't like since cancer dictated what I did or didn't do. Of course, before our meeting, I had anticipated Eason would ask about next steps, but his question tugged at the old me. I wanted what I've always wanted when things got tough. I wanted to run away, far and fast, and feel the velocity of a fast-moving story. I was aware that CNN had a correspondent position open in the Jerusalem Bureau. I picked at my bread roll and asked, "What about Jerusalem? Would you consider sending me to the Middle East?"

This startled Eason. "Israel?" We sat in a beat of silence before he treaded carefully. "Of course you know there's a war going on. Are you prepared to cover a car bomb attack? Is this something you think you. . ." He paused again and chose to be more direct. "Are you prepared to cover families who have lost loved ones. . . so soon after Will?" Eason looked worried, just as

I knew he would. It was a bold ask, but an old twitch of confidence sparked a bit of courage. Yet, the question, once so natural to my workhorse nature, sounded oddly foreign, as if I had voiced someone else's ambition. I let it stand. Eason wasn't going to immediately say no to a grief-stricken widow. I knew if I pushed, CNN would say yes.

"Let's discuss again when you return to Atlanta," Eason said.

If I return, I thought. *If.*

After meeting with Eason, I returned home and took Chloe for a walk to clear my head. I pushed her stroller past rows of charming wooden beach cottages, past the occasional modern three-story glass and stucco tributes to the new money pouring into our quaint community, and past all the doorways painted in whimsical shades of green, blue, or orange.

And lining the sidewalk for the entire ten-block stroll to town were the latest household rage: doormats from Target announcing *Happy Inside*, the words imprinted in hot pink lettering on the thick, coir grass mats. They were a cheerful factory-made declaration of wishful thinking. I was certainly not Happy Inside, but I considered buying one anyway. Of course, the doormats were disingenuous. How many news stories revealed that many people were, in fact, not Happy Inside? A lot of people were Complicated Inside, or even Dangerous Inside. It was more accurate to say I was Waiting Inside but that's not a viral message. It was too sad. Too true.

Friends worried that I had post-partum depression. How would I know? Rick Kaplan called ABC News' Chief Medical Correspondent, Dr. Timothy Johnson, who recommended a psychiatrist in Los Angeles. I said I'd think about it, sure my colleagues thought I had to be going mad. For all that I was going through, they only really knew one woman, the Carol who never let the impossible stop her, the steely woman who never said no.

Another sleepless night followed my meeting with Eason. I rocked back and forth and tried to concentrate on Chloe, who slept soundly on my shoulder. She only had me now. She deserved better. Chloe. Poor, poor girl.

I tiptoed to put her down in her crib, careful not to trip on the empty Pop-Tart boxes and crinkled food wrappers. Sleep had been eluding me like a fugitive. I was desperately tired. But I crossed the hall to where a television sat on another cold floor of another empty room and fumbled at the controls to turn it on.

One gentle push and the DVD clicked. The screen filled with the woman I used to be in the places I used to come alive. Burning flags and checkpoints across Israel and the West Bank, yellow police tape fluttering outside a school shooting. My mom's amateur attempts meant the video skipped and skittered, with clips jumping from one dramatic scene to another. But had life been any different? Hadn't I run from one big story to the next? On television, I was stoically immune to the misfortune that surrounded me.

I wanted to warn myself. *Get out. Run!* Who was this ignorant fool? She was living a con. Her luck was going to run out. Soon, no one will remember she existed. She was just another fallen CNN anchor, lost without the compass of her career.

The picture disappeared with a click.

I padded over to the hallway bathroom mirror, afraid of what I would see. But instead of a haggard specter, I saw dark bangs falling softly over sad brown eyes. In my reflection, I was dead-eyed but with skin still smooth, flush and damp with perspiration, a woman who had created life, fought for life, and still had years to live, still unaware that this grief would light an unexpected fire in me.

And then my baby stirred. And whimpered. Howled. Cried for my body and breast. I was never going to be alone, to grieve in peace. Not for one second. Not even close.

24. OTHER LISA'S

My mom, a daily visitor, was anxious to show her love through random acts of service. She washed, wiped, vacuumed, and cooked, which mysteriously led to more washing and wiping, as if her intent was to clear away the past.

"You need to get out of the house," she said one day, standing at the kitchen sink with her back to me. Her short, permed curls vibrated from the force of her scrubbing a plate taken from a pile of dirty dishes. "You spend too much time by yourself. Chloe needs to see other children."

I looked at Chloe, who lay on the living room rug under a toy arch, batting the monkey and pulling at a stuffed giraffe. She was fascinated with what her little hands could do now. "Mom, she's three months old."

"She's developing," my mom continued because she had raised a daughter, and I had not. "The book says babies' brains are like computers, always taking in information." She paused. "She only sees you."

"What. I'm not enough?

"Carol, that's not what I'm saying."

My mom wiped another plate that was already dry. She finally laid it on the paprika-red Caesarstone countertops, which the architect thought was a clever nod to my Chinese heritage, along with the naturally-stained maple kitchen cabinets. I didn't need decorative touches to be reminded I was a Chinese daughter with a Chinese mother who doubled down on her traditional authority over me.

"She's fine. We're fine," I said, taking a deep breath and then another sip of decaf coffee. Bits of milk floated on the surface of the tepid brown liquid. I was about to check the expiration date on the wax carton when I noticed my coffee mug was chipped. *I should throw it out and get new cups*, I thought. But I couldn't bear to part with anything Will had used. I believed his DNA infused everything around me. His clothes, his shaving kit, and everything in our kitchen that were wedding gifts held bits of him. My chipped cup was a vessel that connected me to my dead husband.

"Ay! So heavy!" My mom had moved on from washing the dishes to the pile of cooking pots by the sink. She weaponized steel wool pads on my Cephalon pans, which she had already complained about ten years ago when we hauled them, still wrapped in gift boxes, to the car after the wedding.

Now, a decade later, she was still complaining. "You need to get smaller pots!" My mom shook the hot, soapy water off her hands and drove in her daggered opinions. "You only cook for one now. You need to be practical. Think about where you are in life now. Don't make things so hard." She held the large pasta pot with two soapy hands and flipped it upside down to peer at its metal inscription. "Bah! Williams and Sonoma. Fancy pots for you!"

"Mom! That's not true. That's mean. Don't say that."

Getting out of the house and meeting new people suddenly sounded like a great idea. I recalled a flyer Adele had left me about a class for new moms and their babies. It was decorated in bright blues and pinks with a bold, white-lettered promise: "Mommy and Me classes bring moms and their babies together uniquely to build lasting relationships!" I was suspicious.

'Unique' was the telltale word in press releases when publicists were unwilling to fully commit to a PR promise.

But there was a class in a couple of hours. I quickly handed the baby to my mom.

"Where are you going?" she demanded as she reached out and awkwardly held Chloe in a half-hunched scoop against her stomach.

"Mom, hold her up! She's going to fall."

I signed up to prove, if only to myself, I hadn't become just a hairy recluse and rummaged through Chloe's diaper bag to take inventory of what I needed for the hour I'd be away. I had chosen my bag for its low-key tan canvas, which felt practical and familiar, like the field bags I used as a reporter. The community center wasn't far, only half a mile; technically, we could walk, but I decided to drive. Out there, beyond my front door, who knew what might happen. I could run out of food or, worse, diapers. Chloe might spit up. *But I can do this*, I told myself. Chloe looked clean enough, even with the spot of breast milk near the zipper of her onesie.

"Where are you going?" my mom repeated as she heaved Chloe to her shoulder.

"Out. I'm taking your advice!" I went downstairs to my closet, where I still had my things in boxes, and rifled through a plastic bin. There you are! I freed a pair of maternity jeans that didn't look too wrinkled. This was my first time meeting new people, so I decided a chunky blue sweater would hide any leaks if class passed my pumping time.

I sniffed my armpits. Oh my gosh, I reeked.

A hot shower felt good. As the warm water hit my face, I brushed my short hair away from my eyes, turned in a circle, and rubbed clean all the essential parts. I quickly toweled off and then struggled to pull my maternity jeans over my damp legs. My hair pancaked flat as I shoved my head into the sweater. *Got to do something about the hair*, I thought to myself. Always the hair. I didn't have time to blow dry and style, so I used a TV trick and flipped my head over, fluffing my hair to damp-dry with my fingertips before spritzing a cloud of hairspray. No time for makeup. Besides, I didn't want anyone to recognize me. I relished that, for one hour, I might hide in plain sight, just another mom with a new baby. The trouble was that I didn't know other moms.

In the mirror, I caught a stray chunk of hair that escaped the initial attack of hairspray and tucked it in, hoping it would hold in place. "Okay, Chloe," I said. "Time to make friends."

I drove Will's old Toyota Camry for good luck. Its faded maroon paint and gray polyester seats were full of memories. The car belonged to Will's dad and had many lives between its heyday in Wichita, Kansas, and its charming decline in Manhattan Beach. I pulled into the community center and parked at the far end, away from the rows of shiny new Jeep Grand Cherokees and Mercedes SUVs. Evidence of mommies abounded in downtown Manhattan Beach. Small bright yellow triangles hung like required parking permits in backseat car windows announcing *Baby on Board*.

I pretended to check my reflection in a car window to sneak a peek inside. Color-coordinated car seats were secured against the soft taupe leather interior. Chloe, in her cute purple polyester onesie, and I stared back, and I wished I had put on makeup after all. I glanced around to see if anyone thought we were stealing something, then spotted a solitary pink balloon drooping by the community center's double glass doors. The automatic doors swung open at our approach and animated the balloon; it bounced wildly and made Chloe giggle. It was love at first sight. Automatic doors never left you stranded clutching a baby and a diaper bag.

I spotted a young woman dressed in black yoga pants signing a clipboard at the front desk. Her blond ponytail was neatly threaded through a clear pink visor that matched her top.

"Is this where the Mommy and Me class will meet?" I asked. She raised her eyebrows in an 'Are you talking to me?' expression and looked me over. Something caught her attention, like I had spinach in my teeth. Then I realized my sweater was on inside out *and backward*.

"Um. Hi," she finally said. "Oh my God! Your baby's so adorable!" Her voice was breathy and anxious, and she smiled with perfect teeth. "Uh, yeah! I think it's over there. . .? Excuse me. . .?" She trailed off with a high-pitched question mark and scooted past me. Was it the sweater? She could just tell me.

Class started in two minutes, so I half-jogged down the short hallway and followed the Question-Mark Mom, who joined her nanny. The nanny cooed with her little charge, quickly swapped places with the mom, and blended into the back of the room while her glossy employer sat down in the circle of about fifteen women who chattered away.

I dropped my diaper bag in the last space left by the door and felt a cold draft, but the circle of moms with their babies closed fast. A large, colorful parachute lay flat at the circle's center. I'd seen on the flyer a game where the moms fluffed the brightly patterned cloth overhead with the babies laughing under the canopy. This was a signature move for Mommy and Me that promised to build important emotional bonds.

"I need food!" one of the women in the circle said and shriek-laughed with the mom sitting next to her. "Oh. My. God. Have you and Matt gone to Mangiamo's for their risotto? To *die* for."

People said this often, about what was worth dying for, but I didn't think they understood what these words really meant. Still, I was shamelessly glued to their conversation.

"I'm asking for a night nanny as my push present instead of a ring," the woman continued. "I'm d*ying* to go out."

Her girlfriend leaned in and laughed like it was the funniest thing she'd ever heard. She was small-boned with chiseled cheeks and a suspiciously smooth forehead. Their high ponytails flicked in unison. Puffy pink lips puckered in delight. I pursed my own dry lips. I could've at least put on some lip color.

Babies gurgled as they lay on colorful, monogrammed blankets. I put Chloe down on hers, the free one the hospital gave us when she came home. We had received some beautiful baby blankets as gifts, but they were pristine and untouched, still tucked in boxes from the move. I quickly pulled my sleeves and spun my sweater around, so the tag sat in the back.

"That happens to me all the time. That's when I even remember to get dressed!" the mom beside me said. Her wonderfully regular, faded baggy jeans and oversized blue button-down shirt made her the most beautiful woman in the room to me. Her brown hair hung in a low ponytail secured by a pink scrunchie. "What's your baby's name?"

"Chloe. . .?" I was so nervous that I started conversing in question marks, too.

"This is Lila."

I leaned toward her baby. "Hi, Lila! I'm Carol."

Lila's mom stuck out her hand. "Lisa. Nice to meet you."

"You too." I squeezed Lisa's hand and smiled, my shoulders relaxing a little.

"Ladies. Lay-deeeeez," said a woman in the circle. "We're going to begin now. WELCOME. I'M ASHLEY!" The leader of Mommy and Me resembled an aerobics instructor. Her cropped yoga top was short enough to show off her impossibly flat stomach. Lisa settled next to me, threw me a glance and mouthed, "Really?" Her eyes crinkled at our inside joke.

Ashley continued in her all-caps lilt. "We will have SO MUCH FUN. Crisscross applesauce, everyone!" All the moms, except me, knew what this meant. They shifted, crossed their legs, and checked on their babies. I mimed them and hoped no one noticed I was two beats behind.

"OKAY! We will start with the icebreaker question to get to know each other better. I know, I know. These early months are SO HARD!" A soft murmur rippled through the circle. "SO. Let's start over here." Ashley turned to the mom on her right. "What's your name, Mommy?"

"Klaire. Klaire with a 'K.'"

"Okay, Klaire, what's the *hardest* thing you've had to deal with since the birth of your baby?" The question sucked the air out of me, but the circle tittered in delight. The mommies liked this one.

Klaire smiled, bit her lip, and said, "I just don't sleep anymore! It's all diapers and dishes. James doesn't like to nap, so the nanny and I take turns rocking him. It's exhausting." The circle vibrated in agreement.

I looked at Lisa, who touched the back of her hand to her forehead and subtly pretended to be appalled at Klaire's dilemma, but I also noted the sympathy in her eyes. We all knew what Klaire meant, minus the part about having a nanny. I gave a hard laugh, but a knot grew in my stomach as the ice breaker question barreled toward me. What will I say? I looked down at Chloe on her blanket. She was busy trying to get baby Lila's attention.

There were five moms ahead of me. One had a husband who complained about the lack of sex. Another's baby didn't latch to breastfeed. The third lost her nanny to another mom in the community. The politics of it all! The fourth mom sought advice about stain removers. The last mom before me wondered whether it was okay to start date nights and leave the baby with a new sitter.

My turn.

"Well, the hardest thing I've had to deal with since having my baby. . ." I stalled for time, parroting the question but still getting stuck. "Um. . ." *Just repeat the main talking point about sleepless nights*, I coached myself. *Or no sex.* There was definitely no sex for me. *Just tell them what they want to hear.* My fingers dug into my thighs, which were stiff with the crisscross that had nothing to do with applesauce. The circle stirred. "My husband died of cancer when Chloe was ten weeks old. I have to decide whether to go back to work. I work for CNN, and I'm talking to them about an assignment in the Middle East, where I think it might be easier to forget. . ." I looked around at a circle of stunned faces, and my last words stumbled out. "You know. Easier to forget the sad part."

The truth didn't just hurt. It went viciously for the jugular. I heard Lisa gasp, but I kept staring at the edge of Chloe's blanket. I couldn't even look at my baby. Her innocence would make this moment feel worse.

I felt Lisa's hand on my forearm, offering an empathetic squeeze, but I was not like Lisa or any woman in this room. I didn't belong. Tears welled up with the fraud of me being here. Someone coughed. Finally, Ashley broke the freeze from my icebreaker response, which probably broke any future I might have had with these women.

"Carol, I'm so sorry. This is AWFUL. And I'm sure all of us in this room wish you ALL THE BEST."

"Right. Thank you," I said. This was worse than a TV live shot gone bad. There was no studio to toss it back to, no camera to turn off, no going to black. I had become the circus act before the parachute song. I scooped up Chloe in her blanket and rose. Lisa got up too, grabbed my diaper bag from the floor, and helped slide it onto my shoulder. She pulled me into a quick hug and whispered, "Every day at two o'clock. Hermosa Valley Park playground. If you want to come."

"Thanks. Bye, Lisa," I said. I didn't mean to be abrupt, but I had to get out of there, "I'm sorry, everyone. Bye."

As I hurried down the hall, Chloe's hospital blanket landed on the scuffed linoleum. I picked it up and tossed it in the trash. Will once told me that when it comes to live shots, no one remembered a reporter's mistake, only how well you recovered. But in my small beach town, people talked. *Oh, did you hear how that CNN anchor fell apart at Mommy and Me?* they would say. Y*ou know Carol Lin? Oh, you don't know her? Yeah, it has been a while. . .*

I drove home for Chloe's nap, but I was too agitated to go through the motions of her sleep routine. As soon as I closed the front door behind us, I let the diaper bag drop and laid down the rug I had bought for a moment just like this—when I'd walk through the door so tired, I couldn't take another step. Had I known my foray to Mommy and Me would be so brief, I wouldn't have brought so much stuff. Chloe rolled back and forth, pleased that she didn't have to depend on me to set herself in motion. I still felt the warmth of Lisa's hand and recalled her whispered words: *Every day at two o'clock. Hermosa Valley Park playground.* If I want to come.

She had invited me, even after she learned I was a widowed, single mother. I stared at the ceiling. Tears fell down the sides of my face. There were probably other Lisa's in that room. I didn't look hard enough. I was too biased, too busy looking for what I expected to see: women who were so much better off than some sad sack like me. Maybe I chose to see only glossy smiles of privilege and willfully ignored signs that they, too, sought to be accepted. Perhaps I missed the stretch marks and dark circles or was too quick to judge ponytails when none of us had time or energy for a shower and shampoo. Who was I to ignore the pressure they might feel to fit into the crop top uniform of a carefree beach mom three months after giving birth in a town where image was everything. When that mother joked about food, it was probably because she was hungry.

No, I wasn't alone in wanting to belong, to understand how beautiful it could be to sing under a colorful parachute. I wasn't alone in wanting to pretend for an hour that it was possible to make sweet memories, like when moms moved as one into "crisscross applesauce, let's begin" and tried to recapture the life we had imagined.

25. RETURN

Dr. Thomas Kerrihard's office had soft amber lighting and the plush upholstery of a designer showroom. It was what I expected from a West Hollywood psychiatrist situated on Robertson Boulevard, a short distance from The Ivy, a restaurant so chic even celebrities dined there to people-watch. The doctor was beautiful too, tall with smooth skin and warm brown eyes that crinkled. He, in his impeccably tailored jacket, sat across from me with hands gracefully folded in his lap. I was nervous and anxious, like therapy was a test. I didn't know if it was the dusky cream tones of his office décor or the languid way he carried himself from desk to chair, but it soothed me to think of this more as a meet-up with a stylish friend. I'd rather ask him about his skin care routine.

"How are you, Carol?" Dr. Kerrihard asked.

That was a big question. "Sad," I said. "I guess I'm just sad."

"It's understandable. You've suffered a great loss." He paused to see what this observation brought to our conversation.

"Mmhmm." I thought I was supposed to nod, so I did. I'd never been to a psychiatrist. Aren't psychiatrists for really distraught people, the kind carted off to a locked facility? Psychiatry sounded so level-up from therapy with a social worker or a psychologist. I maintained eye contact with Dr. Kerrihard in case my eyes were truly the window to my troubled soul. Maybe he could see past the cloud in my head.

He persisted. "What do you hope to get from our sessions?"

"I don't know. What can this do for me? What can you do? What can anyone do?"

I didn't know how sitting in a dark room with a doctor armed with a notepad would make me feel any different, but I suspected psychotherapy was about more than feeling better.

"I'd like you to set the goals, Carol, but we can accomplish many things. First, how are you doing with basic tasks. . . sleeping, eating. . . taking care of yourself?

"There's no 'self' in my day, Dr. Kerrihard. I have a baby. It's pretty much about her now. . ." I trailed off, thinking about Chloe. "She's a little over three months old."

"And how are you doing with her? How is motherhood?" Just like that he zeroed in on my biggest struggle.

"Um. It's okay." I knew it was not completely okay, but I didn't have an experience to compare it to. It was hard. Really hard. I did what the books told me to do, followed the recommendations for how often to change diapers, how to check the color of her poop, when to put her down for a nap, and for how long. I made the pediatric follow-up appointments and tried different techniques for social stimulation: music, reading to her, and talking out loud so Chloe could build language. I told myself she got everything she needed, or. . . well, maybe not everything. I couldn't give her Will. When Chloe and I had locked eyes minutes after she was born, I had connected. I had felt protective. A bond had begun to bloom when she latched on to me. But that fantastic sensation of the baby who had laid on me was inseparable from Will's hand in mine in the delivery room. We were supposed to grow this love together. But the more time Chloe and I spent together, the farther apart I felt from her. With her father gone, Chloe only had half the love she deserved.

"How do I know if I really love her, Dr. Kerrihard? How do I know, if I don't tell her that I do, if I don't say the words?" The words had eluded me. *I love you* felt forced, weighted when it should be lightly given, spontaneous instead of planned. I wanted to tell Chloe *I love you* in the same way I wanted those words from my own mother.

Dr. Kerrihard put his pen down and steepled his fingers. "Perhaps just as important to the bonding process for your baby is knowing you are present. When she is hungry, you feed her. When she is cold, you warm her. She knows she can count on you because you are being present. You have the rest of her life to tell her you love her. The words can come later, perhaps when they will mean more to both of you."

"What if she needs more than I can give her, doctor?" My face burned. "What if I *don't* actually love her when I never tell her that I do?"

"Grief is complex, Carol. You're experiencing the trauma of losing your husband. Your brain is processing a lot of change and a lot of information. Think of your brain like a computer. It has a specific amount of capacity, but when grief and trauma occur, our brains go into overdrive to bring forth the most relevant things we've learned from past experiences."

"So, you're saying my brain does not have room for love?"

"No. I'm saying our brains can adapt based on our past experiences, but brains need time to process new circumstances. I understand you were. . . are. . . a journalist?"

"Yes. I was. Am. I *am* a journalist."

"Analytical? Fact-based? A documentarian?" Dr. Kerrihard pressed me, and I tried to follow his logic.

"I guess? Maybe."

"So, what did you do when you were on a story that wasn't adding up? And what was the emotion that you felt at the time?"

"I pushed harder, knowing the information was there. Someone knew. And, if I'm honest, getting angry makes me dig my heels in even more. I don't like letting a gap of information get the best of me. But that was work. That was me before cancer kicked my ass. It just. . . Will's cancer, it. . . just killed me."

Dr. Kerrihard nodded. "One thing I know is that the brain can heal, given the right conditions and support. We, as humans, are wired with a deep desire to live and thrive. How that wiring gets short-circuited by life is a different conversation. But I've seen in my practice that people with the right support systems can overcome overwhelming obstacles to heal. I think you can, too," he added gently. "If you're asking me if you will ever feel love for your baby, I'm hopeful."

My head throbbed. I was nervous that the beautiful Dr. Kerrihard was judging me as harshly as I had judged myself. Of course, this was ridiculous. He was a doctor, and he made interesting points. "How will I love her if I can't overcome this sadness?"

"Because grief exists on a wide spectrum. The patients I typically deal with are dying. Mostly HIV positive, but some have terminal cancer. Your grief is just as relevant, but some depression is so deep that some of my patients are catatonic. They are traumatized by the fact that they are dying. This is when family and friends become extremely important in the healing process. Mind you, in their case, there is no healing of the body, but there is good work to be done with the human spirit. The most satisfying part of my job is bringing the patient and their loved ones to a good end, to have the strength to face what is about to happen with grace." Dr. Kerrihard paused to let in the notion that, while a part of my life was over, another part had only just begun.

Was I willing to give myself the grace and time to find my future? I was still afraid the years would feel too long and without end.

During my maternity leave, my anchor slot had been capably filled by CNN correspondents who sought a higher profile on the network. My Saturday and Sunday night show, *CNN Tonight*, was the only prime-time evening news programming still produced from Atlanta. After 9/11, CNN moved Atlanta-based talent and show teams to New York, closer to the new corporate owners. CNN, which had once professed that the news was the star, began hiring established names from CBS and ABC.

Jodi called to warn me. "I think you need to get back here and show your face. Have you thought about when you're returning?" Her Long Island accent sounded especially strong that morning. The diesel engine of a truck rumbled in the background.

"Where are you, Jodi?" I asked and then heard the loud crunch of metal.

"Shit! I just backed Sylvia into the tree by your driveway!" Sylvia was Jodi's matte gold minivan. "I'm meeting the movers at your house. Remember? We're packing up your furniture so the renters can move in?"

We had left Atlanta so quickly for Los Angeles to get Will treatment at UCLA that the townhouse I owned had been sitting unoccupied for the last four months.

"Oh no! Oh God, thanks, Jodi. I'm sorry about Sylvia. What's the damage?"

"Hang on! Hang on!" Jodi shouted at the movers. "Sorry. I'm back. Never mind Sylvia. Let's get back to the fact that *you* need to come back to work!"

"I've thought about it. Jim Walton said I could take my time."

"Well, don't take too much time. I'm hearing there may be more layoffs."

It was hard to hear a five-time Emmy-award-winning producer like Jodi worry about losing her job, but AOL, CNN's new corporate owner, wanted to cut costs. "Our show ratings are still good. But Carol, you don't want them too good when you're not the anchor. Come back."

"Okay, I'll think about it. I really will, Jodi. I promise." I couldn't afford not to work. Will didn't have life insurance.

"Babe, I know it's hard. I loved Will, too. But he wouldn't want you to live your life alone like this. I'll be here for you." Then Jodi, always the New Yorker at heart, dropped the sentimentality. "Now get your ass back here! Bye!" And she hung up.

That Jodi. I loved her so much. I looked around my family room, which at least had a sofa now and another soft rug where Chloe rolled around and tried to tug at Billy's tail as it wafted in her face. She crawled over to him, and he let her lay her big head on his belly.

"Billy, you are the fattest, most patient cat on the planet," I said, rubbing his soft ears and feeling his head vibrate with a resounding purr. My baby, the cat, the suitcases, and so many toys—I began to imagine the flight back to Atlanta and what walking into the CNN newsroom would feel like. I visualized my show team's pod of desks surrounded by the hum of developments at both national and international desks. I used to love overhearing the clipped Irish accent of CNN International's editor David Clinch debriefing with someone in the London Bureau; his patient lilt had guided me during my first overseas assignments. I could practically hear the steady murmur of producers and editors organizing the next hour of news and conversations with correspondents worldwide who sought script approval. The studio mood would be casual despite the ongoing top story of the U.S.-led war with Iraq.

Jodi warned me that CNN was moving entire show teams to New York. Jim Walton was not going to wait forever. I waited another week and then let CNN know I'd return the following month. Since elementary school, September had always represented change to me.

"Wonderful!" Senior Executive Sue Bunda had said when I called. Her excitement was warm. "We'll be ready for you. Your weekend show team will be delighted to hear you're coming home."

Sue had likely heard about my conversation with Eason. I was committed to moving to the Middle East. The thought of returning to the CNN Center, where Will and I had worked, was unbearable.

But first, Chloe and I had to return to Atlanta. When I told my mother, she was stoic, but I saw her eyes shimmer before she looked away and offered to take us to the airport in her car that was too small to hold all of us and our bags.

The night before my flight, we cooked and washed the dishes together by hand because it allowed us to stand close but with something to do. After I packed up Chloe's things to return to our house and prepare for the early morning flight, my mom and I stood on the threshold of her back door. Instead of pulling away, she leaned into me when I hugged her. She felt so small now. Her shoulders were slightly bonier, and her head rested under my chin.

"Mom, you're shrinking!" I said.

"Ah! I am!" she said. "Ostah-pro-rosis."

"I think you mean Osteo-POR-osis, Ma."

"Oh Carol, you think you know everything," she laughed, blinking away tears.

"I love you, Mom," I said tenderly. "We'll be back to visit. Often! I promise." And I kissed her cheek, amazed that she accepted my American-style affection and therefore, accepted me.

"Carol, you will come back. I know. Come back soon," she said, pressing her palm to my cheek, a gesture that echoed a moment from her own past. "Come back. When you are ready."

I arrived in Atlanta's Hartsfield International Airport covered in cat hair and cereal crumbs. The process of getting from plane to baggage claim to curb was push and pull, with stroller and luggage cart, and I looked like a sherpa with the giant car seat strapped to my back. Curbside, we hurled ourselves into Jodi's minivan that still had a massive dent in the back.

"It's about time!" Jodi joked. Two months ago, she and Jenny had come to see us in Los Angeles and then double-teamed to get us into a furnished corporate apartment in Atlanta. They had stocked the refrigerator and ensured the place felt like home.

"Helloooo!" Jenny greeted us with a big hug when we arrived, reaching for Chloe while I dragged our suitcases and the cat carrier inside. Jodi, right behind us, chattered about the building, the view, the easy walk to the park, and my return to the show, which was only a week away.

"Everybody says hi. They can't wait to see you. We've got bookings working on the guests. They want to know if you're available for any pre-tapes before the show on Saturday." Pre-tapes were the interviews we recorded before the live show because the guests could not come into the studio on the weekend.

"No, Jodi. I don't think I'm ready," I replied, and dropped to the brown carpet to catch my breath next to Chloe who chewed on a cat toy that I hoped was clean. I was too tired to check. "I'm sorry. Is that okay? Can we just see who we get to come in on Saturday?" I delayed the inevitable.

"You're gonna be fine. But yeah, of course. We can start slow." There was nothing slow about Jodi, but she tried to be patient. "What's up this week? You've got a sitter lined up, right? How's that going?"

"Well, it's not going yet. I've only talked to Jessica on the phone, but she doesn't start for a couple days." Back in Manhattan Beach, I had my mom, neighbors, friends, and people I'd known almost all my adult life to watch Chloe if I needed a break. I was apprehensive about Jessica, even though she had impeccable references.

I changed the subject back to work. "I have an appointment to meet with Jim Walton tomorrow."

"Bring Chloe!" Jenny thought bringing the baby to the newsroom would be a good icebreaker. "She'll make it easier for you."

Babies and work, I thought. *Nothing easy about that.*

The next day, when I got ready to go to the CNN Center, I selected an ivory-colored sheath dress with enough structure to hide the few extra pounds I still carried from pregnancy. As I dressed, I sang to Chloe, who jumped up and down in her bouncy seat on the tile floor. She screamed and laughed because we were going somewhere. Places meant people. And people meant attention. Chloe was a born party animal. Just like her dad.

I put on makeup for the first time since Will's funeral, curling my lashes and smoothing a dark pencil line under my eyes. The makeup was my mask. I was glad I had my CNN ID card to pass security. At least with eyeshadow and lipstick, I physically looked like the old me.

When we arrived at CNN's outdoor parking structure, I buckled Chloe into her stroller and headed for the pedestrian bridge and elevators that lead to the newsroom. A young woman I didn't recognize stopped us.

"Hi," she stammered. "You don't know me, but I know you." This felt creepy. My narrow dress and heels, with baby in tow, would make for a tricky getaway. But she continued. "I work at CNN. And I heard about what happened." Before I could say anything, she pulled me into an awkward embrace and cascaded into a narrative avalanche. "I'm so sorry. This is just awful. Tragic. I mean, your husband died. And you have this baby. And now she's going to grow up alone. Without her father. . ."

I patted her lightly on the back, saying, "My God. I didn't know it was *that* bad!" and tried to disentangle us on a light note because I needed to get to my appointment.

"Oh. Oh!" She sniffed and composed herself enough to release her hold on me.

I stepped back. "Thank you for your kind words. I mean it."

"Okay. Bye. Byyye!" she called after us as Chloe and I fast-walked toward the elevator doors.

When they slid open again, I rolled Chloe through the gray and red space, brightly lit with studio lights, and made our way past editors and producers who glanced up from their phone calls, eyes brightening. I smiled and waved and stepped quickly to a familiar show team pod where Kyra sat in full makeup, ready for her show.

Kyra leaped up and threw herself on me with a hug. "Oh my God, Carol! Welcome back!" She squeezed me hard, careful not to smear her stage makeup.

I had worked with many of her writers and producers before, and now they all stood and gathered around us to say hello.

They murmured their well-intended pleasantries—*So sorry for your loss*, that sort of thing—which felt familiar and yet performative. I knew everyone was at a loss. I held up the baby to give them a reason to smile. Then, some fell back to their work, as others walked up in this gentle tide of grief-and-greet until a supervising producer interrupted the blurry repetition of faces, hands, and smiles.

"Carol, Jim Walton is ready," she said. "Want to head up to his office?"

I left the stroller by the show team pod and carried Chloe across the newsroom to the main stairs that led up two carpeted flights to the floor of executive suites. Ashley, Jim's secretary, greeted us and let us into Jim's office. With the sweep of the glass door, we found ourselves in his hushed space with a large desk and seating area.

"Carol!" Jim strode over for a hug while also trying to avoid Chloe, who furiously squirmed to get down. I instinctively put her on the thick carpet to properly shake Jim's hand. "We've got lots to talk about. How are you, Carol? Welcome back. I hope you're getting settled?"

Before I could respond, I heard Chloe gagging like a cat with a hairball stuck in its throat. She spit up formula in a long goopy thread that landed on a rug so plush that I was sure it was custom-made. Before Jim said anything or called for his assistant, I dropped to my knees and dabbed up the mess with baby wipes I kept in the shallow pocket of my dress—more of a design flourish than practical. The look on the network president's face instantly told me he was not used to babies. Or vomit.

"Excuse me, Jim. I'll be right back." I scooped up the wet wipe, yellow with goo, and carried Chloe out the heavy glass doors to skip-run downstairs back to the newsroom and Kyra's show team. "Kyra, do you mind taking Chloe just for a few minutes?"

"Sure! Come to Kyra, baby!' She reached for Chloe and sat her on her lap, where my baby banged on the computer keyboard. Kyra loved kids. I threw her a grateful look and mouthed *thank you* before I teetered on my heels back upstairs, trying not to trip. Red-faced, I picked up the conversation with Jim.

"I'm so sorry, Jim. Everyone wanted to see Chloe, and I thought. . . you might, too."

"Oh no, please don't be embarrassed. It's nice to see the baby. It's nice to see *you*." Jim was the kind of man people underestimated, only to learn how smart and cunning he was at business. His smile was genuine and warm, in sharp contrast with cool blue eyes that measured everyone he met. His calm was his storm, a man savvy enough to thrive under the Time Warner AOL merger while maintaining his easy-going, shirtsleeves-no-tie demeanor.

I'd anchored at CNN for five years and only occasionally passed Jim in the halls. He'd politely ask how things were going, but I was so immersed in the gritty newsgathering details that my conversations were too granular, and he'd leave our chance meetings reminding me that "I have to let my managers do their jobs." Jim was the big-picture guy; today, I was trying to fit into that picture. I felt positive. Afterall, he did loan me the company jet.

"So, you spoke to Eason? He tells me you're thinking about the Jerusalem Bureau," Jim said somberly. I couldn't tell if he thought my asking to be a Jerusalem-based correspondent was a good or bad idea. The Middle East's second Intifada still raged. Israel was rife with bus and road bombings. Civilian casualties included young people, women, and children. Israeli checkpoints in and out of the Palestinian West Bank grew tighter, and life for Israelis and Palestinians remained dangerous and grim.

"Yes. It's good timing," I said evenly. I wanted Jim to consider me a practical journalist, not a bereaved woman. "CNN has a correspondent opening at the bureau. It's a big story, but not a traveling bureau. It's a family-centric culture. Jerusalem might provide a good work-life balance." Did I say work-life balance? Yup, that's what I said. My word choice troubled Jim.

"Have a seat." He motioned to his small conference table. I felt sweaty. Oh God. What if my eye pencil smudged, and I had raccoon eyes. I glanced around for a discreet reflective surface that could double as a mirror, but there was none. Jim sat and swiveled to face me with his arms folded casually on the tabletop. "It's still a war zone, Carol. Civilians are dying. Are you sure you're in a state of mind where you can deal with that? Won't that be difficult for you?"

I doubled down. "It's work. No different than before when I was covering places where civilians were dying. I can handle it." The bravado was back, or so I thought. But I only told a half-truth. I'd go just about anywhere that didn't have a memory of Will and me. In Jerusalem, I could lose myself in an all-consuming story, the big story I once loved that I thought loved me back. I'd hold the mic again, ask questions, decide what interview drove the story forward, and pick that unforgettable, explosive, opening shot. I told myself, *I did this before; I can do it again.*

Jim looked skeptical. "As your boss, I don't have cause to say no. You're qualified for the assignment. As your friend, I want you to think about this. Let's talk again."

"I have." I didn't want to seem ungrateful, so I promised, "I will."

"I want to bring Sue in on this conversation," Jim said, referring to CNN's Senior Executive Vice President, who had welcomed me back and oversaw an extensive portfolio of CNN's news content, including special events. It made sense to have Sue weigh in. But I also worried. While Sue had reached the executive suite on merit, she was also a local Atlantan and a mother. I had thought Teya would ignore my pregnancy and send me to Iraq, but I was wrong. I had reason to suspect Jim hoped Sue's maternal experience, not her professional judgment, would sway me away from the move. But I was determined to prove I was the same journalist who could handle whatever CNN threw my way. When the producers said jump, I knew to say how high.

I returned downstairs to collect Chloe, whom producers and writers had passed around the pods of tables. She had drooled on the printed-out scripts. It was close to Kyra's showtime, and I felt guilty about recruiting her team to babysit, but everyone smiled, gracious and, no doubt, relieved to hand Chloe back.

"I'm so sorry! Sorry! Thank you. Great to see you. See you soon!" I buckled Chloe in her stroller and walked past the national and international desks, which were all business now. The formalities of saying hi were over.

As the days rolled toward Saturday and my first on-air appearance since returning to work, I imagined what it'd be like to sit in the anchor chair again. Sometimes, tears still welled up without any reason. What if I started to cry in the middle of the broadcast? I didn't have a co-anchor to pick up the slack. No one was next to me to cover if I stumbled. The control room could dump to commercial break only so many times.

I pushed Chloe through Piedmont Park one day when we bumped into Daryn Kagan, CNN's popular late-morning anchor.

"Carol!" she interrupted my thoughts. "I saw you in the newsroom but was on air and couldn't say hi. How are you?"

"I'm okay," I said. "How are you?"

Daryn had always been a bit of a mystery to me. Friendly in a way I interpreted as warm but at arm's length. Daryn was Stanford University-smart, rebelliously stylish, and at ease wearing gold hoop earrings and a sweater set while interviewing world leaders, foregoing the more traditional suit jacket and earring studs. My former co-anchor Leon Harris teased that Daryn dealt with "Man-soons," the torrent of eligible men Daryn attracted. When I first arrived at CNN, we were both morning anchors. My show produced for the East Coast audience, Daryn's for the West Coast. People assumed we'd be rivals, the shortcut summation for two very different women in similar roles. That was never the case.

"This must be Chloe," Daryn said matter-of-factly, looking down but not quite reaching with Kyra's enthusiasm at seeing a baby.

"Yes, this is her, alright," I replied, falling into small talk.

"Your show's tomorrow? How are you feeling about that?" Daryn seemed sincere, so I confessed.

"I'm nervous. I don't know how it's going to go. It's been a while and. . ." This was hard to say, especially to Daryn, who exuded a natural, easy-going confidence. "I'm worried."

Anchoring was a specific performance, different from reporting, more like dining with your audience than dispassionately sharing facts. The audience relied on the anchor to carry them through emotional beats and scenarios, from wars and failing economies to kittens trapped in a sewer. I worked on my performance skills, but I was not a natural anchor. I was a reporter at heart and still more easily saw myself covering a story in the Middle East than leading an hour-long newscast.

Daryn nodded. "Can I give you some advice?"

"Of course."

"You're going to be fine. And I know you'll be fine because you've been through things you absolutely could not control. The anchor chair isn't something to fear, but the one place we are truly in control." Listening to Daryn, my heart, so heavy, lightened a bit. She continued, "When you take that seat and the lights are on and you hear your show's opening music, it's your show, Carol. Remember that. Your show."

Instinctively, Daryn knew what women like me, like us, needed to know: No one can control the news, but there are places, like the anchor chair, where a woman can call the shots.

On Saturday, Daryn's clear-eyed, bottom-line shove put me back on the air. I stepped up to the chair and logged on to my computer while the production assistant handed me my scripts for the six o'clock prime evening newscast. I sat under the studio lights, my first show since Chloe's birth and Will's death about two minutes away from going live and ran through my old rituals, setting the computer screen to the latest news wires, plugging in my earpiece, and clipping my microphone to my jacket lapel.

"Testing one two three, one two three," I said.

"Got you, Carol," Jenny replied in my ear from the control room.

"Let's rock n' roll, baby!" chimed in Jodi, and I smiled, knowing the control room crew watched me curiously across several TV monitors. I pressed the seat lever to add a little extra height, then stacked my scripts so the edges lined up razor straight in front of me. The show music played, the teleprompter adjusted to the first sentence, and I felt something in me release.

Ready. Set. Go.

"Good evening, I'm Carol Lin. Our top story today comes to us out of Iraq. . ."

26. JUMP

Atlanta was still CNN's global headquarters by virtue of CNN International, CNN.com, Headline News, and CNN Sports still broadcasting from the CNN Center, but it was clear after 9/11 that the heart of the network was beating in New York City. The days began with a new morning show based in the city that never slept helmed by a well-known former CBS anchor, Paula Zahn, and the evenings ended with Aaron Brown, who had left ABC News for CNN's promise of his own 10:00 p.m. primetime show. I had no desire to work in New York again. Childcare would be prohibitively expensive. Rolling a stroller through crowds competing for space on broken sidewalks sounded like a nightmare. But I still had my plan to move to Jerusalem as a correspondent covering the Middle East. I wanted to wait a respectful amount of time after my discussion with Jim to demonstrate the great thought I'd put into this decision, when it seemed so obvious to me that it was the right career move. I settled into a steady battle rhythm of researching stories and interviewing guests for my weekend primetime shows and then finally met with Sue.

"What if you went as a trial period?" she asked.

"How long? A month?" *I could do that*, I thought. Once I was there, it'd be harder for the network executives to change their minds.

"Sure, a month. If you went during the holidays, we could assign the special events team and produce some specials. How does 'Holiday in the Holy Land with Carol Lin' sound to you?"

Naming coverage gave it a higher profile and locked in my potential to both field anchor from Jerusalem and report one of the world's biggest stories unfolding in a geographic area less than half the size of West Virginia. It was a war story that kept me close to home, yet reminded me who I was.

Ironically, outside of work, I was in the midst of a bureaucratic identity crisis. Will and I had bought a townhome in Buckhead when, after nearly four years of living in Atlanta, it became clear that we were not returning to California anytime soon. Removing Will from the title to our house, cars, credit cards, bank accounts, and utilities required I curate and keep handy a heartbreaking paper trail. The notarized story went something like this: I was born (birth certificate) and so was Will. We married (marriage certificate), birthed a child (birth certificate), and then he died (death certificate). And sometimes, the updated government paperwork spelled out my trauma in black and white. To Fulton County, Georgia's records division, I held title to my house as a "single, unmarried, widowed woman," as if by law, my new status had to be crystal clear.

Chloe and I rented out that house and moved to a craftsman bungalow in the historic Ansley Park community, notable for its charming in-town urban Atlanta vibe. We could walk to just about anything, including the High Museum on Peachtree Road or the Piccadilly cafeteria for mac and cheese. But then there were the playgrounds where Chloe and I burned off the long hours between naptimes and meals. We started on the swings, moved to the kiddie slide, and finally ended up in the sandbox, ground zero for where small talk turned personal.

"What's her name?" a mom asked one day as she set her baby in the cool sand next to mine.

"Chloe. What's your baby's name?" I warmed up to sound genuinely interested.

"Allie," she sang.

"Oh, what a sweet name!" I sing-song'ed back.

"Yours too. Chloe is such a feminine name!" she chirped. We are birds of a feather now. "Allie has an older brother, Chase. He's four." (Does anyone have just one child anymore?) "Our sitter has him at karate. But the weather's so nice, we wanted to check out the park."

Here it came.

"Does Chloe have siblings?"

"No. Not yet." The lie got bigger from there. "We're thinking about it. I'd like for Chloe to be potty-trained before we add another. Know what I mean?"

"Oh, yes, give it time. We waited three years before having Allie. It's just *so* much work, right? Bob. That's my husband. He *tries* to help?" She sounded like she questioned daddy's abilities but wasn't committed to throwing Bob under the bus. "But you know, they always want mommy!"

"Totally know what you mean," I agreed, lying again. But really, I didn't. I was Chloe's only option. She had woken me at 5:00 a.m. that morning with *Mama—MAH!*, gripping her crib bars like an inmate and pumping her legs in a joyful revolt.

"I'm coming! I'm coming!" I had said and then changed her diaper, made breakfast, fed Billy, and played music on a countertop CD player. Stacks of plastic CD cases littered the kitchen and made it easier to select another set of kid songs with one hand while I held Chloe with the other. But I wanted an extra pair of hands—Will's hands—to hold her.

"What does your husband do?" the mom asked, offering her daughter a Cheerio. Allie reached out with sandy, wet fingers and ate it. I could practically taste the dirt.

"He's in business. Travels a lot," I replied. The traveling part didn't feel as much like a lie. "That's why you don't see him here on weekends."

"I could not imagine if Bob had to travel and leave me with the kids. I wouldn't survive. Do you have help?"

"Yes, some. But I don't mind. I just have the one. For now," I added, fingers crossed behind me.

Let's face it. It was easier to lie, to just fall in line with the usual talking points. Like Jack Nicholson famously said to Tom Cruise, people can't handle the truth. That was clear every time I told it.

Once, I had just put Chloe down in the sandbox in the midst of moms and dads having an animated discussion about whose spouse did more with the kids. The dads wanted their atta-boy's for a midnight diaper change. One, dressed in pressed khakis and a white button-down shirt, beckoned me with a wave of his big hand. "What do you think!? I bet your husband is pretty hands-on. Don't you think us guys deserve more credit?"

Chloe had reached for a plastic castle mold and waved it dangerously close to another baby's head. I caught it before it clocked the kid and blurted, "Oh, I don't know. My husband died. Cancer. Chloe was ten weeks old."

It was as if I'd dropped an F-bomb in front of the children. I clearly did not understand that the sandbox was not the place to share ugly truths. We were growing our children's social network and our capacity for future carpools to T-ball, soccer, and dance classes. Who wanted to share a babysitter for date night with a widow? No, parents wished to suffer together in similar ways and equal measure. Qualifications for this social club included keeping things light. Tragedies need not apply. I stuck to the swings after that, trying to push the loneliness away.

Atlanta's early autumn days were sticky and humid. In the swelter of September, I found a public pool with special hours reserved for parents and babies. It was a short drive from where we lived in the city center to the perimeter highway that fed Atlanta's suburbs.

The community pool was small, but its shallow end allowed me to comfortably stand instead of having to tread water while I held Chloe. It was her first time in a swimming pool and she kicked with delight. Chloe's blue and green two-piece floral swimsuit showed off her round belly and allowed me to easily slip her swim diaper on and off.

My baby was clearly a water baby. Chloe giggled and cooed at the water sparkling in the mid-afternoon sun and blinked away the droplets that clung to her lashes.

"Does she know how to swim?" the mom beside me asked, and I felt the questions coming. "Hi! I'm Michelle. This is my Sadie." Her daughter looked to be about eighteen months old. Sadie was so cute and wore pink inflatable rings around her arms.

"No, this is Chloe's first time in a pool. She's only six months old. What are those?"

Michelle smiled. "They're floaties in case Sadie slips into the water. She knows how to hold her breath, but I just want to be extra safe around the pool. I'm one of those paranoid moms." Michelle neighed with a big horsey laugh while she squeezed the inflatables on Sadie's little arms and reassured me, "Oh, don't worry. I'm just freaky about packing stuff every time we leave the house. My God." She rolled her eyes. "How much more can I put in that diaper bag!"

I liked Michelle. Her laugh was strong, like her features. High cheekbones, broad shoulders, and long athletic arms and hands that playfully dunked Sadie to make her giggle. Michelle's dark blue swimsuit was practical but feminine, with a little ruffle running down the V of her one-piece. Her brown hair looked like she swept it up in a messy bun at the last second, with loose tendrils falling wet across her freckled nose and cheeks.

She balanced Sadie with one arm and pushed her damp hair aside. "I have an extra pair of floats in my bag. Want some? They might be too big though."

I felt guilty looking at Chloe's bare, vulnerable arms. What if she did slip into the water? Well, I'm standing right here. I'd just pick her up. "We're good. I'll keep a close eye on her. But thanks!"

Michelle blew a stray hair with a *pfft!* and brushed her wet bangs away. "Speaking of overloaded diaper bags, I brought snacks for Sadie. We're leaving the house for, like, what, two hours? But the girl can eat. Happy to share." I liked Michelle's sense of humor. She reminded me of the makeup-free women of California's Topanga Beach. I imagined us hanging out at the park, maybe even having Michelle and Sadie over for dinner.

It's like Michelle read my mind. "We're vegetarians, so it's fried tofu. Does that sound like something Chloe would like to try?"

"Oh yeah!" I said as if I made homemade snacks all the time, which I didn't. "Thanks! Why are you vegetarian?"

"I dunno. Meat just freaks me out. And I don't see myself singing, 'and the cow goes moo, moo, moo' and then feeding Bessie to Sadie for dinner." She let out another neighing laugh, thrilled at her own joke. "Just seems a little much, right?"

I laughed and felt the comforting familiarity of a new friendship forming. Chloe made a slight cackling sound and splashed the pool's surface with her tiny hands. I flipped her over and swooped her across the water to play airplane.

"So. Who's the mister in your life?" Michelle asked, eyes bright, ready to share on the next level of conversation.

"Will?" I was distracted by spinning Chloe, and Michelle's question didn't register. "Um. His name is Will." My brain almost defaulted to the lie, but if we were to be friends, I wanted to tell Michelle the truth. "He. . . he passed away from cancer shortly after Chloe was born." I saw Michelle's smile fade and expected the usual condolences to follow, the *I'm sorry's*, and the *I can't imagine's*. . . blah, blah, blah. Instead, Michelle broke out in a big, full belly laugh and then stuttered and gasped.

"Oh my goodness. Oh my goodness, I'm so. . ." Then she just kept laughing. "I can't. . ." She heaved to catch her breath. "I know. I know. This is so awful. Not funny. Not funny!"

I recoiled. I wanted to unhear her staccato sounds that reminded me of gunfire. "I'm. . . I. . . I'll be right back," I said. Chloe sensed the mood changed as I turned and dragged us through the shallow water toward the steps and concrete pool deck. *Step up. Step forward. Walk toward the lounge chair. There's the bag. Reach. I can't.* My arms were full of baby. Chloe squirmed to return to her new friend, Sadie, who was still in the pool.

"Chloe, wait, wait a minute!" I fumbled with her. I couldn't see. Sweat mingled with tears and sunscreen, but my towel was buried at the bottom of the diaper bag. I crouched and patted the concrete. Not too hot. "Chloe, stay here, stay with Mommy." I put her down next to me, freeing me to find the towel.

Michelle called out but sounded far away. "Carol! Come back! I'm. . . I'm sorry!" Her apology was swallowed up by children laughing and mothers bobbing in small talk.

Dammit. I felt wild, pulling everything out of the bag to find my towel. Out came the diaper cream and a small plastic bag of Cheerios that I had neglected to zip tight; the round circles spilled between the plastic slats of the cheap poolside chaise, bounced, and fell into a puddle of chlorinated water that collected at my feet. Where was the damn towel? I stuck my hand under a pile of diapers I had shoved in at the last minute before we left the house and then shook the whole bag furiously until its entire contents flew all around me. Diapers and packaged baby wipes descended with a thud, hitting the chair and flopping onto the wet pool deck. Sunblock, car keys, and little plastic toys scattered to escape my wrath. Finally, I found the towel and pressed it to my face. I inhaled the laundry soap scent and cried like a teenage girl into its plush threads. Dear God, get me out of here!

Wait, I thought. *Where's the baby?* I looked down and spun around. *Where's Chloe?*

"Chloe!" I called out to a watery circus of bright colors, babies, and moms. No one noticed my distress.

Splash. My baby hit the water.

"Chloe!" I ran to the edge of the pool. She was sinking. *Carol, get in the water*. But I didn't feel myself moving.

Jump. Is this real?

Shit. Jump.

The ruffles of her suit wafted with the current. Down, down, down she drifted. Chubby arms reaching for me, tiny toes pointed like a ballerina. Her brown eyes gazing up. What did she see? A woman turned wife. An adulterer. A workaholic, for sure. I was a journalist who planned to flee to a war zone. Add to that list, I was now a mother who watched her baby drift to the bottom of a pool.

Surely, whatever I was, I was not who was best for her. Chloe, you deserve more than me. Aunt Adele and Uncle Jim—they should take you. Chloe, you won't remember me. Will, you're watching. You were supposed to be the parent. Take her, take her now. I can't be the one anymore.

Then, Chloe smiled, just like Will. And I felt. . . breathless. Her eyes, luminous and brown, were mine. *Mama*, they said. That's who she saw.

To Chloe, I am a mother. Her one and only. Her love was absolute.

Jump!

"Chloe!" My hands broke the pool surface, still rippling from when she fell in, and I pulled her out and pressed her small body to mine. How much time had passed? A second? A minute? Or no time at all. Then I held her up and kissed her almond eyes that glistened and sparkled with life.

She blinked and cooed, "Ma-Ma-Ma," delighted to see me.

"Chloe, Mama loves you. Mama loves you. Mama loves you," I whispered again and again. "I do. I do!" My tears mingled with her wet cheek. It had been me, not her; I was the one who had been drowning.

"Ma-Ma-Ma," she replied. I wrapped my baby in the thick cotton towel that had fallen beneath the lounge chair, still littered with diapers and sunscreen, and felt a chill.

"Chloe, it's you and me. Is that okay? Just you and me." Chloe twisted back towards the water and let out a happy yelp.

Michelle walked over to us carrying Sadie. "Everything okay? Carol, I'm really sorry. I don't know why I laughed." Michelle looked shattered. "I feel stupid. I'm stupid, stupid, stupid!"

I turned to avoid making eye contact and focused on my diaper bag mess.

"Can I hold her? Can I help?" Michelle followed me. I had gotten used to hanging out with Jodi and her family who lived through what happened, no explanation necessary, but knew me in happier times too. This was a stranger, and she pressed on. "I didn't expect you to say what you said. And you shared something really important. Kind of brave. I . . . I'm sorry Will died."

"I know," I finally replied.

"Forgive me? Please?" Michelle was not giving up. "Stay. Do you have time for a snack?" She extended her long, tanned arm with a peace offering dripping in soy sauce. Sometimes being hungry was how new moms built friendships. "Tofu anyone? It looks worse than it tastes." Michelle wrinkled her nose, grinned, and held up two fingers in a scout's promise. "Honest, it grows on you. Tastes better once you get used to it."

27. CNN

The CNN Center loomed large as I turned at the corner of Marietta Street and Centennial Olympic Park. Tourists posed in front of the iconic, two-story high, red letters that spelled out the most trusted name in news. The irony of covering the news from inside a Deep South tourist destination used to grate, but as I watched parents lift children on their shoulders and turn with frozen smiles for a photo, I knew I had come to love this daily reminder of our audience. I also knew I would miss them.

All I had ever wanted was to be somewhere big and grand. Breaking news honed my reporting skills and built my identity and self-worth. To be the first on the scene of any news story, the first to report the first plane crashing into the World Trade Center on 9/11, and the first woman to report live from the tribal territories along the Afghan border was everything to me. I had fulfilled my father's American dream and earned my mother's approval. *Carol Lin, American journalist, CNN* on Wikipedia gave my life shape and meaning.

Until now.

After twenty years of saying yes to the news, I realized it was time to say no. No, I cannot move to Jerusalem, even though I had begged for the assignment. No, I will not go to the Middle East with the special events team to shoot a series for the holiday season, even for a month. This was what I came to tell Sue Bunda. As one of CNN's highest-ranking executives,

Sue knew how difficult it was for women to claim their place and keep it after the rocky trail to a professional mountain top.

In the year since Chloe had fallen into the pool, I had decided to stay in Atlanta, knowing that the staff CNN valued most moved to New York. I'd found a therapist because God knows I needed one, and I'd committed to my mental health. I settled down as the weekend news anchor, which I knew was only a temporary placeholder until management found cheaper, pre-recorded programming for my time slot. Even as more layoffs rocked the Atlanta headquarters, I chose the rhythm of children's songs and bedtime routines. Slowly, at first, but eventually, I'd no longer be seen as relevant at a network like CNN.

Sue asked the obvious question: "Why would you do this?"

Of course, I didn't tell her about how I let Chloe fall into a pool or the baptism I had when I realized I needed to commit to professional help to process my grief. But I did tell Sue the truth: "If I move to Jerusalem, I will never be a mother. And that's what I need to be right now." I'd bet a whole paycheck that no one had ever said this out loud on the executive floor.

"But you *are* her mother. Carol. Are you sure about this? Have you thought this through?" She leaned back. "I don't know how I will explain this to Jon."

Jon Klein was CNN's most recently appointed president, the fifth since 1998 when I was hired. Sue had put her faith in me, authorizing my transfer to Jerusalem. I was sure she was taking inventory of what she had already invested in me; the special event unit was ready to deploy to Israel. Now, she had to explain my change of heart. Carol Lin trading a sought-after post for learning how to be a mother was not a good career move for either of us.

"But Chloe would be with you," Sue continued. "You said you had childcare. Wasn't your mom going to go, too? Or something like that?" She trailed off there, less interested in the personal details and more determined to steer me back to the original plan.

"Yes. Something like that," I replied. "But having someone to care for Chloe is different than me becoming her mother."

Sue tried again. "We're ready to go. You said you wanted this—a change, something to look forward to—and it's a high-profile assignment."

"I'm sure," I replied. My heart raced, knowing I had disappointed her. I couldn't tell Sue how much I still wanted this assignment. How I would run to the Middle East if I could, swim the Atlantic, cross the European continent, and then head south to the Holy Land. I wanted to confess that I hungered to work so hard that I'd collapse into a nightly sweet relief of sleep. But I knew, wherever I was, my grief would catch up to me. Running didn't work anymore. I had to be still for my new life to grow. And stepping back at CNN—actually saying no—worked. For a while.

Two years later, *Working Mother* magazine wanted me to write a first-person essay for the magazine's "If You Ask Me" column on what it was like to return to work as a single, widowed mom with a hectic news career. I accepted the challenge because I wanted other women to know that it was possible to live up to the article's title, *"Yes You Can!"* But truthfully, it was the opportunity to go on the record for my daughter. When she was old enough to read my essay, Chloe would know that we left Manhattan Beach, our friends, and family because I wanted to face challenges head-on and return to the work I loved, even though I was heartbroken. *"No matter what happens, Chloe, don't give up. You can still dream."* And yes, I admitted in my essay that I needed childcare as any working mom did, but I had begun to realize the high cost of the 24/7 type of nanny a network journalist needed wasn't making sense to me. Tears fell as I wrote and realized this deep longing to be with my daughter and give Chloe the love of two parents when she had only me. But what did I know? I was still piecing our lives together, in the same way my old investigative producer in Los Angeles used to shoot video first and ask what the story was later. But this I know, I wrote: No one should feel sorry for my girl. Chloe is the daughter of a man who loved her more than life itself, and he will always be part of our story.

So versed in the visual telling of the news, I found an unexpected catharsis in the slower, meticulous process of crafting graphs of thought and emotion. I began to journal, not in any formal way, but steadily, and I also saw a therapist, this time in earnest. I finally understood that I was more than the sum of my career and the collection of awards I earned in the trophy utopia of journalism. I had become a wife who fought for her husband's life and a mother who ensured Chloe would always know how much I loved her. It felt good to declare in that article that the most important thing I would do in my life was be Chloe's mom.

I was substitute anchoring for a weekday show when the supervising producer approached me on set with a message:

"Jim Walton's office called. Please go to his office immediately after your show."

When I entered Jim's foyer, I stood in the same spot where Chloe first spit up on the carpet.

"Carol, thanks for coming so quickly. I appreciate it. How are you?" Jim Walton shook my hand and motioned me to join him at the same side table where I had pitched moving to the Middle East. The man who generously put my family and me on the corporate jet to fly Will to his last chance at cancer treatment was all business now. His eyes were steely, and his posture was formal.

"Let me get to the point. You have a window in your contract coming up. We've decided to exercise it. It allows us to release you without cause or change your assignment."

My chest tightened.

"We'd like you to move to New York and be a full-time correspondent reporting for the evening shows."

"Move? To New York?" I thought he was going to fire me.

"Or you can stay in Atlanta as a correspondent reporting out of the Atlanta news bureau. I know you have childcare and support here. But we are taking you off the anchor desk."

This hurt. Being a full-time correspondent was an honorable profession but meant less airtime, last-minute travel, and odd hours. Most importantly, I'd lose the thing Chloe thrived upon: our routines. Pancakes in the shape of Mickey Mouse, a morning neighborhood walk before daycare, evening bath time, and snuggles in bed. She counted on me to be there for her.

CNN was generous to even consider keeping me on the payroll. At the same time, Jim probably understood these weren't real options for me. I'd known for a while that the fire in my belly dimmed with earlier bedtimes and my no-television rule at home. CNN knew it, too.

"Jim, what would you do if you were me?"

For a moment, I saw his warmth, a spark. Perhaps in this moment, he remembered his sister, who had died of lung cancer, and I was more than a line item out of fifteen-hundred CNN employees. Or maybe he saw what I saw lately: a woman who had finally begun to understand how to be what she needed to be, for herself and her child.

"If I were you. . . ," he started and then paused, "I would find the best goddamn lawyer I could find and have him call me."

This was an offer akin to buying out of the last year of my contract. If I accepted, I would leave my career behind, for no other news organization covered the world like CNN. This was where I had made my name. And for sure, I was no longer mistaken for Connie Chung.

I leaned in and hugged Jim. 'Thank you' didn't begin to describe my gratitude for all he and CNN had done for me and my family. As I heard his door close behind me, I walked down the executive hallway for the last time and prayed for the strength to remember that, yes, I was as good as—hell, I was going to prove I was better than—my last story.

I went to my office to pack up a box. In the nearly four years since Will died, I'd kept less and less there, not even a photo of us, just some notebooks from my favorite assignments. I flipped open a well-worn binder with two dozen research tabs about Afghanistan, the Taliban, and Pakistan's government and its culture. I noted my scribbles and bright yellow highlights of the most important facts. But I also recalled the small details that never made it on the air: my shy translator, Ahmed, who had boldly smuggled us into the tribal territories; the scar-faced warlord who fashioned himself as a benevolent and loving grandfather; and the Pashtun people, descendants of past European conquests dating back to Alexander the Great, who saw the world through amber eyes flecked with gold, green, even blue. As I headed to my car, I hoped my future also held such unexpected beauty.

No one was more surprised than I when my last day at CNN became the beginning of the most rewarding years of my life.

28. TRY

I always loved the ride from LAX to our home in Manhattan Beach: that first lurch into traffic in a musty airport taxi, the driver's hair-raising swerves to avoid the chaos of tourists in crosswalks laden with baggage, and then us finally merging into Los Angeles' diesel-fueled concrete jungle of red lights and black asphalt heading toward the view of the Pacific Ocean and a white sandy beach. This route, our usual one, was brief, only ten minutes from the airport. Taxi drivers hated the long wait at the airport and hoped for passengers who wanted to go as far as possible; long-distance riders were the money. So, it was no surprise that our poor driver grumbled when he got stuck with me, a measly fifteen-dollar fare at most. But I knew from all the rides before, I would surprise him.

We turned off the airport exit onto the Imperial Highway that dead-ended at Playa Vista, "view of the sea" in Spanish, and a familiar thrill rose in me. I loved the sight of Dockweiler Beach at the magic hour, as they say in television to describe late afternoon when surfers sit on their boards on calm waters, silhouetted against the setting sun. It was the movie scene that beckoned the world to come to California.

The driver whispered, "My God. It's beautiful." Yes, the view never failed. Time stopped. Breath slowed.

"I know, right? Turn left and keep going," I said. "Another two miles, please. Okay, Chloe, ready?"

"Mamaaaa! Do it!" she giggled from her car seat. Safety first for my three-and-a-half-year-old.

I rolled down the window and stuck my arm, flat palm down, into the wind and immediately felt a powerful lift that took my hand swooping up and down on an imaginary journey.

"Where are we going, Chlo'?"

"Pear-wiss!" Chloe giggled. She didn't know Paris, except that my plan to see it with her someday made me happy.

"Paris, here we come!" I shouted over the salty breeze that whipped at our hair and sent Chloe's long tresses flying across her face. The messier the better, I said now. Her finger-dried style said we'd rather spend less time fussing in the mirror and more time just having fun.

We arrived home and saw the upstairs sliding glass doors were already open, a handful of familiar faces milling around the deck and living room. Our friends were here. My mom stood on the balcony, too, like a watchman waiting for her daughter's taxi to sail safely to the curb. Had she let everyone in? Since moving back to Manhattan Beach, I'd handed out so many house keys, I couldn't keep track, but it made our house what Will always dreamed it would be: a gathering place. The stark metal rails and walls of glass looked nothing like Will and me, but the architect had convinced us to go modern. When she had rolled out the design plans calling for sharp angles and a flat roof, I wondered whose dream this was, ours or hers.

"We're not cool enough to live in this kind of house," I had told Will.

Will had been brightly optimistic. "Maybe it's not who we are now, but maybe it's who we will be." I think he knew I'd be the one who'd change the most. Now, at sunset, the house lit up like a glass beacon leading me home. And anyway, the architect was right: this design gave us the best views.

My mom met us at the front door and helped pull our bags and car seat inside. "Carol! Too many things! You cannot carry so much!"

"Uh, but I did, Mom. All good!" Yes, I learned to carry more than my weight, more than I ever thought my body could bear. I hugged her tiny frame, afraid to overwhelm her. Was I getting bigger, or was my mom shrinking?

"How was Jodi?" she asked, after hugging me back. She had mixed feelings about me taking Chloe on regular trips back to Atlanta, but Jodi and I pinky swore her boys and Chloe would still grow up like siblings. Plus, Jodi was Chloe's godmother now, which, according to Jodi, made Chloe half-Jewish. "An official member of The Tribe!" she boasted.

I updated my mom on our trip. "Aunt Jodi was great. Her boys had Chloe running around until midnight. At one point, they hid under the beds and went missing, which scared Jodi and me." I gave Chloe my side-eye glance and she giggled.

The next morning, after cleaning up from the previous night's barbeque, Chloe and I made our mini pancakes to the *Shrek* soundtrack, and I considered how our home's oldness had become renewed: the sandy smooth peach stucco, the new windows that had replaced the rotted ones, the original wood shake roof now a matte metal, better able to fend off erosion from the salty ocean air. The second-story balcony, inspired by Will's request to holler at the neighbors when it was happy hour, was where our new puppy, Sparkle, played and pooped; my old reporter reflexes to avoid enemy fire kept Billy, the twenty-five-pound cat, away from the puppy's food.

A lot had changed in the eight months since leaving CNN. Chloe's age, now almost four, would forever measure the time passed since Will died. She was a rambunctious preschooler with my dimples and brown eyes but Will's half-moon chin and smirk. I was teaching at USC's Annenberg School of Journalism and raising venture capital funds for a startup to help cancer patients and their families. If Will had lived, I might still have been in the scrum of news, but I'll never know.

Chloe and I had settled quickly back into our home and returned to morning walks, midday playdates, and new friendships with other mothers, thanks to Lisa's tip about "every day at Hermosa Valley Park, two o'clock." None of this felt like a compromise.

Rather, it was the reward of the big life I had earned and the good life with people who had been there for me all along. When Will first died, I had been so blind with grief that I hadn't seen clearly the friendships that had always surrounded me, thanks to Will. He had made the friends, but now I had found ways to keep them, for Chloe. There were Simon and Alicia, who promised to tail our future teen girl on her first date; Bob and Barb, who had literally stocked my empty kitchen with the essentials in the weeks after Will had died; Dickie and Becky across the street, who said Chloe would learn to appreciate fine wines in their cellar. Chloe was Will's first, but through him, she had become everyone's daughter.

"Mama, is Aunt Adele my real?" Chloe asked as she ate her mini pancakes, always Mickey's ear first. She'd been curious lately about what was true and what was not.

"Your real aunt?" I asked. "Well, there's Aunt Kippie, your dad's sister. She's what we call family. Aunt Adele and Uncle Jim are what we call 'tribe.'" I borrowed from my reporting experience with the Pakistani warlord, who had first impressed upon me what it took to survive hostile forces. "Tribe is just like family, Chloe." I held her tiny chin and kissed her nose while she pondered the similarities.

I looked out the kitchen window and down the street at our neighbor's quaint homes and saw Becky in her garden tending to her roses. Later, Chloe might have a playdate with the neighborhood girls two doors down. Tomorrow, Adele and Jim planned a sleepover with Chloe at their house because they loved spending time with her but also knew it would give me a morning to sleep in. I wanted my daughter to see that we were members of a tribe greater than its individual parts. We looked out for each other. This filled my heart, once so broken after Will died, when I had questioned if I could give Chloe what she needed.

"Mama, let's go!" Chloe climbed off the kitchen chair and pulled on my skirt. She wanted ice cream.

"They're not open yet, silly. It's only eight in the morning!" I laughed as we still headed outside. We sat on the front steps, and as I looped Chloe's sneaker laces into a bow, I realized I had forgotten my keys. "Chloe, there's Aunt Becky. Can you go say hi? I'll be right back." I waved to Becky, who mouthed, "Got her!" and opened her arms for Chloe, hurrying over for a hug. I ran back upstairs, grabbed my keys, and saw that I'd left the news on in the kitchen. Like a siren call, there was the big red breaking news banner. I felt the itch; I always would. But I no longer needed to scratch it.

The year after leaving CNN, I was getting it done—a great kid, meaningful work, a life tethered by heartstrings to a community I loved—when I met Mike. We should have met when we were both history majors at UCLA at the same time. Instead, twenty-five years after graduating, he was an assistant athletic director at our alma mater and trying to contact me, a notable alumnus, to attend the Final Four basketball tournament in Atlanta in the spring of 2007. He didn't know I had already left CNN and was living in Los Angeles.

We initially met over email and then networked in person for the first time over coffee at UCLA. I arrived in a silk kimono-style dress with a wide-sash belt and strappy high-heeled sandals. The outfit suggested an evening date more than a casual coffee though, when I selected what to wear, I truly had only business on my mind. I hurried from the parking lot to Mike's office building, teetering on the heels and tugging at the hem of my dress that suddenly felt too short. I fumbled in my bag for my buzzing cell phone and answered as I pulled open the heavy glass door to the UCLA Athletics lobby.

"Hello?"

"Hi!" Mike's voice exuded confidence. "I see you."

I spun around and saw a tall man with salt-and-pepper hair dressed in a navy-blue polo shirt and pressed khaki slacks.

"Mike Dowling," he said, reaching out and shaking my hand.

"Carol Lin. I'm so sorry I'm late!" I said nervously. Phone still in hand, I clocked myself on the head when I reached to smooth my hair. "Ow! Um. . . " I dumped the phone in my bag and extended a hand. "It's great to finally meet you in person."

Immediately, I envisioned him with a lovely wife and a couple of kids. But my reporter's habit of profiling someone based on a first impression seemed unfair. Plus, I would find out later, I was wrong. He was single.

"Would you like a quick tour through our Hall of Fame? I have a surprise." Mike touched me lightly on the shoulder and steered me toward a museum-like space with glass cases for all the trophies and other UCLA memorabilia. The room celebrated games played long ago. As we rounded the corner, Mike pointed, "Here we are."

A CNN publicity photo of me was propped up in a glass case next to other notable UCLA alumni. It was the airbrushed, hour-in-the-makeup-room, black-and-white version of me. My head rested on my hand in a pose that suggested I suffered from neck pain. It was sweet of Mike to show me this UCLA honor, but I liked that he didn't make too big a deal of it. "Just wanted you to know that your alma mater of nineteen thousand undergrads still remembers you."

I laughed. "Yeah, I feel special."

Mike walked me through campus, and we settled in at the Kerckhoff coffee house. He didn't even mention CNN. Mike was much more interested in my work helping cancer caregivers. He listened intently and perked up when I described Chloe. Though he hadn't married yet, he was godfather to an eleven-year-old girl named Bee. Mike had what police officers described as command presence, a quiet strength and confidence that comes from knowing exactly who he is and what he wants, and it turned out, he wanted me.

A month after we met at UCLA, during which we had more than a few candlelit dinners and late-night phone conversations, Mike came to Manhattan Beach to meet my friends at one of our weekly barbeques. After dinner, Chloe went to bed and the crowd thinned. Those remaining finally left after they gave me a knowing wink at the door. And that's when I realized the night was not over yet. I was alone with a handsome guy, a first since my life with Will. Mike was in my kitchen on a warm August night. I felt a rush of girlish anticipation followed quickly by paralyzing dread. I was afraid of what I'd do next. Then, I was worried I'd do nothing at all.

From a safe distance across the kitchen island, I knew he smelled great, like the end of a perfect summer Sunday—salty and sweaty with a hint of barbeque sauce. There was a dusting of beach sand on his arms, leaning on my kitchen table. I resisted the temptation to reach over and brush off the pale granules, something I reflexively did for Chloe, who was sound asleep in the next room. I fluttered around and nervously spritzed Windex on the polished quartz countertops. He was baffled at my sudden and intense interest in cleaning.

"Have a seat, Carol," Mike said, playfully patting the kitchen stool beside him.

I look up from my damp paper towel, translucent with wear. "Are you thirsty?" I asked, searching for any excuse to drop from view to rummage in the drink fridge. "We have bottled water and. . . oh! Some juice boxes." I'd just offered a grown man a juice box.

Mike motioned for me to come closer and sit down, but as I did, he set the juice box down and reached for my hand. "No thanks. I'm okay." He was on his feet now and inched closer. I'd run out of things to put between us, but I had to stop treating Mike like the enemy. I knew he was a man who might want to love me, not for the TV version of me, but for the woman I had become: mother, teacher, and entrepreneur looking to give back to the cancer community. I didn't have the fancy title or access to special privileges. Far from studio lighting, I was just a single mom with tussled hair and no makeup. And that was enough for Mike, who leaned down, paused, and then pressed his warm, soft lips to mine.

It had been four years since I was kissed. I tried to remember what to do, then pulled back nervously and slid off my kitchen stool. I felt a primal urgency to make a move, not toward the bedroom, but toward the front door, and mumbled about what a great night it had been. This was too much. I needed more time. There was another kiss, this one quick and friendly. I was afraid to see disappointment in Mike's eyes, but all I saw was kindness.

"'Night, Carol. See you soon?"

Mike let me set the speed limit, and he respected that I wanted to travel in the slow lane. When he pulled out of my driveway, I watched his taillights grow small in the distance between us and then went inside to check on Chloe. In the dim glow of her nightlight, there was my little girl, rolled onto her side in a tiny ball, sound asleep with small hands tucked under her chin. My heart felt lighter at just the sight of her.

I leaned against her doorway and recalled how Will had always nudged me toward the courage he knew I had. "Just do it," he had said, about so many things. He would want me to surrender to my intuition. To explore something new.

Everything about Mike was new to me. A man who wasn't trying to convince me of who I was, or what I could be—even what he thought we could be together. His warm gaze, his gentle kiss, the way he patiently waited for my cues. Mike was not interested in telling me what to do. He cared. And he just wanted a chance. It was my choice to give it, take it, or leave it alone.

I said out loud to no one in particular, "It's not going to happen. No way. I'm not ready."

But thoughts of Will flooded my memory. I had promised to love him, always and forever, even when we were far from perfect. But I also wanted more. Would pursuing something new show me that, again, anything can happen and would only add to the love I had already known?

I wondered what Will would say if I told him I wanted this—for me and for Chloe, too.

"Then take it," he would say. "It's yours. It's time to try, Carol. Just try."

ACKNOWLEDGEMENTS

A journalist always begins with the lead: To my handsome husband, Mike Dowling, thank you for lovingly supporting my writing, and for understanding why I had to finish the book I had set aside when we met. I will forever marvel how you fully embraced our girl and became her dad. I love you so much and know Will would have wanted us to become a family.

To Will's family, Kip, Sean, Patty, Ryan and Kristen and his dear friends whom he held close to the end, I loved Will with all my soul. Thank you for understanding that our story does not change that fact.

Thank you to Alle Mudrick, my publisher and dream editor for your badass launching of Third Rail Press and believing that my book could be part of your movement to support women's stories too electric for traditional publishing. You have an uncanny gift to see the story within a story and edited my manuscript with intuitive brilliance, sensitivity, and girl-boss enthusiasm.

My life is abundant because of those who stood by me; Ron and Dianne, Becky and Richard, Gordon and Diane, Jane and Denny, Simon and Alicia, "Book Bill" and "Tile Man Steve," you kept Will laughing until the end, wine in hand, glorious beach sunsets, nightly barbeques to the tune of The Iguanas' "Oye Isabel" blasting. Taking baby Chloe in your arms, you assured me you would be there for all her 'firsts,' and you were.

Adele and Jim, I'll never be able to repay you for opening your home and hearts for Will, Chloe, me, the cat and the menagerie of friends and relatives who walked freely through your unlocked door to help us. I hope our chapters honor our friendship. To my cousin Katrina and friend Yin, please take comfort that writing this book has brought me closer to God. Thank you for your prayers on our behalf.

Pam Sellers, what can I say? My fellow Californian who greeted me on my first day at CNN with the heads up that, in Atlanta, they put cream cheese inside sushi and deep fry it, along with the ice cream for dessert, and that's okay! Together we learned to love new things. You as the ace CNN editorial and guest producer prepped me for tough interviews and made me a part of your family. You, Peter, and your girls, Bella and Sophia, are in my DNA.

Zain Verjee, a woman so beautiful, heads turned when you finished your CNN International show, but off-air, you made me laugh, even as I cried.

If the discipline of memoir allowed for every name and every kindness of those who stuck by me, despite my foibles, this book would be a thousand pages. Thank you for the flowers, cards, filling my empty fridge, lending books, loading up the baby gifts and babysitting, and to this day, keeping Will's memory alive. I like to think Joanne rests in peace, knowing that I understand love the same way she did.

I never thought I wanted to be a mom, but Chloe connects me to my better self. She inspired the medical community to explore every option to extend Will's life, even as they couldn't cure his cancer. My deepest gratitude goes to my cousin, Dr. Vivian Liu Fuller, and Dr. Clark Fuller for making the medical introductions that eventually got us to the team at UCLA Medical Center, especially to Dr. Fairooz Kabbinavar and Dr. John Timmerman, who eventually, years later, provided life-saving Lymphoma treatment for my mom. Your persistent belief in the value of your patients' lives still brings me tears. I hope you know the special place you and your resident doctors and nurses have in my heart.

To my earliest readers, thank you for calling me out when I skirted the uncomfortable chapters, never questioning why I wrote this book. Helen Chavez, Nicole Nishida, Lee Tatum, Jen Thym, Deborah Cooney, thank you for your insights and honesty. Sophia Lin and Justine Stamen Arrillaga, my heart is full, sharing our Hawaii life. Mahalo for being honest about when you thought the story was ready for primetime. Malia Mattoch McManus, my fellow journalist and author, when we met at a Pau Hana dinner, your first words were "How can I help?" Draft after draft, your keen reader's eye challenged me to confront my truth, and the book is better for it.

To my virtual writing community, this book would not exist without The Book Incubator writing program. Mary Adkins, Rufi Thorpe, Harrison Gale, Gayle Brown, Liz Pickart, Connie Richardson, Jos Linder, Alle Mudrick, and Emma Dries, you are inspirational creators, writers, mentors, editors, and teachers.

Thank you, Lindsay Bartels, my fellow Book Incubator memoirist for sharing your infectious optimism that we both would publish our memoirs and so we are with Third Rail Press. I just adore you for so many reasons, including your critiques, comments, edits and deep insights and shared experience on what it means to become a mother.

And then there's you, Liz Logan. I smile every time I think about the great minds at The Book Incubator who matched us to swap manuscripts; you, a young tech whiz and stand-up comic with me, at the gateway of my golden years. I'm lucky to learn from you that female rage is actually a thing.

Last, but never least, to the brave, immensely talented camera crews I've had the pleasure to work with. You geared up and ran toward gunfire and down dark alleys to capture that opening shot. I am so grateful for the privilege of working with you.

The audience should know there are at least thirty field, show team, and editorial producers supporting a single correspondent through logistics, fact checking, editing the video, to playback on the air. CNN had the most women in these editorial leadership positions: Jodi Fleisig and Jenny Wilburn, whom you got to know in the book, Jen Cook, Jen Marnowski, Chandra Whitt, Liz Mercure, Leslie Steinhauser, Stacia Phillips, Nancy Lane, Gail Evans, Judy Milestone, Parisa Khosravi, Rena Golden, Mary Lynn Ryan, Tori Blasé, Clare Schexsnyder, Carol Kinstle, Pam Sellers, Cory Charles, Jill Neff, Joy DiBenedetto, Jen Bernstein, Jennifer Thomas, Vivian Kuo, Diane Dexter, and Diedre Wenokur. These women led with their intelligence, compassion, keen news instincts, and lived experience and reminded each other to sit at the executive table, not the edge of a room. The years have passed, but never once have I forgotten our journalistic sisterhood.